Ferdinand Christian Baur, Allan Menzies

The Church History of the First Three Centuries

Ferdinand Christian Baur, Allan Menzies

The Church History of the First Three Centuries

ISBN/EAN: 9783744669610

Printed in Europe, USA, Canada, Australia, Japan

Cover: Foto ©Lupo / pixelio.de

More available books at **www.hansebooks.com**

THEOLOGICAL
TRANSLATION FUND LIBRARY.

THE CHURCH HISTORY

OF

THE FIRST THREE CENTURIES.

VOL. I.

THE CHURCH HISTORY

OF

THE FIRST THREE CENTURIES.

BY

DR. FERDINAND CHRISTIAN BAUR,

SOMETIME PROFESSOR OF THEOLOGY IN THE UNIVERSITY OF TÜBINGEN.

THIRD EDITION.

The Translation from the German edited by

THE REV. ALLAN MENZIES, B.D.

MINISTER OF ABERNYTE.

VOL. I.

WILLIAMS AND NORGATE,
14 HENRIETTA STREET, COVENT GARDEN, LONDON;
AND 20 SOUTH FREDERICK STREET, EDINBURGH.

1878.

CONTENTS.

PART FIRST.

                                                PAGE

The Entrance of Christianity into the World: Primitive Christianity,   1-43

    The Universalism of the Roman Empire as a preparation for Christianity,   1-5
    Christianity and the old Religions,   6-10
    Greek Philosophy,   10-17
    Judaism,   17-23
    Primitive Christianity: The Gospels,   23-26
    The original Christian Principle,   26-33
    The Kingdom of God,   33-36
    The Person of Jesus—The Messianic Idea,   37-41
    The Death and Resurrection of Jesus,   41-43

PART SECOND.

Christianity as a universal principle of Salvation: the conflict between Paulinism and Judaism, and its adjustment in the idea of the Catholic Church.   44-183

I. The Conflict,   44-98
    The Church of Jerusalem and Stephen,   44-46
    Paul the Apostle of the Gentiles, and the older Apostles,   46-55

	PAGE
The Apostle Paul and his opponents,	56-65
In Galatia,	56-60
In Corinth,	60-65
The Epistle to the Romans,	65-73
The last journey to Jerusalem,	73-76
The height of the Conflict,	76-98
The Gospel of Luke,	77-82
The Paulinism of Marcion,	82-84
The Judaism of the Apocalypse,	84-87
Papias and Hegesippus,	87-89
The Ebionites of the Clementines,	89
Simon Magus,	90-98
II. The Reconciliation,	99-152
Different views on the subject,	99-104
Points of the Reconciliation,	105-106
Baptism in place of Circumcision,	106-109
Peter the Apostle of the Gentiles,	109-111
Influence of Jewish Christianity on the formation of the Church,	112-114
Mediating tendency of the post-apostolic works included in the Canon,	114-136
The Epistle to the Hebrews,	114-121
The Epistles to the Ephesians, Colossians, and Philippians,	122-128
The Pastoral Epistles,	128
The Epistle of James and the First Epistle of Peter,	128-131
The Acts of the Apostles,	131-136
The Apostolic Fathers,	137-142
Justin Martyr,	142-147
Peter and Paul united,	147-152

	PAGE
III. Johannine Christianity,	153-183
The Apostle John. The writer of the Apocalypse and the Evangelist.	153-155
The Gospel of John,	155-181
The complete rupture with Judaism.	155-159
Christ the true Passover,	159-163
The Paschal Controversy,	163-177
The higher form of the Christian consciousness,	177-180
Retrospect. The Ebionites,	180-183

PART THIRD.

Christianity as an ideal principle of the world; and as a real phenomenon existing under historical conditions; or, Gnosticism and Montanism, and their Antithesis, the Catholic Church,   185

Gnosticism and Montanism,	185-255
I. Gnosticism,	185-244
Notion and Essence of Gnosticism.	185-190
Its Origin,	190-193
Its main elements: spirit and matter, the Demiurgus and Christ.	193-199
Different sects, forms, and systems of Gnosticism,	199-236
Cerinthus, Simon Magus, the Ophites, the Perates,	199-204
Valentinus,	204-213
Basilides,	213-222
Marcion,	223-228
The Pseudo-Clementine Homilies,	228-235
The Three Types,	235-236
Docetism,	237-244

		PAGE
II. Montanism,	.	245-256
Gnosticism and Montanism,		245
The Belief in the Parousia,		246-248
Chiliasm and Prophecy,	. .	248-250
Reactionary Tendency,		250-255
Origin of Montanism,		255-256

PREFACE TO THE FIRST EDITION.

A DESIRE has existed for some time and in various quarters to have the results which have been emerging from the most recent critical investigations in the field of primitive Church History brought together in a compendious form. And such a work cannot fail to promote the success of these investigations. On this field of historical inquiry, which requires to be again and again, and more and more thoroughly, discussed, there are many points which, when looked at in themselves, appear unimportant or of doubtful certainty, and which can only be seen in their true light when placed in their proper connection in the history, where the unity of the whole supports and holds fast the parts.

This is the chief object of the following work. But this is not its only object; it is by no means a mere repetition of views which have already been put forward. Even in those sections where, from the nature of the case, little more was necessary than to recapitulate and sum up the main points of my earlier investigations into particular questions, I have not only examined and sifted the materials afresh, and placed the questions under new points of view, but I have also enriched the discussion by the new contributions afforded both by recent examinations of the sources, and by sources which have been recently discovered. Of these latter I have chiefly, to mention the *Philosophoumena*, known under the name of Origen which are of great importance in connection with the history of Gnosticism and of the earliest Christian doctrine; and extensive use is here made of them for the first time in the discussion of these subjects. Another Gnostic work to which little attention has hitherto been paid, but which is also a very remarkable one, is *Pistis Sophia;* and it also has been used here. The principal thing to be mentioned, however, is, that in addition to the work of arrangement and completion which had to be done for these earlier parts, I have in the two last sections of this work advanced beyond the line of my previous works on the apostolic and post-apostolic age. There are certain other sides of the genesis of the Church which have to be taken into consideration in a general description of the Christian Church of the first three centuries, and without which such a description must fall short in completeness and comprehensiveness, as well as in clearness and vividness; and these sides of the subject have also been set forth in this work.

The standpoint which I have occupied for a long series of years is well known. I adhere to it still as firmly and with as sincere conviction as I have always done; and there is no need at this time to enter into explanations on the subject. In my work which appeared last year, Die Epochen der Kirchlichen Geschichtschreibung, Tübingen, 1852, I have stated my view regarding the treatment of Church History in general, and the leading principles by which writers of Church History have to be guided. That work may thus be regarded as an introduction to this one, in which accordingly these general considerations are omitted. My standpoint is in one word the purely historical one: namely, that the one thing to be aimed at is to place before ourselves the materials given in the history as they are objectively, and not otherwise, as far as that is possible. How far I may have succeeded in this is not for me to say; but I am not conscious of having followed any other aim, and this consciousness sufficiently protects me against all insinuations, against those perverted and ill-natured judgments which are unfortunately the fashion of a time which cannot see beyond its own limited party interests. It is needless to refer to writings which bear the most evident marks of one-sidedness, and in which the shallow treatment of history is imperfectly concealed by arrogance of tone. No one can possibly ignore the demands which this, the most important period of the history of the Christian Church, still puts forward for historical investigation. It is confessed on all hands that a great task still confronts us here, and that many questions still await a more satisfactory solution than has hitherto been found for them. Even if we take the best and most accepted works on the history of primitive Christianity, and examine them with a view to see how far they succeed in combining the historical materials which are of so heterogeneous a nature, and have to be collected from such different quarters, to the unity of a whole, how isolated and fragmentary, how destitute of inner principle and motive, how vague and dim do they appear in many respects! And, as we might expect, this want of unity becomes the more apparent the further we go back to those points with regard to which it is first of all required of the historian that he should have made up his mind and formed a definite opinion; since, without definite views with regard to them, no historical conception of the way in which Christianity grew into the Church is possible at all. Every attempt to obtain accuracy and depth in the foundation, which is the first requirement of the historian, and which no one can lay otherwise than as history herself has laid it in her own unchangeable truth, to bring connection, proportion, and unity into the whole woof of the narrative; to separate, according to their different character, the various elements which here co-operate, and the moving forces and principles, the product of which is the result of the first three centuries; to trace the action of these forces and principles upon each other, and to unite, as far as possible into one harmonious picture, all the individual features which belong to the character of a time so rich in life and movement,—every attempt to do all this must, if it at all fulfils the first requirements for the discharge of such a task, derive its justification from no other source than from itself. It is from this point of view that I would have this work judged by those who are sufficiently impartial, and sufficiently acquainted with the subject, to appreciate the importance of the attempt here made.

Whether I shall afterwards go further on the road I have here begun, I cannot yet distinctly say. It is possible that I may, while not attempting a detailed history, yet indicate the points which my studies and investigations, so far as they have gone, lead me to think most important, in order to follow the general course of the development of the Christian Church. In any case the present work forms a history in itself.

TÜBINGEN, *Sept.* 1853.

PART FIRST.

THE ENTRANCE OF CHRISTIANITY INTO THE HISTORY OF THE WORLD:

PRIMITIVE CHRISTIANITY.

In no field of historical study are the whole scope and character of the successive events of which the history is composed so largely determined by the starting-point from which the movement issues, as in the history of the Christian Church: nowhere therefore does so much depend on the conception which we form of that first point with which the whole historical development begins. The historian who approaches his subject imbued with the faith of the Church finds himself confronted at the very outset with the most stupendous of miracles, the fact which lies at the root of Christianity being in his eyes that the only-begotten Son of God descended from the eternal throne of the Godhead to the earth, and became man in the womb of the Virgin. He who regards this as simply and absolutely a miracle, steps at once outside of all historical connection. Miracle is an absolute beginning, and since as such it must needs qualify all that follows, the whole series of phenomena which fall within the range of Christianity must bear the same miraculous character. Historical connection having once been severed at the outset, the same interruption of the historical process is equally possible at any further point. Thus, on the part of those who are interested in the scientific study of history, the desire has naturally arisen to show how the miracle of the absolute beginning may itself be regarded as a link of the chain of history, and to resolve it, so far as the case admits, into its natural elements. This has often been attempted, and the attempts made in this direction have been subjected to many and various criticisms; but whatever our judgment on this point may be, it cannot really alter the nature of our task. Though we go no further than to ask, why the miracle with which the history of Christianity begins was brought to bear on the world's history at this particular point of time, yet we have raised a series of questions which can only be answered by historical treatment. Our first task, then, in a history of Christianity or of the Christian Church, must be to place ourselves at the point where Christianity enters into the stream of the world's history, and to gain a general idea of its relation to the other elements of the history of the time. With this end we have first of all to ask, whether there is anything in Christianity which we may recognise as, on the one hand, belonging to the essence of that religion, and, on the other, expressive of the general character of the age in which it appeared? If any such points of contact can be distinctly recognised, a ray of light will at once be shed on the historical origin of Christianity.

Now some of the early Christian apologists considered it to be a fact of great significance that their religion had appeared precisely at the time at which the Roman empire arrived at the summit of its power, and came to embrace the whole world in its dominion. All that they inferred from this was, that even in the eyes of the heathen a religion could not but appear auspicious whose epoch coincided with the culmination of the prosperity of the Roman empire.[1] Even on this ground the coincidence of Christianity with the universal empire of Rome appeared to them too remarkable to be ascribed to chance. The true point of contact, however, between Christianity and the Empire is the universal tendency which is common to both. It is a consideration of real significance for the history of the world, that the epoch which saw the Roman empire complete the union of all the nations of the world as it then was in a universal monarchy, also witnessed the

[1] Cf. the Fragment of the Apology of Melito of Sardes, given by Eusebius, Eccl. Hist. iv. 26; and Origen, contra Celsum, ii. 30.

beginning of the religion in which all religious particularism disappeared and gave way to universalism. Christianity thus stood, in respect of its universalism, at the stage which had already been attained by the power and genius of Rome in its world-wide monarchy. In fact we may say that the time had come when the human spirit was to make this momentous advance. As the barriers and divisions between different countries and nationalities were dissolved before the ever-advancing power of the Romans, and their general subjection to a common head caused men to be aware of the unity in which their differences disappeared, the whole spiritual consciousness was proportionately enlarged, and found itself led more and more to disregard the distinctions and exclusiveness which separated men from each other, and to lay hold of what was universal. The general tendency of the age towards an all-embracing unity, in which all that was separate and exclusive might be taken up and disappear, found its greatest and most imposing expression in the universalism of the Roman empire. But this universalism was the very goal to which the history of the world had been tending for centuries before. The conquests of Alexander the Great had opened to the West the portals of the East, and the new routes to the East had developed an active traffic which brought men of all races in contact with each other, and thus diffused the Greek language and culture over the whole of the known world. It was but another step in the same path of historical development when the dominion of the Romans cast over the nations of the world the new bond of political unity. The forms which made this unity possible had never existed before: it arose on the broad basis of Roman civilisation and law, and operated through the vast and well-articulated organism of the Roman state. The nations thus found themselves placed in relations to each other which tended inevitably not only to melt away the stiffness and unsociableness of their previous attitude to one another, but even to obliterate all merely national or individual distinctions, and to produce a broad sense of universality in which minor differences ceased to be felt. The union was not a merely political one : it also bound the different races of the world together in a new bond of mental sympathy. The influence which was working to this end was not to be escaped even by that race which had always been most broadly distinguished from the rest by its peculiar national character, and which had always maintained its own national peculiarities most obstinately and persistently. By the double destruction of their state the Jews were cast out among other nations throughout the wide world. When the successors of Alexander founded their kingdoms, the Jews became an important element of the new population which arose in these new towns, which were to be the chief centres of the political and intellectual intercourse of different races. Here they became Hellenists, and assimilated all the various elements of Greek culture. Finally they were drawn into the ever-widening net of the Roman dominion : and so it came about that Christianity, arising as it did on Jewish soil, stood even at its birthplace in contact with the power that was destined to be its forerunner on the road to the conquest of the world.

Thus the universalism of Christianity necessarily presupposes the universalism of the Roman empire. But in considering how these two great powers now came into contact with each other, we must not rest content with the ordinary view, which starting from the standpoint of teleology, considering merely the outward circumstances and relations amidst which Christianity entered into the world, sees in them the special favour of divine Providence, which, it is thought, could have selected no fitter time than this for the accomplishment of its designs. In this view the great fact in connection with the subject is thought to be nothing more than that the opening up of so many new routes for traffic facilitated the diffusion of Christianity throughout the provinces of the Roman empire, and that the protection of the Roman police and civil order removed many hindrances which might otherwise have obstructed the progress of the messengers of the gospel.[1]

[1] Cf. Origen, in *loc. cit.* To the objection of Celsus, that the sun first displays himself by illuminating all other things, and that the Son of God ought to have

But the bond of connection between the religion and the polity is a much deeper and more intimate one than this, and is to be looked for in the general spiritual movement of the time of which both are manifestations. What we have to keep in mind is, that Christianity never could have been that general form of the religious consciousness which it is, had not the whole development of the world's history, up to the time when it appeared, been preparing for it. First came the general intellectual culture which the Greeks made the common property of the world, and then the Roman rule uniting the nations, and introducing political institutions, which served as a basis for universal civilisation. By these agencies the barriers raised by national sentiment had been broken down, and many differences softened which had tended to keep the nations apart from each other, not only in their outward relations, but in the inner sphere of thought and feeling. The universalism of Christianity could never have become a part of the general consciousness of the nations, had not political universalism prepared the way for it. The universalism of Christianity is essentially nothing but that universal form of consciousness at which the development of mankind had arrived at the time when Christianity appeared.

displayed himself in the same way, Origen answers, that such had been his manifestation. "Righteousness arose in his days, and the fulness of peace was at hand from the moment of his birth: while God was preparing the nations for his doctrine, and providing that all men should obey the one Roman emperor: lest, if there were a number of kings and nations strange to each other, it might be more difficult for the Apostles to do what Jesus commanded them, saying, Go, teach all nations. It is well known, however, that Jesus was born under the reign of Augustus, who had bound together in one empire the great multitude of the dispersed inhabitants of the world. A plurality of kingdoms would have been a hindrance to the free dissemination of the doctrine of Jesus throughout the whole world; both from what we have said above, and especially because men would have been obliged to make wars for the defence of their particular countries: as had been the case before the times of Augustus and even earlier, when war was unavoidable between the Peloponnesians and the Athenians, and in the case of other nations also. How then could this peaceful doctrine which does not even allow men to revenge the injuries of their enemies, ever have made way, had not the affairs of the world been composed, at the time of the advent of Jesus, to a more peaceful state?"

Thus, when we place ourselves at the point at which Christianity enters into the world's history, and inquire into its general historical bearing, we find that it is a universal form of the religious consciousness which answers to the spirit of the age, and for which the history of the nations had long been preparing. But how comes Christianity to be this universal form of religion ? Its claim to be so called is founded on the fact, that it has more and more pressed back the other religions, resolving them into itself, and has risen above them to the most wide-spread dominion over the world. As against those special forms of religion it is therefore the absolute religion. But what is it in Christianity that gives it its absolute character? The first and obvious answer to this question is, that Christianity is elevated above the defects and limitations, the one-sidedness and finiteness, which constitute the particularism of other forms of religion. It is not polytheistic like Paganism : it does not, like Judaism, attach itself to outward rites and ordinances, nor identify itself with the positive authority of a purely traditional religion. To speak broadly, it is a more spiritual form of the religious consciousness than these are, and stands above them. This, however, is saying very little: this is self-evident as soon as we begin to compare Christianity with the two other religions which it had to encounter. When Christianity first made itself felt as a power of permanent importance, Judaism and Paganism had long fallen into decay. They had lost their deeper application to the religious life of their peoples, and had become mere external forms, devoid of substance and vitality. Paganism had sunk into the mindless religion of the vulgar. With all educated men belief in the old gods had become more or less disconnected with the religious feelings. The myths in which the simpler faith of the earlier world had found expression for its fairest religious intuitions, seemed now mere fables, in which there was no spiritual bond to join form and contents in harmonious union : or they were mere symbols to represent ideas which had arisen on a totally different soil. What alone continued to engage men's interest in the maintenance of the national religion, was, that as the religion of the State it was closely intertwined with all the functions of the national life, and could only with great difficulty have been separated from them. Judaism, no doubt, had a deeper religious foundation to rest on. To the Jew the religion of his fathers was never a mere name: there was no failure of the veneration with which the worship of the temple, with its vast array of elaborate ceremonies, was regarded. But the appearance of numerous sects and parties, at variance with one another on the most fundamental questions, showed unmistakably that here also the national religion was tending to dissolution. These two religions had thus been making way for a new religion; and if we look at the subject from the teleological point of view, we cannot but hold it to have been by the special arrangement of divine Providence that Christianity appeared precisely at the time at which there was so great a void to be filled up in the religious life of the ancient world. But this view fails, as much as that to which we formerly referred, to give us any further insight into the connection in which Christianity, as a new form of the religious consciousness, stands to the previous development of religion.

Now the main connection between the old religions and Christianity has generally been taken to consist in the absence from the former of what Christianity supplied. In many respects, it is said there is a positive antagonism between it and them. But apart from this, we may find the point of connection in the religious feelings and cravings which the old religions failed to satisfy. The unbelief and superstition which were present in Paganism and Judaism were certainly opposed to Christianity; yet there were elements present in that unbelief and superstition which facilitated a transition to Christianity, arising as they did from a state of feeling which was very favourable to its reception. There were various kinds of unbelief. There was an unbelief which sprang from a craving for belief which received no satisfaction from all that the philosophy and religion of the old world gave. The human heart has a desire which will not be denied to know and to have intercourse with the supernatural. The prevalence of an all-denying scepticism does not quench the desire, but rather intensifies it. The same was the case with the correlative of unbelief, superstition. At the root of much of it there lay a need which looked for satisfaction, and which could find it only in Christianity, the need of deliverance from the deep-felt schism within, and of atonement with an unknown God. This was what men were seeking, whether or not they were consciously aware of it.[1]

Here we are referred to the immediate religious sense as the ground why men were prepared to receive Christianity. Now Christianity indubitably has its roots, as every other religion has, in this primary ground of all religious life. But to refer Christianity to nothing but this is no explanation at all of the general question: this is merely a vague and general speculation how individuals might be affected. The question is not what peculiar frame of mind or position of circumstances might dispose this or that individual to adopt Christianity. We have to regard Christianity not as it affected individuals, but objectively, as an influence affecting the world. It must have had some connection with the previous religious development of the world, not merely in the way of difference, but also in the way of similarity and of adopting what it found. And we have to inquire what this connection was. We have seen that the universal tendency of Christianity presupposed the universalism to which the general consciousness of the age had broadened out under the influence of the Roman empire. Now, if this be the case, it must be no less true that those elements of Christianity which make it an absolute as well as a universal religion stood in the same vital and necessary connection with the previous religious and spiritual development of the world. Here, however, it is of the first importance not to take up any narrow or one-sided notion of what the absolute character of Christianity consists in. Some

[1] Compare Neander's General History of the Christian Religion and Church, i. 5, sq. and 46. (Bohn's translation.)

have thought to find it in the fact that Christianity gives so full and welcome a satisfaction to man's longing for belief, or in the fact that it is a supernatural revelation, a system of universal efficacy for the reconciliation of man with God, or in the fact that it places before us in the person of its founder one who is the Son of God and the God-man, in the sense in which the Church uses these words. But this only leads to the question what there is in these features of Christianity to place it so high above the old religions. For in one way or another these elements of religion were believed to be present in them all. Every religion claimed to be a supernatural revelation; there was no want of arrangements for bringing about the reconciliation of man with God, and the communion of man with God was believed before Christianity to be provided for by beings whose functions were nearly the same as those of the Christian Son of God. What is it, then, that gives Christianity its peculiar and specific superiority above all that more or less resembled it in the ancient world? Again, Christianity may be regarded under various points of view, each of which will only exhibit to us one of its various sides. But what is Christianity itself? What common unity underlies these different aspects, and combines them into a whole? We answer in a word, its spirituality. We find Christianity to be far more free than any other religion from everything merely external, sensuous, or material. It lays its foundations more deeply in the inmost essence of man's nature and in the principles of the moral consciousness. It knows, as it says of itself, no worship of God but the worship in spirit and in truth. When we inquire what constitutes the absolute character of Christianity, we must point to its spirituality. In this wide view of the absolute nature of Christianity, let us inquire what points of contact it presents with the movement prior to or contemporary with its appearance. What features do we find in the general advance of the human mind during those ages that may be said to be akin to Christianity, and to have been essentially preparing the way for its reception?

Decay and dissolution, as we have said, had completely seized on the old religions. At the time when they came in contact with Christianity, no one who had become aware of their imperfection and finiteness, or who had seen them as they really were, could escape the sense of an infinite void, or fail to feel a craving for a contentment which nothing in the whole range of these religions could give, and a need for something positive to which the religious instinct might attach itself. But what had so thoroughly broken up the old faiths? They were crumbling into ruins before Christianity came to touch them. Some other power must have been at work on them which was stronger than they. It is a mistake to think that ages of transition, like that immediately preceding the appearance of Christianity, are simply times of decay and disintegration, when all spiritual and religious life is completely moribund. At such a time the old forms in which religion used to move do indeed decay. What used to fill them with life and reality departs from them, till the hollow forms alone are left. But the very cause of this process is, that the spirit, whose religious feelings the forms once served to express, has expanded and risen beyond them. Where an old system decays we may be sure it is because the new truth which is to succeed it is already there; the old would not decay if the new had not arrived, be it but in germ, and been long labouring to undermine and eat away the existing structure. It may be long before a new kind of spiritual life takes such shape as to arrest the notice of the world. But the plastic spirit is active all the while, though unobserved; the leaven is working deep out of sight, and the unresting vital process cannot be stayed, but goes evenly and regularly forward, in its successive stages, until it has produced a new creation.

The decay of Paganism is not to be dated from the time when Christianity appeared, and can in no way be said to have been brought about by Christianity. It had been in course of progress ever since Greek religion began to be accompanied by Greek philosophy. Not only did this philosophy deal with the popular mythical beliefs in the way of critical reflection, and so place itself above them, but it created a new world which arose in total independence of the popular faith, in the realm of pure thought. In this world the spirit which could no longer find its adequate expression in the myths of the popular religion, found a new sphere for its thought and intuition. Thus, next to the religious teaching of the Old Testament, Greek philosophy forms the most important spiritual antecedent of Christianity. And its relation to Christianity has always been one of chief points taken up in the attempts that have been made to estimate the true position of Christianity in history. But here also it has been customary to urge the negative rather than the positive side of the relation; and only in the case of Platonism is it perceived that along with much which was defective and one-sided it possessed elements which prepared the way for Christianity. It spiritualised religious thought; it turned away from the many gods of Paganism, and pointed to a certain spiritual Divine unity above them; it struck out many ideas which are akin to Christianity, as that of a redemption, in the sense of deliverance from the blind power of nature which opposes the divine; it gave the elevating conception of a divine life which stood above the influence of the Nature-powers. Much more unfavourable judgments are passed not only on Epicureanism but even on Stoicism. It is self-evident, we are told, that a system like the former, offering atheism for theology, and making happiness the highest good, is utterly alien to Christianity. And it is urged that there is the strongest possible contrast between the humility of the believing Christian and the proud self-sufficiency of the Stoic sage. Such indeed must be our judgment, so long as we confine our attention to the points where the contrast is most evident and extreme. But our task is not to attend to mere particulars. We have rather to attempt to interpret all the phenomena in question as parts of the great historical development. The question we have to ask is, how Greek philosophy, such as it was from its principal epoch downwards, was related to Christianity?

In how different a light does this question appear when we call to mind the well-known parallel drawn by so many writers between

Socrates and Christ! The parallel is certainly not without justice. Christianity closes a movement which arose upon the soil of Pagan religion and philosophy, and the seed of which was sown by Socrates. And if this be the case, then each of the principal forms assumed by Greek philosophy during this interval must have been a step in the preparation for Christianity. An investigation of the course taken by Greek thought during this most important period will contribute much to make it clear to us why Christianity entered into the world at this particular time and at no other. Those who hold the essence of Christianity to be its character as a supernatural revelation, can see little need for expatiating over so wide a field in inquiring after its origin. To go back to the epoch of Socrates must seem to them superfluous. But in any case Christianity must be acknowledged to have a genuinely human side; and when we try to form a distinct conception of its first beginnings, of the manner in which it made its way into the world and sought to win an entrance to men's hearts, its genuinely human character comes clearly before us. The words in which it first announces itself to the world, its call for $\mu\epsilon\tau\acute{a}\nu\omicron\iota\alpha$, its bidding men go into themselves, this at once defines the relation which it takes up towards man, and the stand-point from which it interprets the relation between man and God. It begins with an earnest call to man to direct his gaze within, to turn in to himself, to become acquainted with himself in the deep places of his own self-consciousness. In this way he is to learn what his relation to God is, and what it ought to be, and to become aware of those needs in his moral nature out of which the cry for redemption proceeds, in all their depth and intensity. Looking away from all that is unessential, and asking what is the element in Christianity which makes it a religion in the absolute sense, we find that it rests on man's knowledge of himself as a moral subject. Had not man's moral consciousness been already fully developed in all those bearings which lend it its profounder interests, Christianity could not have gained a footing in the world in its peculiar character as an essentially moral religion.

Now when and how was it that man first recognised himself as a moral being? It was when he awoke to the idea of himself as a subject, a being essentially distinct from and independent of the world without: when he first grasped the principle of subjectivity, that the true standard of thought and action is in the inner life. Socrates marks an epoch, because this step of progress is due to him.[1] He first urged, that man should come back to himself, and search his own being: the mind was to withdraw from the outward world, and to concentrate itself on the world within. Thus, occupying himself with the contents of pure thought, man would find himself face to face with the only real and true existences. In the same way, in the practical sphere, by referring virtue to knowledge, by following the command 'know thyself,' and turning the moral consciousness back upon itself, man was to find in the conviction which arose out of his own nature his rule of action. From this point forward we have a long and uninterrupted series of philosophical developments. First the Platonic and Aristotelian theories of knowledge, which aimed at determining the general nature of things, then the ethical systems of the Stoics and Epicureans, and following on the last, the Sceptical and Eclectic movements, in all of which practical interests were more and more preferred to theoretical, and the moral nature of man was regarded in the same light as Christianity regards it, and made the chief object of philosophical reflection. More directly and earnestly than any other schools, the Stoics and Epicureans applied themselves to discover man's moral end, and the conditions under which it is attained. All those questions to which so many discussions were devoted, concerning the idea of the good, the highest good, the relation of virtue to happiness, the value of moral action, etc., are but the ethical expression of the problem laid before man by Christianity as a question of religion. Divergent as the two systems were, the very opposition between them served to rouse

---

[1] Cf. my Essay: Das Christliche d. Platonismus, oder Socrates und Christus, p. 20; in the Drei Abhandlungen, Leipzig, 1875, 247 *sq*. Zeller: die Philos. d. Griechen, 2d edition, ii. 78; p. 100 in Reichel's translation.

moral thought. The moral consciousness of the age was so enlarged and educated in every direction by these discussions, that Christianity found the ground prepared on which its higher moral and religious task could be accomplished.

Stoicism, on the ground of the strictness and purity of its principles, may seem to claim an unquestionable superiority over Epicureanism. But it has justly been acknowledged[1] that the latter system, leading man away from the outer world, and bidding him seek his highest happiness in the fair humanity of a cultivated mind content with itself, did a useful work; that by its mildness, no less than Stoicism by its austerity, it contributed to develop and diffuse a free and universal morality. Both schools started from the common leading idea of the post-Aristotelian philosophy —the postulate, that man should withdraw himself within the sphere of his inner consciousness, and seek for his perfect contentment there. The vocation and happiness of man, according to the one, are found in that submission of the individual to the reason and the law of the universe, which is virtue. According to the other, they consist in independence of all external things, in consciousness of this independence, in the undisturbed enjoyment of the life a man has to live, in freedom from pain. Thus, although by different ways, both sought to reach the same goal, namely, the freedom of the conscious self: and this led them at once to a position which is quite inconsistent with the fundamental religious sentiment of Christianity. The wise man of the Stoics, and the wise man of the Epicureans, are ideals equally strange to Christianity. The common endeavour of the two systems to make man free by bidding him rest on nothing but himself, to confer upon him, in the infiniteness of his thought and self-consciousness, complete independence of all without him, involves both in the same contrast with the Christian feeling of dependence. But even the Stoic saw himself compelled to descend from the height of his moral idealism, and to recognise its limita-

[1] Zeller: die Philos. d. Griechen, ii. 263; Stoics and Epicureans (Dr. Reichel's translation), p. 445 sq.

tions in the presence of practical needs. And as we mark how Scepticism was the next stage at which Greek philosophy arrived in its development out of these systems, we see that that unbounded freedom of the inward consciousness which they claimed led to nothing but the discovery of the essential limits of knowledge. The opposing tendencies were found to be mutually destructive, knowledge was despaired of, and the mind withdrew into itself. But though drawing back into itself and seeking to suffice for itself without the support of outward positive truth, the mind could not remain so entirely inactive as not to turn to one alternative or another as the more probable. Thus Scepticism in its turn gave birth to Eclecticism. This mode of thought escaped from the harshness and one-sidedness of the earlier schools by choosing the best that it could find, and removing the features that it desired to retain from their logical connection in the systems to which they originally belonged. And we are concerned to notice that Eclecticism readily lent itself to promote the union of religion with practical interests. At the Christian era it was more widely diffused than any other way of thinking, and had grown into a popular philosophy and natural theology. The writings of its chief representatives, Cicero, Seneca, Epictetus, and Marcus Aurelius, contain many elements allied to Christianity. Indeed, so much is this the case that their views and doctrines might appear to be something more than merely the approved result of all the ethical discussion that had gone before, as it had learned to meet the practical wants of the age. In reading their writings we seem to be upon the ground of Christian moral and religious teaching. We come upon sentences the Christian tone of which surprises us.

The fixed first principle of Eclecticism (which, like other systems, required a standard whereby to test different opinions) is with Cicero, the best known and most popular writer of the school, the immediate consciousness of man, his inner self-assurance, the natural instinct for truth, or innate knowledge. The germs of morality are implanted in us. Nature has not only given us the moral faculty, but has bestowed on us the fundamental ethical conceptions, as an original endowment, and prior to any instruction; our task is merely to work out these innate conceptions. The nearer a man stands to nature the more clearly will these original ideas be reflected in him: it is from children that we learn what is in conformity with nature. The belief in God rests on a like foundation. By virtue of the affinity of the human spirit to God, the knowledge of God is given to us along with the knowledge of ourselves. Man need but recollect his own origin, and he is led to his Creator. Nature itself, therefore, tells us of the existence of God: and the strongest proof of this truth is its universal recognition.[1] In these few sentences we see clearly traced the outlines of a natural theology, the construction of which was afterwards continued within Christianity and on a genuinely Christian foundation. The view which declares that the consciousness of self is also, and at once, the consciousness of God, will naturally arrive at the conclusion that man's original knowledge is a thing given him from without, and will look to receive in the immediate consciousness itself, but from some source of knowledge higher than our finite selves, the revelation of Deity. It was in such a longing for a higher communication of truth and an immediate revelation that Greek philosophy finally terminated its course in Neo-Platonism.

[1] Cf. Zeller ii. 585. The natural theology which arose upon the foundation of Stoicism appears in its purest form, and attains its closest analogy to the doctrines of Christianity, in the writings of Seneca. Cf. my dissertation, Seneca und Paulus: das Verhältniss des Stoicismus zum Christenthum nach den Schriften Seneca's; (originally in Hilgenfeld's Ztschr. 1858, p. 161, 441—now re-published in the "Drei Abhandlungen" cited above). I have there pointed out a peculiar characteristic of Seneca's Stoicism, viz., his tendency, in proportion as he departs from the old system of the Porch, to approach the Christian religious position. I have considered this tendency under the following heads: 1. God and the feeling of dependence. 2. Man and his need of salvation. 3. The relation of man to his fellow-men. 4. The belief in a future life. 5. The difference of principle between the Stoic and the Christian views of the world. I have tried to show the groundlessness of the conclusion, that the above-mentioned tendency must be ascribed to Seneca's having made acquaintance with Christianity as it was preached in his neighbourhood.

Thus our survey of the progress of Greek thought shows us that Christianity, which we are considering in its relation to Paganism, entered the general stream of history at an epoch when preparation had been made for it in many and important ways. It came at a time when the heathen world had come to feel the profound significance of the moral consciousness, and all that was most spiritual and most practically important in the results arrived at during the whole long course of Greek ethical speculation had become the common belief, the essential contents of the mind of the age. All men now recognised the truth that man was a moral being called to devote his life to fulfilling a definite moral task. In Christianity the various tendencies which had hitherto been seeking the same end by different ways meet together to be fixed in definite notions and presented in the fullest and richest expression. Such, when approached from the side of Paganism, is the position of Christianity in the chain of history. As the absolute religion, however, it unites both the older religions. Let us therefore consider that element in it which lies towards Judaism, and observe how on this side also it embraces in itself the highest spiritual attainments which Judaism had made.

Christianity arose on Jewish soil, and it is connected with Judaism far more closely and directly than with Paganism. It professes to be nothing more than spiritualised Judaism: it strikes its deepest roots into the soil of the Old Testament religion. In Paganism, Greek philosophy had developed the moral consciousness till it reached a stage at which Christianity could combine with it: in Judaism religion arrived at the stage at which Christianity could adopt it. The special superiority which distinguished the Hebrew religion from all the religions of the heathen world was the pure and refined monotheistic idea of God, which from the earliest times had been the essential foundation of the Old Testament faith. In its consciousness of God, therefore, Christianity feels itself at one with Judaism as with no other faith. The God of the Old Testament is the God of the New, and all the teaching of the Old Testament concerning the essential distinctness of God from the world, and the absolute majesty and holiness of his nature, is also an essential part of Christian doctrine. But on the other hand the Old Testament conceived God as the God, not of the human race, but of a particular nation. And the particularism, the limitation of the blessings and hopes of religion to the Jewish race, which was partly the cause and partly the effect of this conception of God, stood in the strongest contrast to the spirit of Christianity. If the Old Testament notion of God was ever to be a sufficient form for that consciousness of God which belonged to the universal and absolute nature of Christianity, it was necessary that it should first be freed from this national one-sidedness and defectiveness. It was necessary that it should discard all that belonged only to the narrow range of vision of the Jewish theocracy, and that it should no longer, in accordance with the conceptions of antiquity, ascribe to God a human form and human passions.

The historical experiences of the Jews had an important influence on their religion. Not only did their religious conceptions undergo various modifications, their religious consciousness itself did not stand still, but became gradually wider and more spiritual. On the other hand, however, the hard fortunes of the people only made them cling more strongly to their belief that they alone were the people of God, and to their national prejudices and traditional observances. In this respect the circumstances by which the Jews were surrounded in the kingdoms founded after the death of Alexander, especially in Egypt, and in such a city as Alexandria, first brought a radical change. Here first took place that transformation of Judaism by which it passed beyond the barriers of its national and political exclusiveness, and accepted the influence of new and formerly alien and repugnant ideas.[1] The dispersion of the Jews among foreign nations had before this brought into existence a new class in whom Judaism was mixed, as the circumstances would have led us to expect, with Greek culture and manners. These formed a link, such as had hitherto been wanting, between Jew

---

[1] Cf. Georgii: die neuesten Gegensätze in Auffassung der alexandrinischen Religions-philosophie, insbesondere des jüdischen alexandrinismus. Illgen's Ztschr. für hist. Theologie, 1839, Nos. 3 and 4.

and Gentile, a circumstance which could not fail to have the most important bearing on the intellectual and religious development of mankind. But the Hellenism which had thus arisen only acquired its full significance when it gave birth to an entirely new form of thought in the Græco-Jewish philosophy which sprang up at Alexandria. At such a place the Jews experienced the full power of the Greek spirit, and the desire to gain a closer acquaintance with the ideas and doctrines of Greek philosophy was not to be resisted. The mere existence of such an interest implied that they had advanced beyond the standpoint of pure Judaism; and the more they occupied themselves with Greek philosophy, and became conscious of its charm, the more did they necessarily find themselves in conflict with the religious views and feelings of their race. On the one hand, they could not shake off their interest in the new ideas; on the other, their ancestral faith affirmed its old indefeasible authority. How was the contradiction to be overcome? The reconciliation was accomplished, as is well known, by allegorical interpretation applied to the Scriptures. According to the Jew's view of his sacred books, nothing could be true which was not to be found in them. They were the source of all truth: they must, therefore, be the source of the ideas which he had now adopted. All that was necessary was to find the right key for the explanation of the books of the Old Testament, and then exegesis could bring forth out of those books the ideas which the commentator himself had unconsciously put into them. In this way there arose an entirely new form of Judaism. Men fancied that they were keeping a firm hold of the old faith, but in reality they had substituted entirely new ideas in its place; and while it was supposed that the new matter was contained in the Old Testament, the words of the text were turned into mere vehicles of a doctrine of which the writers had never dreamed. The peculiar character of this Alexandrine Judaism consisted in this, that the limits of the old Jewish particularism were broken through and set aside, as far as this could possibly be done without completely abandoning the standpoint of the Old Testament religion. The doctrines of this religion received a form, modified in many respects, and generally freer and more spiritual; new ideas were introduced which involved an entirely different theory of the world from that of Judaism; and above all, the Old Testament conception of God was freed from all those elements which belonged merely to the narrow sphere of the Jewish theocracy, and raised to a much higher plane of thought. The profound influence which the Alexandrian philosophy of religion came afterwards, in its highest and most elaborate form as it appears in the writings of Philo, to exercise on Christian theology, shows distinctly that the mode of thought on which it was based must have had great affinity with the spirit of Christianity.

Our task, however, merely requires us to trace its influence in that narrower sphere where it came into close contact with the very earliest Christianity. From this point of view the two sects of the Therapeutae and the Essenes, especially the latter, are a very noteworthy phenomenon.[1]

The Therapeutae are the intermediate link between the Hellenistic Judaism of Alexandria and the Essenes of Palestine. The latter however, closely as they are related to the Egyptian Therapeutae, cannot be classed with them, but must be reckoned among the sects into which the Judaism of Palestine was divided. They represent Judaism in the form which it assumed when the Jew of Palestine came to find in the Graeco-Alexandrian doctrine, what his brethren abroad had already found in it, a deeply religious conception of life. This is what places the Essenes in so close a

---

[1] On the Essenes, cf. Zeller, iii. 235, Ritschl, Theol. Jahrb. 1855, p. 315, sq., and die Entstehung der alt-kathol. Kirche, 2d ed., 179, sqq., traces Essenism to an endeavour to realise the ideal of the priestly kingdom held up before the people of Israel, Exod. xix. 6, and to form a society of priests answering to it. Zeller opposes this view, and argues (Theol. Jahrb., 1856, p. 401, sq.) for the common supposition of a connection between Essenism and the Orphico-pythagorean discipline and view of life which were so widely diffused in the ancient world, and were not without influence upon the Jews. The considerations which he adduces are enough to confute Hilgenfeld's view, that Essenism owed its origin to the apocalyptic prophecy which was so rife at the time (Die jüdische Apokalyptik in ihrer geschichtlichen Entwickelung; Jena, 1857, p. 245, sq.), and are likely to assert themselves against any similarly eccentric theories which may yet be put forth.

relation with Christianity. Of course it cannot be thought for a moment that Christianity itself sprang from Essenism; yet it is impossible not to see that the religious view of life held by the Essenes is far more closely allied to the original spirit of Christianity than any of the peculiar doctrines or practices which distinguished the sects of the Pharisees and Sadducees. They certainly attached great value to certain outward practices, yet they were not entangled either in the ordinances and traditions of the Judaism of the Pharisees, or in the purely external forms of the Levitic temple worship. Their religious feeling was more spiritual and inward than that of the other sects, and had a thoroughly practical tendency. The highest object of life was to them to elevate themselves above the material and sensuous, and to turn their whole activity into a constant exercise of all such practices as could bring them nearer to this great end. The name Essenes indicates that they claimed to be physicians of souls. As such they proceeded on the principle of making use of all means which seemed adapted to promote the soul's healthy and vigorous life, and to keep it ever open to receive the influences and revelations of the higher world. Essenism has many features which remind us of the spirit of primitive Christianity; such as its prohibition of oaths, the zeal it encouraged in the practice of the duties of benevolence, and its community of goods. A peculiarly characteristic trait, however, is its principle of voluntary poverty. The view taken of poverty is, that it is better to be poor and possess as little as possible in this world, in order to be so much the richer in the good things of the world to come.[1] This is the same love of poverty which we find in Christianity when its first disciples are called blessed because they are poor in spirit. We may very reasonably assume that in addition to those who carried out all the outward practices which appear in the description of the sect, Essenism had many friends

---

[1] Cf. my Comment. de Ebionitarum origine, et doctrina ab Essenis repetenda, 1831. Notice the passages which I have there quoted from Philo, Quod omnis probus liber, ed. Mang. ii. 457, de vita contempl. p. 473; and from Josephús, de Bello Jud. ii. 8. 3. See also Dähne: die jüdisch-alexandrinische Religionsphilosophie, i. p. 476.

and sympathisers who did not think it necessary to declare their adherence in this way. It was not only a sect, but a widely diffused way of thinking and a view of life which was carried out with various modifications, in one case with more and in another with less of the element of discipline. We may say that all those who shared in the deep and general tendency of the religious spirit to leave what was outward and concentrate itself upon the inward, were touched more or less by the Essene spirit. If this be so, then Essenism is undoubtedly one of the deepest and most truly spiritual points of contact between Judaism and Christianity. And even when we look at merely outward relations, how near do these allied phenomena of the religious life lie to each other. The Essenes had their settlements in those same Jewish border-lands inhabited by a population mixed with Gentiles, in which Christianity first began to preach the blessedness of the poor. Where else could the gospel which was preached to the poor have found hearts so ready to receive it, as among those meek ones of the land, whose style of piety was in so many ways akin to the attitude of mind out of which Christianity itself proceeded?

Thus we find that all these various movements, starting as they do from such widely different quarters, meet each and all at the same point. When placed in its position as connected with the history of preceding times, Christianity appears as the natural unity of all those elements. Various and manifold as they are, they belong to one and the same process of development. As this process moves gradually forward, and eliminates more and more completely all that bears the stamp of particularism and subjectivity, we see that it can have no other issue than at the point where the origin of Christianity is found. On what grounds then can we regard Christianity itself as a phenomenon purely supernatural, as an absolute miracle introduced into the world's history without the operation of any natural causes, and therefore incapable of being comprehended as belonging to any historical connection, when we find in every direction, wherever we turn, numerous points of connection and affinity in which it is linked with the most intimate bonds to the whole history of the development of mankind? It contains nothing that was not conditioned by a series of causes and effects going before; nothing that had not been long prepared in different ways, and carried forward towards that stage of development at which we find it in Christianity; nothing that had not been previously recognised in one form or another, as a necessary result of reasoned thought, or as a need of the human heart, or as a requirement of the moral consciousness. What room is there then to wonder that that which had so long been in different ways the goal of all the endeavours of the human reason, and had been forcing itself upon the opening and growing human consciousness as its proper and necessary contents, which could not be denied, should at last have found its simplest, purest, and most natural expression in the form in which it appeared in Christianity?

When, however, we go on to consider the nature of Christianity itself, we find it presented to us under many very different aspects, which do not admit of being all placed under the same point of view. The question thus arises, whether what has been said holds good of Christianity in its whole scope and extent, or only of one particular side of it, and if it applies to that which we must regard as the true core and centre of its organism? When Christianity is considered from the point of view which we have set forth, it is of course obvious that the side of it which is meant is that on which all those points of connection and of affinity are to be found which bring it into so intimate and vital a relation with the whole preceding history of human development. But, it may well be asked, is it on this side that we find the original and substantial essence of Christianity? is it not rather a secondary and subordinate feature of it on which we have been dwelling? Is it possible to speak in any real sense of the essence and contents of Christianity without making the person of its founder the main object of our consideration? Must we not recognise the peculiar character of Christianity as consisting in this, that whatever it is, it is simply on account of the person of its founder? And if this be so, is it not a matter of very slight importance to seek to understand the nature and contents of Christianity in the light of the connection it may have had with the history of the world? Is not its whole meaning and significance derived from the person of its founder? Can our historical consideration of it set out from any other point than this?

To answer these questions we require to go back to the sources of the gospel history. The most recent critical investigations declare that a great distinction has to be drawn between some of these sources and others.[1] The sources of the Evangelical history are the four gospels. Now the great question is, in what relation we are to place the fourth to the first three. It is impossible to ignore the fact that the conception we form of Christianity will be radically and essentially different, according as we on the one hand take it for granted that the four gospels agree with each other throughout, or on the other recognise the divergences between the Johannine gospel and the three Synoptics as amounting to a contradiction which renders a historical unity impossible.[2]

---

[1] Cf. my work: Kritische Untersuchungen über die kanonischen Evangelien, Tüb. 1847. Köstlin: der Ursprung und die Composition der synoptischen Evangelien, Stuttgart, 1853. Hilgenfeld: die Evangelien nach ihrer Entstehung und geschichtlichen Bedeutung, Leipzig, 1854.

[2] The question which has to be dealt with at this stage is not the authenticity of the Johannine gospel; whoever the writer of the gospel may have been, whether the Apostle John or some other man, it is a plain matter of fact and cannot be denied, that the evangelical history of the fourth gospel is an essentially different one from that of the first three. Now as this historical difference must either be admitted or denied, and no third alternative is possible, we have here the parting of two roads which lead in totally different directions, and issue in totally different conceptions of the whole of Church history. The student who in the strength of dogma overlooks this difference will read the whole history of the Church with other eyes than he who does not regard the interests of dogma as supreme, but makes it his principle that the materials which history has to deal with are to be treated in a strictly historical way. As for the question of authorship, the more the critical dilemma of the Johannine authorship of the gospel and of the Apocalypse is insisted on (as is well done by Lücke in the second edition of his Introduction to the Revelation of John, 1852, p. 659-744), the less will any sophistry be able to prevent the great preponderance of evidence from inclining to the side of the Apocalypse, when the external testimonies for the Johannine origin of the two works are fairly and impartially weighed.

If it be assumed that the four gospels agree with each other and are capable of being harmonised, then the absolute importance which the gospel of John assigns to the person of Jesus must determine our whole view of the gospel history. We must then regard Christianity as consisting in the fact of the incarnation of the eternal Logos : it is a miracle in the strictest sense, and absolutely. The human is lost in the divine, the natural in the supernatural. Whenever the first three gospels disagree with the fourth, the authority of the latter must be held to be decisive. This, however, amounts to a complete abandonment of all historical treatment of the gospel history. The history is so determined and absorbed by the element of miracle, as nowhere to afford any firm footing for the scientific inquirer. And more than this : to uphold the claim of the absolute miracle of the one gospel, the historical credibility of the other three is brought down to so low a level that they virtually forfeit their position as historical sources. The only way of escape from all these difficulties is to admit the conviction that the gospel of John stands in quite a different relation to the Synoptics from that which is generally assumed. Whether we look to its differences from the Synoptics, or to its general spirit and character, we see that it is impossible to allow to such a gospel as the Johannine the character of a historical narrative, even in the limited sense in which the Synoptics can be called historical. When the different accounts disagree we shall accordingly take our stand on the side of the Synoptics. In this way we escape the consequences which follow inevitably when John is placed on the same level with the Synoptics ; namely, that difficulties and objections are raised on each side, and with equal right, and the whole gospel narrative brought into suspicion. We now obtain a firmer historical basis. But even here we are warned by criticism that the ground on which a trustworthy history can be constructed is narrower than we thought. Recent investigations into the relations of the gospels to one another show us that the Synoptics cannot simply be placed side by side as of equal value. The gospel of Mark is so largely indebted to the other two that we cannot regard it as an independent source at all.[1] The gospel of Luke is coloured by the Paulinism of its author, and cannot be regarded as an impartial narrative. We are thus thrown back on the gospel of Matthew as comparatively the most original and trustworthy source of the Evangelical history.

An examination of the contents of this Gospel shows us that there are two distinct elements present in it: the doctrine, and the purely historical narrative. The early tradition about Matthew states that he wrote down the λόγια, the sayings and discourses of Jesus, for the Hebrews, and in the Hebrew language. Now the Greek Gospel of Matthew which we have answers to this description. The great bulk of its contents, the body of the work, consists of the discourses and sayings of Jesus. His public ministry opens very significantly with the Sermon on the Mount. We may justly conclude from this that the author's original and leading idea was to treat the life and the whole manifestation of Jesus from this point of view. There is another narrative which deals largely in the discourses of Jesus. The discourses of John's Gospel, however, turn as well as the rest of that work on the person of Jesus and his superhuman dignity, as the theme which they all help to illustrate. Such is not the case here. The whole scope and spirit of the Gospel are different. What the discourses of this Gospel present to us is the human and familiar element of Christ's teaching, the direct appeal to the moral and religious consciousness, the simple answer to the question which naturally came up first of all—in what state of mind he must be, and what he must do, who would enter into the kingdom of God. We do not mean to deny that the gospel of Matthew also ascribes its full significance to the person of Jesus. Even in the Sermon on the Mount there are some hints of such a doctrine. But in the thought and imagery of the Sermon on the Mount the personal element remains as it were in the background of the scene; the discourse does not derive its importance from the person; it is

---

[1] Cf. my work: das Markus-evangelium nach seinem Ursprung und Character; Tüb. 1851. Theol. Jahrb. 1853, p. 54, sq. Köstlin, op. cit. p. 310, sq.

rather the profound and weighty discourse that reveals to us the true character and greatness of the speaker. It is the thing itself that speaks here; it is the inner force of truth making its way straight to men's hearts, which here announces itself in all its significance for the history of the world.

Now what does this direct and original element, this principle of Christianity, consist in, as we find it expressed both in the Sermon on the Mount, and in the parables, and in the whole of the doctrinal contents of the Gospel of Matthew? It may be shortly summed up under the following heads:—

It is in the beatitudes of the Sermon on the Mount that we obtain the deepest and most comprehensive insight into the fundamental way of looking at things, the fundamental mood, out of which Christianity proceeded. What is it that finds expression in all those utterances in which blessedness is said to belong to the poor in spirit, to those who mourn, to the meek, to those who hunger and thirst after righteousness, to the pure in heart, to the peacemakers, to those who are persecuted for righteousness' sake? It is religious consciousness which is penetrated by the deepest sense of the pressure of the finite and of all the contradictions of the present, and yet is infinitely exalted, and knows itself, in spite of this, to be far superior to everything finite and limited. The most pregnant expression for this, the original Christian consciousness, is the poverty of the poor in spirit. They are rightly placed at the head of all the different classes who are called blessed.[1]

But the poor here spoken of must not be taken to be, as the ordinary interpretation has it, merely those who feel themselves inwardly poor and empty from a sense of their spiritual needs. We shall have an inadequate idea of what this poverty denotes if we do not take outward bodily poverty as an essential part of the conception. We are not at liberty to overlook this feature of it, since, in the first place, the parallel passage in Luke (vi. 20) gives us not the πτωχοὶ τῷ πνεύματι of Matthew, but

[1] Cf. my Kritische Untersuchungen, p. 447, sq.

simply πτωχοί; and in the second place, the history of the Gospel shows us that it found its first adherents almost exclusively among the poor. This being so, we see that this poverty of spirit is a poverty which, when looked at in a spiritual way, is exactly the opposite of what it appears to be outwardly. Since these poor ones accept their poverty gladly and voluntarily, and of their own free-will elect to be just what they are, their poverty becomes to them a sign and evidence that, though outwardly poor, they are not poor in reality. Here they are the poor and those that have nothing; but there they are all the more certain to be the opposite of what they are here. They are the poor who have nothing, and yet possess all things. They have nothing, since their bodily poverty consists in having none of the goods that go to make property in this world; and what they may regard as their possession in the world to come is for them a thing entirely in the future. They having nothing, they live and move in an atmosphere of longing and desire for that which they have not; but, in this longing and desire, they virtually possess that to which their yearning and desire are going forth. Their having nothing makes them to be those who have all things; their poverty is their riches; the kingdom of heaven is even now their sure and peculiar possession, because as surely as they have nothing here, so surely they have all things there. In this contrast of having and not having, poverty and riches, earth and heaven, the present and the future, the Christian consciousness attains its purest ideality; it is the ideal unity of all the contradictions which force themselves upon the consciousness, as long as it confines itself to visible objects. All that the most developed dogmatic consciousness can comprise is already present here; and yet the whole significance of the early Christian idea consists in the fact that it has not ceased to be the immediate unity of all antitheses. All the beatitudes, variously as they sound, are but different expressions of the same original idea and mood which lie at the root of the Christian consciousness. What they express is the simple feeling of the need of redemption, which contains in itself implicitly, though as yet undeveloped, the antithesis of sin and grace, and is its own sufficient evidence of the reality of the redemption which it longs for. It is because all antitheses are here held together in their unity that this original Christian consciousness is so vigorous and rich in thought. It is not only a deep and intense self-consciousness; it is also a lofty and commanding world-consciousness. We see this from the words which Jesus uses immediately after the beatitudes, where He calls his disciples the salt of the earth, which must never lose its savour if the world is not to be deprived of the power which, in deed and truth, holds it together, and preserves it from decay; and the light of the world which must not be set under a bushel, but must shine before the whole world, that men may see the good works of those who let their light shine, and may glorify their Father which is in heaven.

The beatitudes of the Sermon on the Mount express, in an absolute manner, what constitutes the inmost self-consciousness of the Christian, as it is in itself, and apart from external relations. The original and radical element of Christianity appears further in the form of absolute moral command in the controversial part of the discourse which is directed against the Pharisees, and in other parts of it. In the Sermon on the Mount Jesus insists emphatically on purity and singleness of heart, on a morality which does not consist merely in the outward act, but in the inner disposition; and upon such an earnest and moral observance of the law as can admit of no arbitrary exception or limitation, nor tolerate any false hypocritical pretences, or any dividedness or want of singleness of heart. Here, however, the question may arise whether this principle be new or peculiar to Christianity. Jesus declared at the outset that he was not come to destroy the law and the prophets, but to fulfil them, and might thus appear to have taken up an entirely affirmative position towards the Old Testament. It might be said[1] that the difference

---

[1] Cf. Ritschl, die Entstehung der alt-katholischen Kirche, Bonn 1850, p. 27, sq. Ritschl changed his views in the second edition, but this fact does not invalidate

between the teaching of Jesus and the law, or the Old Testament, is one not of quality, but of quantity. On this view no new principle is advanced in his teaching; all that is done is to widen the application of the moral precepts which the law contained, and assert their authority over the whole extent of the moral sphere to which they are capable of referring. That is given back to the law which should never have been taken away from it. The law is declared to be capable of expansion in its meaning and its range of application, and this is said to be done. This interpretation of the Sermon on the Mount appeals to the fact, that in the further discussion of the subject, individual injunctions of the law are taken up, and each of them brought back to the original meaning of the law, or interpreted in a sense which satisfies the moral consciousness. But though there is no enunciation of a general principle which is to apply to all cases alike, yet when we consider what is said to be the true fulfilling of the law in each separate instance, and see how in each instance what is done is to contrast the outward with the inward, to disregard the mere act as such, and lay stress on the disposition as that which alone confers any moral value on a man's acts, we cannot but recognise in this a new principle, and one which differs essentially from Mosaism. What the law contained, it is true, but only implicitly, is now said to be of most importance, and enunciated as the principle of morality. The expansion of the law quantitatively amounts to a qualitative difference. The inner is opposed to the outer, the disposition to the act, the spirit to the letter. This is the essential root-principle of Christianity; and, in insisting that the absolute moral value of a man depends simply and solely on his disposition, Christianity was essentially original.

In this way the affirmative relation which Jesus assumed towards the law involves in itself the opposite relation of antithesis to the law. If this be so, it is certainly difficult to

the accuracy of the position described in the text as one which has been and may be held.

understand how Jesus could say that not the least jot of the law, not one of its least commandments, should be taken away. How could he say this, when the very opposite came about so soon afterwards, and the whole law was declared to be abolished? How can we imagine him to have affirmed the permanent validity of all the injunctions of the law, when we think, for example, of the one injunction of circumcision? It is impossible to think that Jesus was so little aware of the principle and spirit of his own teaching as this would indicate; and the only choice left to us is, either to suppose him to have spoken exclusively of the moral law, and not to have had the ceremonial law before his mind at all, or to suppose that it was only later that his words received their strong Judaistic colouring. But it was not only to the Old Testament that Jesus took up as affirmative as possible an attitude. Even with respect to the traditions of the Pharisees, and their additions to the law, he did not carry his opposition to the point of encouraging open disregard of them. He paid no heed, it is true, to their exaggerations; against these he asserted what was reasonable in itself, as having indefeasible and incontrovertible authority. This was his position with regard to the acts which were impugned as breaches of the Sabbath law, Matt. xii. 1-14, and in defending himself against the charges of opponents, as at Matt. ix. 11; xv. 1. Yet he recognised the Pharisees as the legitimate successors of Moses. It is they and the Scribes, he says, who sit in the cathedra of Moses, the seat of the teacher and legislator, and the people are bound to follow their precepts, if not their example. Nor does he reject out and out even the pettiest regulations which the scrupulous spirit of Pharisaism had devised for the keeping of the law, Matt. xxiii. 1, *sq.*, 23. It is none the less true, however, that he declares their requirements to be heavy and intolerable burdens, a mode of expression which shows that he would not have allowed the oppression under which the people suffered to continue, Matt. xxiii. 3. He also said, when speaking against the Pharisees, that every plant which his heavenly Father had not planted should be rooted up.

Matt. xv. 13. And his actions were in a great measure directed to this end. One of his chief tasks was to contend against the influence and tendencies of Pharisaism as often as any occasion for doing so arose. This shows how wide the difference really was, and enables us to understand how Jesus could feel that it was unnecessary for him to set forth the antagonism of principle expressly, in all its length and breadth, or to show what it led to, and could be sure that, as the spirit of his teaching came to be understood and realised, it would be worked out to all the results which it necessarily involved. That he himself was thoroughly aware not only of the antagonism of principle, but of the consequences to which it could not fail to lead, appears very distinctly in the saying, Matt. ix. 16, where he not only declares the spirit of the new teaching to be incompatible with that of the old, but also intimates that though he himself had held as far as possible to the old traditional forms, thus putting the new wine into the old bottles, he had done this with a distinct consciousness that the new contents would soon break up the old form. But what was there in the new principle to make it break through the old forms, and supersede all that had gone before? What but its going back to the inward disposition, to that in the consciousness of man which declares itself as its self-existent and absolute contents. As the disposition is to be pure and simple, free from all self-seeking; and as it only is the root from which the fruit of good can spring, so man's consciousness is to be directed to that alone which it recognises as its absolute contents. This is the fundamental idea which runs through the whole of the Sermon on the Mount. The sayings in it which strike us as most significant are, when we examine them, just those which express most directly this absolute character of the Christian consciousness. This consciousness rejects—so the sayings at Matt. vi. 19-24 require —all half-heartedness and dividedness, all sense of separation and limitation; and in the light of it alone does the requirement at vii. 12, in which so many have looked for the root of Christian morality, receive its meaning as a principle. If the Christian is conscious of his absolute standpoint, he must be able to abstract from himself, from his own ego, and to know himself as so much one with all others, that he regards each other man as one who possesses equal rights with himself. And this is what Jesus means when he says of the requirement we are speaking of, that it is the law and the prophets, or equivalent to the Old Testament command, "Thou shalt love thy neighbour as thyself." He who loves his neighbour as himself must renounce everything egotistical, subjective, or peculiar to himself; above the purality of separate subjects, each of whom now is the same as we are, there comes to stand the objective universal, where everything particular and subjective is done away. This universal is that form of action in accordance with which we do to others what we wish that others should do to us. The morally good is thus that which is equally right and good for all, or which can be the object of action for all alike. Here then we meet again the characteristic feature of the Christian principle. It looks beyond the outward, the accidental, the particular, and rises to the universal, the unconditioned, the essential. It places a man's moral value only in that region of his life where he is in the presence of absolute considerations, and his acts possess absolute value. The same energy of consciousness which refuses to find the substantial essence of morality anywhere but in the inmost core of the disposition, asserts itself in the demand to do away with the individual ego by raising it up to the universal ego, the general self, that humanity which is present and is identical with itself in every separate individual. All the difference between this requirement and the commandment of Christ is, that in the latter the former appears in its simplest and most practical expression.

Thus do the absolute contents of the Christian principle find their expression in the moral consciousness. What gives a man his highest moral value is simply the purity of a disposition which is genuinely moral, and rises above all that is finite, particular, or merely subjective. Now, this morality of disposition is also the determining standard of man's relation to God. That which gives him his highest moral value also places him in the adequate relation to God which answers to the idea of God. When man is regarded in his relation to God, the supreme task of the moral consciousness appears in the requirement to be perfect as God is perfect (Matt. v. 48). In this requirement the absolute nature of the Christian principle comes to its most direct expression. Christianity has no other standard for the perfection of man than the absolute standard of the perfection of God. If man is perfect as God is perfect, then, in this absolute perfection, he stands in that adequate relation to God which is expressed by the notion of righteousness. Righteousness in this sense is the absolute condition for entering into the kingdom of God. In the connection in which righteousness is spoken of in the Sermon on the Mount, it can mean nothing but the perfect fulfilment of the law; a fulfilment of the law, however, in that sense only in which Jesus considers the law to possess permanent validity. If it be asked how man can attain this righteousness, we find it to be a peculiarity of the teaching of Jesus, that it simply takes for granted that the law can be fulfilled, and the will of God done on earth as it is in heaven, so as to attain that righteousness which places man in his adequate relation to God. It appears, however, that a forgiveness of sins on God's part, by which the shortcomings in man's conduct may be balanced and made good, is an essential element of this adequate relation; for in the Lord's Prayer the forgiveness of sins is the object of a separate petition. Man must have his faults and sins forgiven, else he cannot enter into the relation which God's will requires. And as the doctrine of Jesus is led by its fundamental principle to estimate a man's whole position as a moral being, not by what he does outwardly, but by what he is in his heart, it can place this righteousness, in which consists the adequate relation of man to the will of God, nowhere but in his inner disposition. Man has this righteousness when he comes into such a frame of mind that he entirely renounces his own will, and devotes himself unreservedly to the will of God. This is worked out in the doctrine of the kingdom of God, which is to be found principally in the parables. In the kingdom of God the will of God is, in the first place, what every individual feels himself required, with the force of an absolute command, to fulfil; and, in the second place, the common task of a certain definite association. All the members of this association are to co-operate to realise the object which the will of God sets before them, and the more closely they are united with each other the more will that object be realised among them. The social element, which is an essential part of religion, is also the leading and essential feature of the kingdom of God. In the doctrine of Jesus we find the Old Testament notion of the theocracy in a spiritualised form; the relation of man to the kingdom of God is based upon none but moral conditions. So exclusively do moral considerations here prevail, that we hear nothing whatever of any of those external means which afterwards came to be considered as the doors which alone could give admission to the kingdom of God or to communion with him. It is taken for granted here that a man's partaking of all the blessings of God's kingdom depends simply on himself, on his own choice, on his own susceptibility to moral influences. How clearly and vividly is this simple truth presented to us in the parable of the sower! What makes a man fit for the kingdom of God is the Word, a term which comprises all those doctrines and precepts, by attending to which a man comes to realise the will of God. The Word is given to man; he can hear and understand it, but everything depends on the reception which he accords to it. And on this point what does ordinary experience show? That as the scattered seed cannot spring up nor bear fruit unless it fall on soil that is suited for it, so men are very differently constituted in respect of their capacity to receive the Word of God. There may be few who receive the Word in a right spirit; yet it is the fault of man himself if the Word does not produce in him all the effects which, for its own part, it is capable of producing. The reason lies simply in the want of a disposition to receive the Word, and this can only be corrected by man's own will. Nothing else is necessary than his will; so simple is man's relation to God. Whether or not he will enter into the kingdom of God depends entirely on himself, on his own will, on his own natural capacity and readiness to receive. This being so, the whole relation of man to the kingdom of God can only be conceived as a moral one; and it is of the first importance that man should recognise this, and not think that any but purely moral conditions can avail to admit him to a part in the kingdom of God. The first requirement, then, which is made upon him is that he renounce every pretension on which he might rely as giving him an outward claim upon God's kingdom—that he should simply go back into himself, and seek nowhere but in himself, in his inner nature, in his moral consciousness, the evidence of his fitness for the kingdom of God. If he thus renounces everything that might place him in a merely external relation to God's kingdom, and takes up this humble and unpretending attitude towards it, which he cannot but assume when he retires simply into his own soul, then he will be fit for the kingdom. His fitness will consist in this, and this alone, that he is entirely receptive for what the kingdom has to give him. This is the meaning of the words in which Jesus deals with pretensions, such as the ideas the Jews held about the kingdom of God frequently led them to put forth—Matt. xviii. 3 : "Except ye be converted, and become as little children, ye shall in no wise enter into the kingdom of God." To become like a little child is to cease wishing to be independent, and to remain in that purely natural relation out of which the sense of dependence and need at once arises. The less a man has in himself that which he ought to have, the purer is the longing for that which only the kingdom of God can give, and the more surely will the kingdom of God be recognised as possessing transcendent and absolute value. This truth is symbolised in the parable of the pearl, for the sake of which the merchant parts with all his other property, Matt. xiii. 45, *sq.* There can be no doubt that the parables which deal with the attitude men take towards the kingdom of God, and which set forth the moral conditions of participation in it, are, together with the Sermon on the Mount, the most genuine and original remains which have come down to us of the teaching of Jesus.

If the ideas on which we have been enlarging are the earliest and most essential element of the teaching of Jesus, it appears to be purely and entirely moral in its tendency, and what it aims at is simply to throw men back on their own moral and religious consciousness. A man has only to become clearly aware of that which announces itself in his own consciousness as his highest moral end, and he can realise it by his own efforts. When we thus look back to its earliest elements, Christianity appears as a purely moral religion; its highest and most peculiar distinction is that it bears an essentially moral character, and is rooted in the moral consciousness of man. The Gospel of John insists on faith in the person of Jesus as the indispensable condition of the new relation with God to which man is introduced by Jesus; faith in the person of Jesus is there the first and most essential requirement of the gospel. In the original Christian doctrine no such requirement is put forward. There are other elements which belong to the character and the contents of Christianity, and the relation which these bear to its original and simple beginnings may be variously determined; but there can be no question that the purely moral element which lies at its first source has ever been its unchangeable and substantial foundation. Christianity has never been removed from this foundation without denying its true and proper character. To this foundation it has always been forced to return as often as it went astray in that exaggerated dogmatism, whose logical conclusions were found to undermine the very foundations of moral and religious life. The element which appears at the outset with all the significance of far-reaching principles, which has always remained the same though other parts of the religion changed, and which contains in itself the evidence that it is true,—this surely must be held to be the proper substance of the whole.

And yet had Christianity been nothing more than such a doctrine of religion and morality as we have been describing, what would it have amounted to, and what would have come of it? True though it be, when we regard Christianity in this aspect, that it comprised and summed up those pure and simple truths which utter themselves in man's moral and religious consciousness, and that it opened up these truths to the common mind in the plainest and most popular style, yet more than this was needed. A form was needed for the religious life to grow up in as a concrete structure. A firm centre was required, around which the circle of its disciples might rally, so as to grow into a fellowship which should be able to win dominion over the world. When we consider the way in which Christianity grew up, it is plain that it could have had no place nor significance in history but for the person of its Founder. How soon must all the true and weighty precepts of Christianity have been numbered with the faint echoes of words spoken by many a friend of humanity and philosophic sage of ancient times, had not its doctrines been made words of eternal life in the mouth of its Founder? But we cannot help asking, with regard to the person of Jesus, what is to be considered as the secret of the importance it has attained for the whole of the world's history? However powerful we may conceive his personal influence to have been, it must have acted from a certain point or fulcrum supplied by the circumstances of the place and time. Without this it could not have produced that effect on the mind of the age, which enabled the work and influence of an individual to set on foot a movement so extensive and profound, and exercising such an influence on the whole history of mankind. Here, then, is the point where Christianity and Judaism belong to each other so closely, that the former can only be understood in the light of its connection with the latter. To put it shortly: had not the Messianic idea, the idea in which Jewish national hopes had their profoundest expression, fixed itself on the person of Jesus, and caused him to be regarded as the Messiah who had come for the redemption of his people, and in whom the promise to the fathers was fulfilled, the belief in him could never have had a power of such far-reaching influence in history. It was in the Messianic idea that the spiritual contents of Christianity were clothed on with the concrete form in which it could enter on the path of historical development. The consciousness of Jesus was thus taken up by the national consciousness, and enabled to spread and become the general consciousness of the world.

The Gospel history supplies us with abundance of evidence to show that, at the time of Jesus, the Messianic expectations had not only engaged the attention of pious souls here and there, but become a prominent feature in the belief of the people at large. As the political position under which the people was suffering at the time was flagrantly inconsistent with the theocratic idea which enters into the whole history of the Jewish race, men were led to gaze intensely into the past. There they discerned one point at least at which the theocratic ideal appeared to have been realised, though but for a short time. From that point downwards the history of their nation had been very different in fact from what it should have been. Yet they did not despair, but expected with all the greater confidence that the near or distant future would bring what the past had so long failed to realise,—that promise given to the fathers, which generation had long handed down to generation as the object of their yearning. It is an important and peculiar characteristic of Judaism that, by the constant and ever-widening contrast between the idea and the reality, and as the belief in the Messiah was a belief in one who was still to come, it came to be mainly a religion of the future. Thus no important movement could take place upon the soil of the history of the Jewish people and religion without either being introduced by the Messianic idea or becoming involved with it at a later stage. The way which Christianity had to take was thus foreshadowed. The synoptic account of the Gospel history brings Jesus before us accompanied by all the miracles which were to announce him to the world as the long-promised Messiah who had now appeared, and as the Son of God, according to the Jewish notion of that dignity.

From the standpoint of historical criticism we can only ask how it came to be an established fact in Jesus' own mind that he was called to be the Messiah? There are three points in the

Gospel history which seem to offer light upon this point and deserve attention, the name of υἱὸς τοῦ ἀνθρώπου which Jesus applies to himself; the group of narratives comprising the confession of Peter, the scene of the transfiguration, and the first announcement by Jesus of his approaching death; and his appearance in Jerusalem. The manner in which Jesus applies the name υἱὸς τοῦ ἀνθρώπου to himself is so peculiar that whatever account of its precise meaning we accept, we must suppose him to have intended some reference to the Messianic idea when he used it.[1] Such a reference is, however, more evident in the second particular which we spoke of. If we follow the Gospel history up to the point where we find those narratives (which are not only placed together by the evangelists, but are intimately related to each other in matter and import), we see distinctly that a very important crisis has here been reached in the progress of Jesus' cause. Both he and his disciples have now arrived at the clear conviction that he is actually the Messiah.[2] It is certainly quite incomprehensible how this belief could still require further confirmation, when the Gospel history has already narrated a multitude of indisputable proofs of Jesus' Messiahship. This, however, only makes it the more remarkable, and for the historian the more gratifying, that even in such a narrative as that of the synoptics there should have been preserved the steps which led to a belief which was not yet at that time fully formed. The most unequivocal proof, however, of Jesus' belief in himself as the Messiah is furnished by his appearance at Jerusalem. Even had the triumphal entry been wanting, the significance of his going to Jerusalem remains. After his long and uninterrupted ministry in

---

[1] It is very doubtful if this expression was a current name for the Messiah at the time of Jesus. With regard to the use of it by him, the most likely explanation is that it indicated an antithesis to the Jewish υἱὸς θεοῦ, and the ideas associated with that title, and an emphatic assertion of the truly human character of Jesus' coming and vocation. Cf. Baur die Bedeutung des Ausdrucks ὁ υἱὸς τοῦ ἀνθρώπου, in Hilgenfeld's Zeitschr. für histor. Theol. 1860, 3, p. 274).

[2] Cf. Theolog. Jahrbücher, 1853, p. 77, sq.

Galilee,[1] and after all the experience he had gained of the acceptance of his doctrine among the people and the opposition made to it by his adversaries with whom he had already come in contact, he comes to the resolution to leave Galilee and go to Judea, to appear in the capital itself, at the seat of those rulers, against whose whole system and traditions his ministry up to that time had been the most distinct and outspoken protest. Such a momentous step can only have proceeded from the conviction that it was absolutely necessary for his cause, now ripe for decision, to be at once decided. The time had come for his doctrine and person to be either accepted or rejected; the whole nation must be called on to declare whether it would persist in that traditional Messianic belief which bore the stamp of selfish Jewish particularism, or if it would accept such a Messiah as he was, and had shown himself in his whole life and influence to be. This was the question which could receive no answer but one; the answer to which he had long ago made up his mind with all the calmness of assured conviction.

Never was that which bore the outward appearance of ruin and annihilation turned into such signal and decisive victory and so glorious a passage into life, as in the death of Jesus. Up to this time there was always a possibility that he and the people might come to agree on the ground of the Messianic faith: the people might acknowledge him to be the person to whose advent the national expectations pointed; the disagreement between his idea of the Messiah and the Jewish Messianic faith might still

---

[1] The duration of the Galilean ministry is one of the many unsettled points in a life of the outward outlines of which we know so little. The usual assumption that it continued for three years has no other basis but the number of the festival journeys mentioned in John, and this depends on the way in which the Johannine question is settled. The great weight of the tradition of the early church is to the effect that Jesus taught only one year. This one year, however, is the ἐνιαυτὸς Κυρίου δεκτὸς of the prophet Isaiah lxi. 2, cf. Luke iv. 19, and is doubtless nothing more than a dogmatic assumption. It is not in itself probable that the public ministry of Jesus extended over so short a period. Compare Hilgenfeld die clementinischen Recognitionen und Homilien, 1848, p. 160, sq. Kritische Untersuchungen über die Evangelien Justins', 1850, p. 337. My Kritische Unters. über die Kanon. Evang., p. 363, sq.

be peaceably adjusted. But his death made a complete and irreparable breach between him and Judaism. A death like his made it impossible for the Jew, as long as he remained a Jew, to believe in him as his Messiah. To believe in him as the Messiah after his dying such a death involved the removal from the conception of the Messiah of all the Jewish and carnal elements which were associated with it. A Messiah who died, and by his death put an end to all that the Jew expected his Messiah to accomplish—a Messiah who had died to the life in the flesh—was no longer a Χριστὸς κατὰ σάρκα (2 Cor. v. 16) such as the Messiah of the Jewish national faith was. Even to the most faithful adherent of the cause of Jesus, what could a Messiah be who had fallen a prey to death? Only two alternatives were possible: either with his death the faith which had gathered round him must be extinguished, or this faith, if it were firm and strong enough, must break through the barrier of death itself, and force its way from death to life. Nothing but the miracle of the resurrection could disperse these doubts which threatened to drive away the faith of the disciples after its object into the eternal night of death. The question as to the nature and the reality of the resurrection lies outside the sphere of historical inquiry. History must be content with the simple fact, that in the faith of the disciples the resurrection of Jesus came to be regarded as a solid and unquestionable fact. It was in this faith that Christianity acquired a firm basis for its historical development. What history requires as the necessary antecedent of all that is to follow, is not so much the fact of the resurrection of Jesus, as the belief that it was a fact. The view we take of the resurrection is of minor importance for the history. We may regard it as an outward objective miracle, or as a subjective psychological miracle; since, though we assume that an inward spiritual process was possible by which the unbelief of the disciples at the time of the death of Jesus was changed into belief in his resurrection, still no psychological analysis can show what that process was. In any case it is only through the consciousness of the disciples that we have any knowledge of that which was the object of their faith; and thus we cannot go further than to say that by whatever means this result was brought about, the resurrection of Jesus became a fact of their consciousness, and was as real to them as any historical event.

Great, however, as was the importance of this fact, and certain as it seemed to bring the minds of the disciples who believed in Jesus into direct conflict with Judaism, the idea was still too narrow to accomplish much. Had the belief in the risen one continued to be what it was at first, that he had passed from death to life and risen from earth to heaven, to return after a short interval, the same as he had been before, only seated on the clouds of heaven and clothed with all the power and majesty that belonged to the Son of man, to realise at last what his early and violent death had left unaccomplished,—had the belief not risen above this form, what could it have achieved? As the first disciples conceived that the very next step after the departure of the Lord from the earth was to be his second coming which was to be the consummation of the whole of the world's history, their faith in the risen one was simply a new and stronger form of the old Messianic expectations. Had no new development taken place, the only difference between the believing disciples and their unbelieving fellow-countrymen would have been that to the former the Messiah would have been one who had come already, and to the latter one who was still to come. The Christian faith would have become the faith of a mere Jewish sect, in whose keeping the whole future of Christianity would have been imperilled. What was it then that invested the belief in the risen one with a higher significance, and made it possible for the principle which had entered into the world in Christianity to develop itself in the great and imposing series of phenomena in which its history was unfolded, and to triumph over every influence which opposed it and threatened to hinder or obscure the all-commanding universalism of its spirit and aims?

PART SECOND.

CHRISTIANITY AS A UNIVERSAL PRINCIPLE OF SALVATION: THE CONFLICT BETWEEN PAULINISM AND JUDAISM, AND ITS ADJUSTMENT IN THE IDEA OF THE CATHOLIC CHURCH.

I.—THE CONFLICT.

It is a proof of the strong faith of the disciples, and of the great confidence they had already gained in the cause of Jesus, that during the period immediately succeeding his death they neither dispersed about the country nor agreed to meet at any more distant spot, but made Jerusalem itself their permanent centre. Here it was that the first Christian church was formed, and the Church of Jerusalem continued to be regarded by all Jewish believers in Jesus as the headquarters of their religion. Recent critical investigations show that the statements given in the Acts of the Apostles afford but a dim and confused picture of this early community of believers, and yield little to the historian in the way of trustworthy or consistent materials. It is not till we come to the appearance of Stephen and the persecution of which he was the occasion (Chap. vi. and vii.) that we stand on firmer historical ground. Here there are two things to be remarked. The charge brought against Stephen, which is strikingly similar to that brought against Jesus at his trial, and cannot in the latter case any more than that of Stephen have been an entirely baseless statement on the part of the false witnesses, shows us the early beginnings of an opposition which could only find its further development in Paulinism. The more spiritual worship of God which Stephen opposed to the externalism of the existing temple worship, could not fail to lead beyond Judaism. The whole appearance of Stephen suggests that the cause he pleaded was one which would justify us in calling him the forerunner of the apostle Paul. It is important, however, to notice, that this opposition to Judaism to which Stephen was the first to draw public attention, seems to have existed in the Church of Jerusalem for some time, and to have divided the church into two different parties. Stephen was a Hellenist, and it cannot be thought accidental that this more liberal tendency appeared in one who was a Hellenist. The fact of which he is an example, that the primitive church at Jerusalem numbered Hellenists among its members, is confirmed by the express statement of the Acts (viii. 4, xi. 19, *sq.*) When the members of the Church fled from the persecution to which Stephen fell a martyr, and were scattered abroad throughout the regions of Judea and Samaria, not only did these fugitives carry Christianity to Samaria, to the towns of the sea-coast, and even to Cyprus and Antioch, but at Antioch some of them, men from Cyprus and Cyrene, and of course Hellenists, took the important step in advance of preaching the Gospel to the Gentiles. Antioch thus became the seat of the first church of Gentile Christians, as Jerusalem was the mother church of the Jewish Christians. It is stated in the Acts (viii. 1) that only the apostles stayed in Jerusalem at this persecution; but this is improbable. If we may judge from the occasion out of which it arose, this persecution was not aimed at the Church as a whole, but rather at the Hellenists who sympathised with Stephen in his more liberal views and his consequent hostility to Judaism. Thus the history of Stephen affords clear evidence to show that the Church of Jerusalem had all along consisted of two parties, the Hebraists and the Hellenists, who now effected a complete separation from each other. From this time forth the Church of Jerusalem consisted entirely of Hebraists. The Hellenists, however, were widely diffused even before this time; and though the more liberal tendency only found its first expression in Stephen, yet we cannot be wrong in thinking that it had been at work before, and that it was due to its influence that Hellenism was already giving birth to Gentile Christianity. It was the apostle Paul, however, in whom Gentile Christianity found in the course of these same movements, of which the proto-martyr Stephen is the centre, its true herald, and logical founder and expositor.[1]

The history of the development of Christianity dates of course from the departure of Jesus from the world. But in Paul this history has a new beginning; from this point we are able to trace it not only in its external features, but also in its inner connection.

What the Acts tell us of the conversion of the apostle can only be regarded as the outward reflection of an inner spiritual process. The explanation of this process is to be found in the apostle's own individuality as we have it set before us in his epistles. In speaking of the period immediately preceding the great turning-point of his life, he says that he was a great zealot for the traditions of the fathers, and that he went beyond many of his contemporaries in the Jewish religion. The reason of this must have been simply that he saw more clearly than many others how completely the new doctrine would undermine Judaism if it prevailed. The characteristic feature of Christianity appeared to him no doubt to be what the main charge brought against Stephen, and against Jesus himself, had indicated, namely, its refusal to regard true religion as a thing bound down to special ordinances and localities. This refusal naturally and at once impressed on the religious consciousness a tendency to detach itself from the ground of traditional Judaism. Thus it arose out of the natural logic of his character that as when a Jew he had thrown all the vigour of his intellect into the persecution of Christianity, so when converted to Christ he should become the most trenchant opponent of the very principle of Judaism. Accordingly the history of his conversion, as he himself gives it to us (Gal. i. 15, 16), presents us with the remarkable circumstance that the revelation in which God revealed his Son in him, and the

[1] Cf. Baur's Paul, his Life and Works, his Epistles and his Doctrine. T. T. F. L. Williams and Norgate, 1875-76.

call which he then received to preach the Gospel among the Gentiles, were to his mind one and the same spiritual act. He did not merely become a disciple of Jesus, like other converts to the Christian faith: the consciousness sprang up in him that he was an apostle of Christ such as the older apostles were; and yet quite different from them, since he felt that it was only in the Gentile world that his apostolic mission could be accomplished. Thus, not only was he the first to lay down expressly and distinctly the principle of Christian universalism as a thing essentially opposed to Jewish particularism. From the first he set this Christian principle before him as the sole standard and rule of his apostolic activity. In his Christian consciousness his own call to the apostolic office and the destination of Christianity to be the general principle of salvation for all people were two facts which were bound up inseparably in each other, and could not be disjoined. We cannot call his conversion, his sudden transformation from the most vehement opponent of Christianity into its boldest preacher, anything but a miracle; and the miracle appears all the greater when we remember that in this revulsion of his consciousness he broke through the barriers of Judaism and rose out of the particularism of Judaism into the universal idea of Christianity. Yet great as this miracle is, it can only be conceived as a spiritual process; and this implies that some step of transition was not wanting from the one extreme to the other. It is true that no analysis, either psychological or dialectical, can detect the inner secret of the act in which God revealed his Son in him. Yet it may very justly be asked whether what made the transition possible can have been anything else than the great impressiveness with which the great fact of the death of Jesus came all at once to stand before his soul. From the moment of the revelation in which the Son of God was revealed in him, he lives only in contemplation of the Crucified One: he knows no other, he is crucified with him, his whole system of thought turns on this one fact. The death which was to the Jews a stumbling-block, and to the Greeks foolishness, for him contains and expresses all salvation, and that as no ideal death, but in its most obvious and material aspect as a fact, as the death on the cross from which Christianity itself is named the word, the preaching of the cross. In what other way can he have overcome his hatred and repugnance towards Christianity but by being plunged, almost against his will, in a high-wrought and intense frame of spirit, into contemplation of this death? To the Jewish imagination a crucified Messiah was the most intolerable of ideas. His mind, however, accustomed as it was to deeper thinking, came to see that even what was most repugnant to man's natural feelings might yet prove to be the most profoundly and essentially true, and so the idea ceased to be intolerable. Death, he came to see, can be transfigured into life. A Messiah who has died in the flesh cannot indeed be a $Χριστὸς κατὰ σάρκα$ in the sense of the Jewish national ideas. Yet all the more surely may he be discerned as one who has died to the flesh and been transfigured to a higher life and stands as a Redeemer high above all the limitations of Judaism. A death which ran so directly counter to all the facts and presuppositions of the Jewish national consciousness, could not be confined in its significance to the Jewish nation, it must have a scope far transcending the particularism of Judaism. There can be no doubt that this was the thought in which the apostle first discerned the truth of Christianity. It was certainly the thought which lay at the root of his view of the person of Christ, and from which the whole dialectical development of Pauline Christianity proceeded. Now the Christian universalism which thus became a certainty to the apostle before any other of the disciples had reached it implied from the first a much deeper breach with Judaism than we might have supposed. This is the only possible explanation of the fact, that from the time of his conversion the apostle Paul went his own independent way, and avoided intentionally and on principle all contact with the older apostles.[1] He made a short visit to

[1] Cf. the work of Dr. A. Holsten, Inhalt und Gedankengang des Briefs an die Galater, Rostock 1859, p. 4, sq., 17, sq. This work is markedly superior to ordinary commentaries in its logical precision, and its luminous development of the apostle's thought. See also Holsten on Galatians in the Protestanten-Bibel, Leipzig, 1872, p. 700, sqq.

Jerusalem, during which he was with Peter, but he leaves us without any clear information as to his intercourse with him beyond what may be gathered from the certainly significant expression that he only came there to make Peter's acquaintance. After this short visit he seemed to turn his back on Judaism for ever (Gal. i. 17-24).

But the apostle takes up an attitude of so great freedom and independence not only towards the older apostles, but towards the person of Jesus himself, that one might be inclined to ask whether a view of his relation to the person of Christ can be the right one which would make the apostle Paul the originator and first exponent of that which constitutes the essence of Christianity as distinguished from Judaism. Is there not too great a distance between the founder of Christianity and one who made his first appearance altogether outside the circle of the first apostles? The difficulty is great if we are to suppose that this apostle derived no assistance from the original apostles, but did of himself what no one had done before,—introduced Christianity to its true destination as a religion for the world, and enunciated, with a full sense of its vast significance, the principle of Christian universalism. Here, however, we shall do well to attend to the two elements which we found in the person of Jesus, and to their relation to each other. First, there was the moral universal in him, the unconfined humanity, the divine exaltation, which gave his person its absolute significance. On the other side there was the cramping and narrowing influence of the Jewish national Messianic idea. The latter was the form which the person of Jesus was obliged to assume if the former element was to have a point of vantage from which to go forth into the stream of history, and to find the way on which it could pass into the general consciousness of mankind. What, then, could be more natural than that one set of his followers should hold to the national side of his appearance, and attach themselves to it so firmly as never to surmount the particularism of Judaism at all, while the other of the two elements, which in the person of Jesus were combined in a simple unity, found in another quarter a much more distinct and energetic expression than the first set of his followers ever could have given it?[1] In this way the natural starting-point of each party is found in the life and work of the founder. The only question comes to be how the apostle Paul appears in his Epistles to be so indifferent to the historical facts of the life of Jesus. He seldom appeals to any traditions on the subject, though his apostolic activity, as well as that of the other apostles, would have been meaningless without them. He bears himself but little like a disciple who has received the doctrines and the principles which he preaches from the Master whose name he bears. But this only shows us how large and how spiritual his conception of Christianity was. The special and particular vanish for him in the contemplation of the whole. Christianity stands before him as a great historical fact which can be understood and grasped only in its unity and its immediateness as a divine revelation. The great facts of the death and resurrection of Jesus make it what it is. Around these facts his whole Christian consciousness revolves; his whole Christian consciousness is transformed into a view of the person of Jesus which stands in need of no history to elucidate it. Why should he go to eye-witnesses and ear-witnesses of Christ's life to ask what he was according to the flesh, when he has seen himself in the spirit? Why should he ask whether what he is teaching agrees with the original teaching of Jesus, and with the discourses and sayings which have been handed down from him, when in the Christ who lives and works in him he hears the voice of the Lord himself? Why should he draw from the past what the Christ who is present in him has made to be the direct utterance of his own consciousness?[2]

[1] Cf. my work, Die Tübinger Schule, 1859, p. 30, sq.

[2] Nothing could be more paltry than the attempts some scholars have made to fill up the supposed gap in the evidence of the apostle's legitimation. This is done by collecting from his works as many quotations as possible of the words of Jesus. It is also asserted that the confidence the apostle expresses that he had not run in vain must mean that he had an accurate acquaintance with the teaching of the historical Christ. Otherwise, it is said, he must have been proclaiming himself as a second and better Christ, a sort of Montanist Paraclete. See Paret, Jesus und Paulus. Einige Bemerkungen über das Verhältniss des Apostels Paulus und seiner Lehre zu der Person, dem Leben und der Lehre des

Fourteen years had passed since the apostle's conversion; he had entered into his sphere of apostolic activity, had planted churches of Gentile Christians, and founded at Antioch a metropolis for the whole body of Gentile Christian believers, when a question which it appears had never yet been stirred, and with regard to which Jesus had had no occasion to declare himself, all at once rose into the most serious practical importance. Up to this time Paul and his apostolic fellow-labourers had not scrupled to invite the Gentiles to the Gospel. Nor had they thought of making it a condition of their participating in the Messianic blessings that they should submit to circumcision, and in so doing become bound to observe the law. But as the number of converts from heathenism increased, and as the efforts of those who carried the Gospel to the Gentiles diffused it more and more widely throughout the Gentile world, the Christians of Jerusalem became alarmed. They could not look on with indifference, when they saw a Gentile Christian Church arising over-against the Church of Jerusalem in utter dis-

geschichtlichen Christus. Jahrb. d. deutschen Theol. 3, 1858, p. 1, *sq.* The attempt to make out quotations is very defective and unsatisfactory, and it is impossible to help thinking that had the apostle himself felt the need of such credentials for his teaching, he would have expressed himself quite differently in his epistles. Nor would it be easy to understand, on such a hypothesis, how at the very time at which it must have been his chief concern to gain as accurately as possible a knowledge of the teaching of Christ, he could maintain an attitude of such indifference towards the older apostles. The teaching of Jesus was to be found nearest its source with them, and if he wished to have the best and most trustworthy information on the subject he should have frequented their company. Now Gal. i. 11, *sq.*, shows us distinctly that he recognised no obligations to the older apostles with regard to his gospel. He would have regarded their communications as a purely human medium, and could not have brought them into connection with the immediate ἀποκάλυψις Ἰησοῦ Χριστοῦ which had taken place in his own consciousness. From this we cannot but conclude that we should have a totally false notion of what his apostolic consciousness was if we supposed that he reached it by the processes on which our own historical information is dependent, and which render it so limited and so uncertain. We have only to consider what is involved in the claim he advanced to be not merely a disciple of Jesus, but an apostle, with the full autonomy of the apostolic authority. Compare the discussions (which the author of the above-named dissertation has left quite unnoticed) which I gave in my contributions to the explanation of the Epistle to the Corinthians, on the apostle's principle of authority. Theol. Jahrb. 1852, p. 32, *sq.*, and on the ecstasies of the apostle, 1850, p. 182, *sq.*

regard of the ordinances and privileges of Judaism, and yet putting forth a claim to equal place and dignity with themselves. Members of the Church of Jerusalem came to Antioch, as the apostle himself tells us (Gal. ii. 1, *sq.*) He calls them false brethren, intruders, who jealously spied out the liberty that was enjoyed and claimed as a Christian right at Antioch, and made it their aim to bring the Christians there into bondage under the law. The matter appeared so important to the apostle that he felt he must himself go to Jerusalem[1] and have the question discussed on the spot where it had arisen, and where alone it could be decided. The direct practical issue of the question which had been raised was whether or not Gentile Christians required to be circumcised. The apostle therefore took with him not only Barnabas but also Titus, an uncircumcised Gentile Christian, that there might be a case before the Church at Jerusalem, in which the strength of the resistance to the demand that had been made there might be visibly demonstrated. But who were the opponents to whom Paul and Barnabas had to offer so strenuous a resistance? Who else than the elder apostles themselves? We should have a strange conception of the Church at Jerusalem and the position the apostles occupied in it, if we thought that a question of such importance as this could arise in it, and that the apostles took no part in the discussion, the originators of the dispute being merely certain extreme Judaists, with whose assertions and demands the apostles themselves did not agree. Had such been the case, how easy would it have been to arrive at an understanding! This view is clearly contrary, not only to the nature of the case, but to the plain meaning of the apostle's own words. It has often been repeated,[2] but it can never amount to anything more than an un-

[1] Ἀνέβην κατὰ ἀποκάλυψιν, says the apostle, Gal. ii. 2. Here we see very distinctly into the psychological background of such ἀποκαλύψεις, in which Christ himself appeared to him.

[2] A principal authority for this view, which is so totally opposed to sound historical insight, is Lechler's Prize Essay, which was crowned by the Teyler Theological Society, Das apostolische und nachapostolische Zeitalter mit Rücksicht auf Unterschied und Einheit zwischen Paulus und den übrigen aposteln, zwischen Heidenchristen und Judenchristen. Haarlem, 1851. In the second and revised

warrantable claim to set aside the original account, which bears the direct impress of the facts as they occurred, and to set above it a narrative which is inconsistent with it, and is manifestly governed by the writer's desire to give a new version of what had occurred.[1] We need only consider the phrases which Paul selects to describe his opponents, and which are carefully designed to indicate only their own view of the position which they held. He calls them οἱ δοκοῦντες, δοκοῦντες εἶναί τι, οἱ δοκοῦντες στύλοι εἶναι, thus showing us that the older apostles themselves were the authorities for the view with which he had to contend. Then we may remember how deliberately and with how full a sense of the independence of his own position he confronted the apostle Peter himself (ii. 7, *sq.*), and lastly, what the result of the whole conference was. The three principal representatives of the Church of Jerusalem did indeed give to Paul and Barnabas the right hand of fellowship, but the agreement which was arrived at consisted simply in recognising that each party had a right to go his own way, separate from, and independent of the other. Thus there were now two Gospels, a Gospel of the circumcision and a Gospel of the uncircumcision, a mission to the Jews and a mission to the Gentiles. The two were to go on side by side, separate and independent, without crossing each other's paths. The only bond to

edition (Stuttgart 1857), Lechler has simply repeated his former assertion, as was to be expected; he has brought forward no better evidence or arguments in its support. Cf. Hilgenfeld, der Galaterbrief übersetzt, in seinen geschichtlichen Beziehungen untersucht und erklärt (1852), p. 128. Zeitschr. für wissensch. Theol. i. 1858, p. 54, *sq.* 317, *sq.* No recent writer has exposed the unPauline view of the passage with greater logic and acumen than Holsten, in the work mentioned, p. 48.

[1] This is one of the points where the question of the relation between the narrative in the Acts and the apostle's own statements is of most importance. On this subject there is nothing to be added to what will be found in my work on the apostle Paul and in Zeller's work on the Acts. Here if anywhere there is a conflict of principles, which cannot be carried further. The two views simply confront each other as the critical view and the uncritical. The former is based upon differences which lie actually before our eyes. The latter seeks, in the interests of the apostles, to adjust these differences. But the adjustment will only be satisfactory to those who can accept the implied assumption that the interests of the apostles constitute a standard of historical truth. See my Paul, his Life and Work, i. p. 105, *sqq.* Zeller, Acts of the Apostles, ii. p. 8, *sqq.*

connect the Gentile with the Jewish Christians was to be the care for the support of the poor of the parent Church. So decided an attitude of opposition did the two standpoints now assume: on the one side was the apostle Paul refusing with immovable firmness to be shaken even for a moment in any point which his principles required him to maintain, or to yield any compliance to the proposals addressed to him : on the other side were the older apostles clinging tenaciously to their Judaism. During the long period of years which had elapsed they had not made a single step that would have carried them beyond their Jewish particularism. They were still asserting the principle of the indispensableness of circumcision as a qualification for the Messianic community. They could not shut their eyes to the success which had attended the preaching of the Gospel to the heathen, nor deny, what the event had proved, that God's blessing rested on that enterprise. This, and the cogent arguments of the Pauline dialectic, left them without any reasonable objection to bring forward against the prosecution of the mission to the heathen. Yet the concession which they thus appeared to make did not arise from any root of conviction in their minds, and was out of harmony with their religious feelings. In fact the relations of the two parties to each other were now such that the line of demarcation which had been drawn between them could not possibly be long observed. This was proved to be the case in the encounter between Peter and Paul at Antioch, which took place soon after the right hand of fellowship had been given. On this occasion a very outspoken declaration of quite a different character was made. When Peter came to Antioch he at first ate with the Gentile Christians. But some persons came there from James, and by the mere fact of their presence reminded Peter so strongly of the principles which were so rigorously upheld at Jerusalem, that he gave up sitting at the same table with the Gentile Christians as he had hitherto been doing. In drawing this distinction between the Jewish and the Gentile Christians he practically declared that he no longer recognised the latter to be on the same level with the former. The apostle of the Gentiles felt this double-faced conduct to be an attack upon his principles, and took up the matter so warmly that he confronted the chief of the older apostles with a very pointed remonstrance before the assembled church. The apostle Peter's action showed that the alternatives left open to Jewish Christians by the treaty of Jerusalem were either to do away with the distinction between Jewish and Gentile Christians altogether, or to continue to be Jews, and deny to the Gentile Christians any privilege which would place them on the same level with the Jewish Christians. The apostle Paul also took a step which could not fail to have further consequences. With incisive energy he pointed out to Peter how his inconsistent and halting Jewish Christian position, which sought to hold both faith and the law at once, was a logical as well as a moral blunder, a contradiction in which he stood self-condemned. He then went on to demonstrate his own position, and showed what the Christian principle led to, when followed out consistently. Though the law is taken away, Christ is not the minister of sin, and he, the apostle, instead of building up what he had himself destroyed, was through the law dead to the law, that he might live to God.[1] The words and the whole tone of the apostle bear witness how sharp the personal collision between him and Peter must have been, and we are not surprised to find that the scene at Antioch made a deep impression on the mind of the age, and left very lasting effects behind. Throughout all the Epistles of Paul we do not find the slightest indication that the apostles ever drew nearer to each other in after years. The Acts passes over the occurrence at Antioch with a resolute silence, which shows clearly enough how far what was remembered of the subject was from harmonising with the reconciling tendency of this work. From a work written in the second half of the second century, the pseudo-Clementine Homilies, we gather that even then the Jewish Christians had not yet learned to forgive the harsh word which the apostle Paul had spoken of the man whom they regarded as the chief of the apostles.[2]

---

[1] For the exegesis of the passage, Gal. ii. 15, *sq.*, cf. Holsten, *op. cit.* p. 22, *sq.*

[2] Hom. 17-19. Εἰ κατεγνωσμένον με λέγεις, Θεοῦ ἀποκαλύψαντός μοι τὸν Χριστὸν κατηγορεῖς, Peter says to Simon Magus, with an obvious allusion to the

We have seen that at the very outset of the controversy, as soon as the question of circumcision had arisen, men once and again appeared on the scene who had come from the Church at Jerusalem, and openly sought to bring about a reaction (Gal. ii. 4, 12). We meet with the same phenomenon in the Gentile Christian Churches planted by Paul. Judaists of the same stamp appeared in these churches, and made it their business to bring Pauline Christianity into discredit, and to destroy what the apostle had founded and built up as his own work, without the law and in opposition to the law, in order to rear it up again on the basis of the law. The first actual proof of this systematic opposition to the apostle Paul appears in the Epistle to the Galatians, which was occasioned by that very opposition. It was written a few years after the occurrence at Antioch, after the apostle had made his second missionary journey. The whole arrangement and tendency of the Epistle show that the apostle deemed the matter to be of great importance, and saw that his principles were at stake in the contest. He therefore thinks it necessary to give a circumstantial account of his whole relation to Christ and to the earlier apostles, from the time of his conversion onward. He simply narrates the facts, and in this way he considers that he furnishes an irresistible proof, that from the very outset he has asserted distinctly, and in various ways, the independent right of the Gospel which he preached, and that his claim has been allowed. The opponents who had taken the field against him in the Churches of Galatia were but a new detachment of the opposition with which he had had to contend before. They had perplexed the conscience of the Galatian Christians by asserting that the work of their salvation was built

words of Paul, Gal. ii. 10, κατὰ πρόσωπον αὐτῷ ἀντέστην, ὅτι κατεγνωσμένος ἦν. The tradition of the church which brought the apostles together again places the final reconciliation of the two at the end of a long period of separation. Post tanta tempora, the Predicatio Pauli says in the passage which has been preserved in the treatise de Rebaptismate, appended to the works of Cyprian (Cypr. Opp. Ed. Baluz. p. 365, sq.) Petrum et Paulum post conlationem evangelii in Jerusalem et mutuam cogitationem et altercationem et rerum agendarum dispositionem postremo in urbe quasi tunc primum, invicem sibi esse cognitos.

upon a totally wrong foundation if it did not include the observance of the law; and the Galatians were on the point of falling away from the teaching of the apostle, and suffering the whole yoke of the law, circumcision and all, to be imposed on them (v. 2). So great an impression did those Judaists produce even in a church which was mainly composed of Gentile Christians, and which, the apostle declares, had received his gospel of freedom from the law with the most lively interest and the warmest expressions of affection for him personally (iv. 12, sq.) No other Epistle affords us so deep an insight into the grave significance of the rapidly widening struggle, and into the religious motives which operated on each side. The Judaists maintained it to be the absolute privilege of Judaism that only by the law and circumcision could any man be saved; while the apostle Paul set up the counter-proposition, that whoever was circumcised, Christ would profit him nothing (v. 2). According to the former it is in vain to be a Christian without being a Jew also. According to the latter it is in vain to be a Christian if, as a Christian, one chooses to be a Jew as well. And as it is impossible to be a Jew without accepting circumcision, and with circumcision the obligation to keep the whole law in all its particulars, it is evident at once how the man who takes this road must contradict himself, and be divided in his own mind. But the apostle is not content with exposing this contradiction to the Galatians, and showing them how unjustifiable and irrational the step was which they were about to take. He goes to the root of the matter, and attacks Judaism itself, showing that its being a religion based on law, far from giving it any distinction, reduces it to a subordinate and secondary place in the history of the religious development of mankind. Even within the sphere of Jewish religious history, the law is not the primary and original element. Above it stands the promise given to Abraham, which points forward to a time when the same faith which was counted to Abraham for righteousness will become the blessing of all nations. This promise can only be fulfilled when the law, whose curse passes upon all who do not continue in all things that are written in the law to do them, gives way to faith. By faith, faith that is to say in him who has redeemed us from the curse of the law, we receive that which was the object of the promise made to Abraham, namely, the spirit. Thus the apostle has placed the law and the promise in such direct opposition to each other, that he is obliged to ask what the law is, what purpose it serves, when, owing to its want of power to give life, righteousness could not come by it. The answer which he gives to this question is that the law was interposed between the promise and the time when faith should come, because of transgressions, not to prevent them, but that in them sin might attain to its full manifestation and reality. This was the interval of the schoolmastership of the law, when mankind, being concluded under sin, was to be detained in ward till it had become of full age, being set free from the law to receive the sonship of God through faith in Christ.

Thus Judaism is nothing more than the religion of the law in contradistinction to Christianity, which is the religion of the spirit. Both its position in the world and its inner constitution declare that the function of Judaism is that of effecting a transition, of filling up an interval. The object it is there to serve is to exercise the stern severity of a watcher set to mark transgressions, and to keep the promise and the fulfilment apart, till the period which God has fixed for this event in the order of the world arrive (the πλήρωμα τοῦ χρόνου, Gal. iv. 4), and the promise reach its fulfilment. Nay, the apostle places Judaism even lower. Not only does it make men liable to the yoke of the law. Like Paganism, it has its religious institutions and forms of worship which are bound to particular times, to days, and months, and years. Thus it makes man dependent on the same elemental and material nature-powers, the adoration of which is characteristic of Pagan nature-religion; and on this side at least stands on no higher stage of religious development than Paganism does.[1] As surely then as

---

[1] The apostle's object in this passage is simply to define the position which is due to the law in the divine government of the world. Cf. the very acute and

it is a law of the divine government of the world, that there is a progress from the minority and the restriction of boyhood to the majority and the maturity of manhood, from bondage to freedom, from the flesh to the spirit, so surely does Christianity stand high above Judaism; and it can only be regarded as an irrational inversion of the relation which God has ordained, to fall back from Christianity into Judaism. So lofty is the standpoint on which the apostle here appears to us when we see him for the first time setting forth in logical order the arguments with which he resisted the claims of his Judaising opponents! Not only does he repudiate, as utterly unjustifiable, the demand which they had made with regard to circumcision, he denies that the law possessed that absolute right which the Jew ascribed to it. He places Judaism and Christianity together under the light of a great religio-historical contemplation, and of a view of the course of the world before the universal idea of which the particularism of Judaism must disappear. The demand of circumcision which was made upon the Gentile Christians amounted to a claim that, in submitting to that rite, they should acknowledge the absolute superiority which the Jewish nation as God's chosen people possessed over all the other nations of the world. This claim the apostle's wide and comprehensive view of history sufficiently disposed of. The cardinal point of his dialectical polemic, however, is to be found in the passage where he draws the conclusion from the previous discussion regarding the law and the promise, that all who are baptized into Christ enter at once, in that very act, into a new community, in which all the causes of division between man and man, which are to be found in the outward circumstances of life, are at once removed, so that there

accurate analysis of the course of the apostle's thought here, in Holsten, *op. cit.* p. 30, *sq.*, where the result is summed up as follows:—The law cannot be considered as the absolute purpose of God, but it is a relative purpose: it is taken up into his absolute purpose as a means. Thus, while it is distinguished from the promise, its unity with the promise is maintained. In God's purpose of salvation the νόμος is distinguished from the ἐπαγγελία, but in the economy of salvation they are in unity with each other. (ὁ μεσίτης οὐκ ἔστιν ἑνός—ὁ νόμος οὐκ ἔστιν κατὰ τῶν ἐπαγγελιῶν τοῦ Θεοῦ.)

is no difference any longer between the Jew and the Greek, between circumcision and uncircumcision, but all may regard themselves as children of Abraham. All are one in Christ, in the same faith which manifests itself by love.

The inner force of truth and the acuteness of his logical demonstrations give the apostle an unquestionable superiority over his Judaistic opponents. But what could all this avail, if the evidence of the truth of Christian teaching was to be sought for, not in the teaching itself, but in the apostolic authority of the teacher? and if, when Paul was compared with the earlier apostles, they were seen to be the immediate witnesses of the truth declared by Jesus, while his apostolic authority was founded on no external warrant or commission whatever, but simply on the assurance of his apostolic consciousness in his own mind? Accordingly, we can discern plainly enough, even in the Epistle to the Galatians, that he was well aware of the intimate and inseparable connection between these two things—the truth of his Gospel, and the assertion of his apostolic authority. He could only maintain the former by securing his position with regard to the latter: by establishing his right to the position of an apostle as against the older apostles. What then are his apostolic credentials; and if he affirmed that he alone was the true apostle of Jesus Christ, how stood the case with the older apostles who put forth the same claim for themselves? The dispute which had arisen about the necessity of circumcision and the permanent validity of the law, necessarily opened up further issues.

Whatever may have been the result of Paul's Epistle to the Galatians, and of his controversy with his opponents in the Galatian Churches, the dispute did not end there. Not long after that Epistle was written, we meet with opponents of the apostle in a different quarter of his sphere of labour, whose attacks upon him seem to be dictated by the same motives, and to be carried on in the same spirit. There can be no doubt that the Epistle to the Galatians was written in the earlier period of the apostle's residence at Ephesus, which is to be placed in the years 54-57.

The composition of our first Epistle to the *Corinthians* belongs to the latter part of his residence there. It was occasioned by news from Corinth which showed him that he had to expect a renewal of his Galatian experiences in the Corinthian Church. Judaizing teachers had made their way into this Church also, and had unsettled the faith of the apostle's converts in his Gospel. Several divisions and parties had arisen; but the main controversy about which they were ranged originated in a party which bore the name of Peter, although there can be no doubt that Peter never was at Corinth at all, and set itself in opposition to those members of the Corinthian Church who remained faithful to the principles of Pauline Christianity.[1] The party-interests which now came to operate in various ways on the Corinthian Church arose undoubtedly out of the same great controversy which forms the subject of the Epistle to the Galatians. It is very remarkable, however, that in the two Corinthian Epistles the subjects of the law and of circumcision, which formerly occupied the forefront of the battle, have completely disappeared. A very personal question has now come to the front, a question which could not fail to be raised sooner or later, namely, the apostolic authority of Paul. What authority could he claim? in whatever way he had come to his present position, it certainly could not be said of him that he had become an apostle in the same way as the older apostles; was it not doubtful whether he could be regarded as a true and genuine apostle at all? The apostle does not address himself directly to this most important question till the end of the second Epistle; but it can easily be perceived that, throughout the whole course of the two Epistles, he never loses sight of it, and that he takes advantage of every opportunity to clear the ground, and give all the explanations necessary for the proper understanding of what he had to say for his own personal interest; so that when he takes up the personal

---

[1] I am still of opinion that the only view of the Corinthian parties which will explain Paul's Epistles and the nature of the parties at Corinth generally, is that the party of Cephas and the so-called party of Christ were essentially one and the same. See Paul: vol. i. 257, *sqq*.

question he can meet his adversaries with all the force of a direct and outspoken denial of their charges. He asserts in the most emphatic way that he is an apostle as well as any other, and not a whit behind the so-great apostles whose authority was held up against him. Of the outward advantages of Jewish race he will only speak in irony, though in these also he can measure himself with them;[1] but the arguments on which he rests his case are very real and substantial ones. They are the actual results to which he can point, in the ever-widening sphere in which he had preached his Gospel, then all those painful experiences, in which he had approved himself as a servant of Christ, and finally, the visions and revelations of the Lord, of which he could boast. The apostle could not leave this last point unnoticed, when once the question of his apostolic calling had been so pointedly raised. He might appeal with the greatest justice to the success of his missionary activity;[2] that was a thing which could not be denied; yet it was evident that no one could be an apostle of Christ who had not been called to that office by Christ himself. In the first Epistle he had insisted emphatically on the fact that, as he was an apostle, he had also seen the Lord (ix. 1). The visions and revelations of the Lord, of which he speaks at the close of the second Epistle, are intended in like manner as a proof of his apostolic calling. They are to him what the direct call addressed to the older apostles by Jesus himself during his life on earth is to them. To the apostle himself this was the most direct and most convincing proof of his apostolic calling. But, on the other hand, he could have brought forward no evidence more subjective or with less force for others. He spoke of ecstasies, of things that he had seen in his own spirit, facts of his consciousness which could not possess the same objective reality for any one else as they had for him who was the immediate subject of them. And

[1] 2 Cor. xi. 5, 21, 22.
[2] Cf. especially such passages as 1 Cor. ix. 1, *sq.*; xv. 10; 2 Cor. ii. 14, *sq.*; iii. 2, *sq.*; x. 13, *sq.*; xi. 23. In the same way in the Epistle to the Galatians he cites it as a proof of the actual reality of his apostolic calling, that ὁ ἐνεργήσας Πέτρῳ εἰς ἀποστολὴν περιτομῆς, ἐνέργησε καὶ ἐμοὶ εἰς τὰ ἔθνη.

we cannot wonder that opponents who could never bring themselves to grant the truth of the apostle's doctrine, should also have refused to grant the premisses on which it was based. It was at this point that they chiefly directed their attacks: and here the apostle could not but feel the poison of their darts, as he could not conceal from himself that on this side his attitude towards his opponents was somewhat peculiar. The excitement and irritation which he betrays when writing against them on this subject is to be interpreted as arising mainly out of his uneasiness in having to do a thing which was impossible, namely, to prove as an objective matter of fact a thing which was purely subjective in its nature. This impossibility confronted him most painfully just at the point where his dearest personal interests were involved.

When we look at the matter from this point of view, the case of the apostle's opponents appears in a very different light from that in which it has generally been regarded. They have generally been judged entirely by the very unfavourable description which the apostle gives of them. Now it may well have been that human passion and party spirit did contribute an element of baseness and selfishness to the opposition they carried on against the apostle; but why should we judge that all the wrong was on their side in opposing the claim which Paul put forward, when we remember that he not only claimed to be an apostle himself, but in carrying out his argument to its logical issue, placed his own apostolic authority above that of all the older apostles together? If he appealed to the inner certainty which he possessed regarding his vocation by Christ, and to his apostolic consciousness, they, on the other hand, stood on the historical ground of their actual connection with Christ. Thus principle stood opposed to principle; and only the future development of Christianity could decide which of the two principles would acquire the predominance over the other. In the meantime, the attacks made upon the person of the apostle, and on his apostolic authority, form a new and a noteworthy epoch in the controversy in which Judaism and Paulinism had now come to be engaged. The deep earnestness which the apostle throws into his contendings with these opponents is enough to show the importance they had in his eyes. We should have a very mistaken notion of them did we hold their movement to have been a mere isolated phenomenon, the undirected and arbitrary action of certain individuals who were stirred up by merely fortuitous and personal motives to create disturbance and throw obstacles in the apostle's way in his own sphere of labour. Everything combines to show that they had a great party behind them, and knew themselves to have a right to appear as the agents and emissaries of that party. Not only was the name of the apostle Peter the standard under which their efforts were carried on,—a name which showed what spirit they were of, and made their cause appear to be the common cause of all Jewish Christians. We learn from the apostle himself (2 Cor. iii. 1) that they had brought letters of recommendation with them, which left no doubt as to the party they belonged to. From whom could such letters of recommendation proceed but from men who had such a position in the mother Church, that they could count on their authority being recognised in foreign Churches too? These letters prove to us how party spirit was growing, how the two parties were being ranged in a position of antagonism to each other, how efforts were being made by each party to counteract the other locally. They also represent to us, in a new and striking way, the radical difference between the two principles which are here contending with each other. They exhibited to the Corinthians the contrast between the two conflicting principles of authority. The authority of the one party having been outwardly communicated, was capable of being delegated by such credentials. Against this outward authority the apostle had nothing to affirm when it came to the point but his own independent self-consciousness. This is his position in the passage where he speaks of these letters of commendation of his opponents (2 Cor. iii. 1-18).

In dealing with his opponents at Corinth, he takes up, as he did in the Epistle to the Galatians, the standpoint of the higher religio-historical contemplation. Judaism and Christianity are related to each other as the old and the new διαθήκη; the old one is antiquated and extinct, but the new one is bright and luminous. In this distinction between the two dispensations, and in the spirit as the principle of the Christian consciousness, is to be found the justification of his apostolic authority. The character of Judaism is that of a religion of concealment and restraint, the religious consciousness which belongs to it is narrow and finite, but Christianity is the opposite of this; in it the religious consciousness has opened up to perfect clearness and self-certainty, and does not need to rely on any material aids. And this is the principle of his apostolic authority too. With those who refuse to recognise him as an apostle he can use no other argument than that their religious consciousness is imperfect, that they are at a standpoint at which the veil, the symbol of Mosaism, still lies upon their Jewish consciousness, and does not allow them to perceive the fact that the end of the old religion is now come. The principle of Paulinism could not be expressed more simply and accurately than is done by the apostle in this same passage, when he sums up his argument against the old covenant and those who had gained the Christian consciousness, and yet remained standing under it, in the words (2 Cor. iii. 17): The Lord is the spirit: and the spirit is liberty. That is to say, the principle and essence of Paulinism is the emancipation of the consciousness from every authority that is external or exercised through human means, the removal of all confining barriers, the elevation of the spirit to a standpoint where everything lies revealed and open in luminous clearness to its eye, the independence and immediateness of the self-consciousness.

Thus the apostle meets the opponents of his doctrine and of his apostolic authority by demonstrating the imperfection, the narrowness, the finiteness of the religion of the Law. But to get rid altogether of that particularism which was so closely interwoven with Judaism, that national pride which led the Jew to think that because he was a Jew he was better and more highly privileged than all other men, it was necessary to attack it more directly, to lay the axe more sharply to its root. This could not be done without a profounder and more searching appeal to the moral consciousness than could be made by a discussion which after all belonged to the sphere of abstract and theoretical contemplation. It is in the Epistle to the Romans that we see the apostle proceed to this, the third and most important stage of the long and hard struggle which his principle had to support as it forced its way through all the forms of opposition it encountered. Regarded from this point of view, the Epistle to the Romans appears in the light not merely of a compendium of Pauline dogmatics, but as a historical source of the first importance.[1]

What was it that led the apostle to write to the Roman Church, and to address that Church in such an epistle as this? As a rule he wrote only to Churches which he himself had founded. The Roman Church was not one of his, but neither is it known that any of the other apostles was directly concerned in its foundation. What naturally suggests itself as the probable account of its formation is, that it grew up of itself in consequence of the frequent intercourse which the Jews in Rome, long before this a numerous body, maintained with Judea and Jerusalem.[2] It was not even a Gentile-Christian Church, it was at least mainly composed of Jewish Christians, and its prevailing character was Jewish Christian. It has indeed been generally supposed that the Christians at Rome to whom the apostle wrote must have been Gentile Christians; but when we look at the whole tendency of the Epistle, at the aim to which it is directed, and at the nature of the greater part of its contents, it should be impossible any longer to question, that the apostle is dealing mainly with Jewish Chris-

---

[1] Cf. my essay on the object and the line of thought of the Epistle to the Romans, in the Theol. Jahrb., 1857, p. 60, sq., 184, sq. See also Paul, etc., i. 308, sqq.

[2] A clear proof of the impulse which was inherent in Christianity to communicate and propagate itself. With regard to the spread of Christianity locally, we should not ascribe too much to the personal exertions of the apostles. There seem to have been a great number of Christian Churches at a very early date in countries which there is no evidence that any of the apostles ever visited.

tians. This very fact must have been the immediate occasion of the Epistle to the Romans: the apostle addressed himself to them because they were Jewish Christians, and because he saw in them the Church which both in virtue of its position in the metropolis, and from the number and influence of its members, stood at the head of all the Churches out of Palestine, and might be taken as representative of all the Jewish Christians who lived among the Gentile races. And another circumstance which may have helped to fix the apostle's attention on this Church for some time back, and even made him wish to visit it, as he says i. 13, was the unembarrassed position which he occupied towards it. He had not come into any such personal conflict with opponents in it as in the controversies he had waged in the Galatian and Corinthian Churches. The discussions in his earlier Epistles had been disturbed by a great deal of personal matter, which added nothing to the argument, but, on the contrary, introduced irritation. But in writing to the Roman Church he could take up the same questions again, and deal with them calmly and with an objectivity which had not been possible before. He could place the great argument in new points of view, so as to add immeasurably to the profoundness, and suggestiveness, and thoroughness of the discussion, and bespeak for it a much more favourable judgment on the part of those whom he was seeking to convince. Even at the cardinal points of his argument we find him expressing himself in a much milder, more conciliatory, more sympathetic tone than had hitherto been the case. This, certainly, is only one side; the other side, apparently very different and yet intimately connected with the first, in the thought on which the whole is based, is a keenness of dialectical polemics which presses deeper than in any of the previous Epistles, and seems bent on severing once for all the very roots from which Jewish particularism derived its justification. These two features, the kind spirit with which he comes to meet his opponent, and seeks to place himself at his point of view, and not to judge him too severely, and the keenness with which he confutes him, are what give the Epistle to the Romans its peculiar interest. Hence moreover it comes, that this Epistle contains the deepest and most comprehensive argument for Pauline universalism as against Jewish particularism. For this, and nothing else, is the true theme of the Epistle.

There might be many who no longer clung with the old tenacity to the privilege which attached to the circumcision of the Jews as against the uncircumcision of the Gentiles, who could no longer conceal from themselves the insufficiency of the law for salvation, who were not offended at the admission of the Gentiles to the Messianic blessings, and who could even dismiss from their minds the scruples and objections with which the apostolic calling and authority of the apostle had formerly been regarded. But even for them there was still a point which could not but give rise to some uneasiness. What a disproportion was arising, since the conversion of the Gentiles had come to be on such a scale and went on with still increasing strides, between the heathen and the Jewish world! How was it to be explained that though the Jewish people was the ancient and chosen people of God and the object of God's promises, yet a great part of that people had no part in the salvation which had appeared in Christ, and the Gentiles were pressing in to occupy the place which God's own people had left empty? This question sums up the claim to which Jewish particularism still clung, and which it imagined to be indefeasible. It was not a question of material rights so much as a question of faith, and the apostle would have been stifling his own feelings of patriotism in an unnatural way, had not this question moved him to the very depths of his heart. The question appeared to him to be so important that he made the attempt not merely to remove the hindrance which it presented to the frank reception of the universalism of Christianity, but also to come to an understanding on the subject with his fellow-countrymen. He goes into the question with the deepest interest in the salvation of his own people, but the deeper he goes into it the more does he become aware that what he is dealing with is simply another form of that old claim of a national privilege which is the general assumption of Jewish particularism. Is it really the case, he asks, when the question is considered from the moral-religious point of view, that the Jew as such is better and entitled to higher privileges than other men? Or do not all the advantages he has had over others in the history of his nation rather increase his responsibility before God? This is the point from which the apostle sets out in his Epistle; at the forefront of his argument he places as his guiding thought the contrast between the righteousness of God and the unrighteousness of men, which appears on the very surface of history as a notorious fact among Jews and Gentiles alike. In this respect, Jews and Gentiles are on the same level. If what makes the immoral actions of the Gentiles inexcusable and worthy of punishment is, that they did those actions against their own better knowledge and conscience (i. 19, sq.), the same is true in the case of the Jews. If there be any difference, it must arise out of the different degree of light men have when they do what they ought not to do; but this difference does not turn out to the advantage of the Jews. The Gentiles are not without a law; they have the law of their conscience; and if the Jew has the advantage of another law in addition to this, all the distinctions of which he boasts in reliance upon it only tell against himself. He is not better than the Gentiles are: he is only so much the worse, so much the more worthy of punishment, in proportion as his knowledge places him above them, and as he knows clearly and perfectly out of his law what he ought to do, while all the time he does the contrary. Since then the true moral worth of man consists in his doing that which he feels that he ought to do, this one consideration makes an end of the distinction between Jew and Gentile. Uncircumcision is as circumcision, and circumcision as uncircumcision. The important matter is not what the Jew is outwardly, but what he is inwardly in his heart before God (ii. 25-29). Should the Jew still seek to have some advantage over the Gentile, he must be referred to the Scripture, which itself attests that Jews and Gentiles are under sin; and what the Scripture or the law says, it says to them that are under the law. All the passages of Scripture which speak of the depravity of men are applicable to the Jews first of all, and all combine to prove that no one can be justified before God by the deeds of the law. What comes by the law is only the knowledge of sin. If then there be a righteousness, it is only the righteousness of God by faith in Jesus Christ, by which all boasting is excluded. Faith alone corresponds to the universal idea of God. If it were possible to be justified and saved by the deeds of the law, as the Jews suppose, then none but the Jews would have this righteousness, and God would be the God of the Jews only. But he is the God not of the Jews only, but of the Gentiles also (iii. 21-31). In faith then, the distinction between circumcision and uncircumcision disappears, and as certainly as the universal sinfulness of mankind makes it impossible that there can be any other way of salvation than the righteousness of God by faith, so certainly is the universalism of Christianity established in its full significance, as the apostle expresses it in the words, that God is not the God of the Jews only, but of the Gentiles also. This universalism is founded deep in the fact of the moral consciousness which will not be gainsaid, that Jew as well as Gentile knows himself to be a sinner, and under the judgment of God.

Now the whole force of the apostle's argument depends on the assumption of the objective truth of that new way of salvation which he announces. His Epistle has therefore to address itself to the further task of adjusting this way of salvation to the religious consciousness of Jews and Jewish Christians, and removing the scruples and objections which still stood in the way of its reception in their minds (iv. 1—viii. 39). There are three steps in this argument: 1. The Jewish religious view of the world contains in itself all the positions on which the apostle's doctrine is based. The history of mankind from Adam to Christ divides itself into two great periods. These periods form a contrast with each other: each has its own peculiar principle, by which every separate part of it is determined. It thus appears as an absolute postulate of the history of the world and of revelation, that there is not only a condemnation to death, but also a justification to life (iv. 1—v. 21).

2. It is not the case, as the opponents of the doctrine of faith assert (cf. iii. 8), that it takes away the force of the moral requirement of the law. The believing Christian and sin have nothing whatever to do with each other: the death of Christ has severed absolutely the bond which connected man and sin, and as absolutely is man dissevered from the law through which sin comes to life (vi. 1—vii. 6). 3. At the same time sin and law are not identical. The law is in itself good and holy, in its inmost essence it is spiritual, and only in its relation to nature and to the human consciousness does it give rise to a conflict between flesh and spirit. In this conflict the religious ego of Judaism remains in the condition of an unhappy consciousness, and cannot break through the barrier which separates Judaism from Christianity. Only in Christianity is the flesh encountered by the spirit, the principle which has power to overcome the flesh. Thus only when he receives the spirit is man placed in the relation of sonship to God; and here, in his unity with Christ, there is an end of all that holds man apart from God, so that nothing can separate him from the love of God in Christ. Delivered from the dominion of the powers which ruled in the pre-Christian world, the flesh, sin, and the law, and set free to live the life of the spirit, man can now, by reason of the spirit which dwells in him, know himself as spiritually one with God (vii. 7—viii. 39).

It is at this point (ix. 1, *sqq.*) that the apostle, looking back on all the blessed and saving effects of faith which he has been describing, turns to consider the case of his own fellow-countrymen. On the one hand, he uses the tenderest expressions of sympathy towards them, and labours with all his heart to show them that the participation of the heathen in the kingdom of God does not take place at the expense of Israel. But on the other hand, he cannot do this without denying out and out that primacy of the Jews over the Gentiles with which he has all along had to contend. He meets it at every point on which it relies, and disallows it even in its mildest aspect, in that purely theocratic form where it appeals simply to the faithfulness and truthfulness of God.

For what advantage has the Jew over the Gentile, if there is no such thing as righteousness by the deeds of the law? It is true that the promises of God cannot remain unfulfilled; yet they are fulfilled without any human co-operation. What claim can man assert against God, if God can do what he will according to his pleasure, and can make of man either a vessel of mercy, or a vessel of wrath! Apart from faith, man can only be reminded of his absolute dependence on God, and if faith be taken into account, it is faith that is the stone of stumbling for Israel. All guilt consists simply in unbelief; and though the apostle expresses a hope that finally, after the fulness of the Gentiles has been gathered in, the promises will be fulfilled by the conversion of Israel, yet he grounds this hope, with which, as a born Israelite, as a descendant of Abraham and of the tribe of Benjamin (xi. 1), he finds it hard to part, not upon Jewish nationality and what is connected with it, but on the general truth that sooner or later all things must return to that God from whom and through whom all things are, and in whom all things have the final purpose of their being and subsistence (chap. ix.-xi.).[1]

So utterly is Jewish particularism devoid of every justification, outward or inward. The absolute nullity of all its claims is the great idea which pervades the whole discussion, and which forms the connection between the two great sections of the Epistle (i.-viii. and ix.-xi.): a connection which is not merely external, but internal. From the analysis of its contents which we have undertaken it at once appears, that its great significance lies not so much in its doctrinal discussions about sin and grace, as in its practical bearing on the most important controversy of these times, the relation between Jews and Gentiles. How could the two elements ever have been combined in the unity of one Christian Church,

[1] This is a part of the universalism through which the apostle looks upon the world. The ἥττημα of the Jews and the πλήρωμα of the Gentiles arrive at the same end, because each has its own period, and as God has concluded all in unbelief, so he will have mercy upon all (xi. 32). The apostle can imagine no consummation but the salvation of all. The doctrine of eternal punishment belongs only to Judaism.

had not the work been done which this Epistle was designed to do? It was necessary that the particularism of Judaism which opposed to the heathen world so repellent a demeanour and such offensive claims, should be uprooted, and that the baselessness of its prejudices and pretensions, of the privilege and the superiority it asserted, fully exposed to the world's eye. This was the service which the apostle did to mankind by his magnificent dialectic.

We do not know what impression this Epistle produced upon the Roman Church, nor whether any practical result was at once attained. But we can scarcely be wrong in assuming that, in a Church in which, as we may infer from the Epistle itself, the antagonism between the two parties had already been in some degree softened down, an Epistle of so weighty and comprehensive a character did not fail to produce the fruit which the apostle desired to see.[1] It must also have helped to impress upon the Roman Church that freer, more conciliatory, and mediating tendency in consequence of which it afterwards attained so commanding a position. In spite of its controversial keenness the Epistle has unmistakably a conciliatory character: it bears upon its face not only the deep interest the apostle felt in the salvation of his fellow-countrymen, but also the profound desire which constrained him to try to approach them in every possible way, both of the reason and the affections, and to clear away completely, if it might be, everything that continued to estrange them from him. It is as if the apostle had turned to the Roman Church in the conviction that it was peculiarly fitted to undertake the part of a mediator, as it were, in the great question of his apostolic calling, in which he was still confronted by so many bitter opponents and persecutors. It appears the more likely that the apostle was occupied with thoughts like these, and was seeking to do everything that lay in his power, to get the cause for which he was

---

[1] The two last chapters of the Epistle are not genuine, but an addition by a later hand. Thus the long list of persons to whom questions are addressed in the last chapter affords evidence that the Epistle of the apostle did not fail to attain its end.

working looked at in a conciliatory and loving spirit, and so brought nearer to a final decision, when we consider the circumstances in which the Epistle was written. It was during his last residence at Corinth that he wrote it. He was on the point of setting off for Jerusalem once more—a journey which was undertaken in connection with a piece of business in which he had for some time taken a deep interest, as he saw in it a means fitted to draw the Gentile and Jewish Christians closer to each other, and to make his peace with the Church at Jerusalem. In the Epistle to the Galatians he states (ii. 10), that ever since the assembly at Jerusalem he had never lost sight of a work by which the Churches now divided might be reunited, namely, the support of the poor in Jerusalem. In the period during which the two Epistles to the Corinthians were written, he had given special attention to this undertaking (1 Cor. xvi. 1, sqq., and 2 Cor. chap. viii. and ix.). As the subsidy was important for the object of his journey, he naturally desired that it should be as large as possible. It must have been his uncertainty on this point that made him think at first of sending the contributions by delegates to be chosen by the Corinthians, who should carry an Epistle from him to the Christians at Jerusalem. He adds, however (1 Cor. xvi. 4), that if the affair be worth while, that is, if the contributions prove to be so considerable as to be likely to help him with the end he had in view, he would go with them himself. That the object he thought of was not merely the material sustenance of the poor, that he had another aim much more closely connected with his own apostolic calling, he himself states very distinctly in the Second Epistle, ix. 12, sq., where he says that the undertaking of this service is not only one that supplies a want, there is also a surplus in it by reason of the many thanksgivings which are offered to God for it. The Christians of Jerusalem praise God that the confession of the Gentile Christians is so entirely subject to the Gospel of Christ, that they seek to be nothing but the confessors of the Gospel of Christ. And as they recognise in this gift the heartiness of the fellowship which the Gentile Christians bear to them, their heart turns to them, their prayers for them express the yearning that they feel towards them, because the grace of God has been manifested in them in so superlative a way. An attempt was to be made, then, to remove the wall of partition which still subsisted between the Jewish and the Gentile Christians, and to win for Pauline Christianity that recognition which was still denied to it. The apostle believed that the mistrust and prejudice which the Jewish Christians still felt were due entirely to the old relations, which had now passed away, and that the love-offering which the Gentile Christian Churches were now to send to the Church of Jerusalem in token of brotherly unity, would produce such an impression as to remove these feelings altogether. It was no doubt in furtherance of this design, and with the contribution which had been collected, that he soon afterwards set out on his journey to Jerusalem. But how painfully was he disappointed in these hopes!

It is not necessary to enter in detail into the circumstances under which the apostle met his well-known fate at Jerusalem. There is one question, however, which possesses special interest, namely, who were the authors of those tumults in which the Roman military authorities had to interfere in order to rescue the apostle from the rage of his opponents? Were these tumults caused by Jews, or by Jewish Christians? They were zealots for the law, men who saw in the apostle a transgressor of the law, an apostate, a declared enemy of the national religion. But not only the Jews were zealots of this description, the Jewish Christians also shared this spirit, and carried it even further than the Jews. In their case the mission to the Gentiles had raised the question of the law into a matter of the keenest party interest. And accordingly we can discern, even in the narrative of the Acts, in which the true state of the case is as far as possible concealed, that the Jewish Christians were by no means so unconcerned in the outbreaks of hatred to which the apostle fell a victim, as is generally supposed. Protected by his Roman citizenship the apostle was removed to Rome, after two years' imprisonment at Caesarea. According to the Acts his imprisonment at Rome lasted for a further period of two years: but we are not told when or how it terminated. Even assuming the genuineness of the Epistles which profess to have been written by the apostle during his captivity at Rome, we have no certain or noteworthy information about this period. The most remarkable fact is that the termination of these two years coincides with the date of the great Neronian conflagration, and the persecution of the Christians to which it led. Nothing can be more probable, than that the apostle did not survive this fatal period.

Up to the time when the apostle disappears from the scene of the history, we have before us nothing but differences and oppositions, between which no certain way of compromise or reconciliation yet appears. It was upon that side, from which the great division had proceeded, which broke in upon the common religious consciousness, which Jews and Jewish Christians had hitherto enjoyed together, that a certain need was first felt for approximation and reconciliation between the two parties. But the advance did not meet with such a response as might have been expected from the other party. There were as yet only Jewish Christians and Gentile Christians, with divergent tendencies and interests. There was no ecclesiastical association to combine the two. Nor has history been able as yet to point to any considerable cause which can be said to have effected the filling up of the great gulf which since the events at Antioch had continued to exist between Peter and Paul, the heads of the two parties. All we can say is, that there must have been reconciling elements in the Church of Rome. This was the case before, and the influence which Paul had over this Church, both by his Epistle and by his personal residence there afterwards, must have strengthened this tendency. And how could the martyrdom with which the great apostle of the Gentiles certainly in one way or another finished his work in that city, fail to leave behind it a healing influence for the future of the Church? A legend of much significance, which however arose at a much later time, connects the brotherly unity of the two apostles with this death. This is accordingly a fixed point in the history of the further development of these relations. But the interval which elapsed between the death of the apostle Paul and that point contains many movements in many different directions, and the development of the history will conduct us to that goal by a longer road than might have been supposed.

The main tendency of the period must have been, as we may infer from the result which we have mentioned, to bring the two opposing parties nearer to each other, by a process of smoothing down their differences, and finding the mean between their opposing principles. This tendency must, from the very nature of the case, have become more and more general and predominant. But if we are to follow it in its whole range, we must first of all obtain a clear view of those points where the existing antagonism is most extreme. This is of course the case, where the antagonism is conscious and designed: there it is most bitter: each of the two parties makes it its chief end to assert that in which it differs from the other. The antithesis is wilful and resolute, and the goal of a possible union is removed to a distant future. Are there then, we have to ask, phenomena of such a kind after the death of the apostle Paul? Do we find instances in which Paulinism takes the offensive against Jewish Christianity? do we find instances in which Jewish Christianity keeps up the same keen opposition against Paulinism with which the Jewish Christians had originally set themselves against the apostle Paul?

Next to the Epistles of Paul, the Gospel of Luke[1] is the purest and most important source we possess for the knowledge of Paulinism. It contains special reference to the destruction of Jeru-

---

[1] Cf. my Krit. Untersuchungen über die kanon. Evangelien, p. 427, and my work on the Gospel of Mark, p. 191, sq. Köstlin, Ursprung und Composition der synopt. Evang., p. 132, sq. Hilgenfeld: die Evangelien, p. 220, sq. Köstlin does not see in this Gospel the sharp and outspoken opposition to the Judaism of the Gospel of Matthew that I do. I consider this to be a defect in his view of that work. On the other hand, the unknown author of the work: Die Evangelien, ihre Verfasser und ihre Verhältniss zu einander, Leipzig, 1845, appears to me to have stated this antithesis too broadly. But the merit belongs to him of having been the first to put the question clearly and in the full light of the issues it involves.

salem, so that its composition must at any rate be later than the year 70. From the earliest times it has been held to be a Pauline Gospel, but it is only very recently that the Pauline character which distinguishes it from the other two synoptic Gospels has been clearly and accurately recognised. This point is so closely connected with the question as to the composition of the Gospel that we can only touch on its more general aspects; yet, even here, we shall find unmistakable evidence of its Pauline tendency. The spirit and tendency of the Gospel of Luke can only be understood by the light of its relation to the Gospel of Matthew; and so the Judaism of the latter supplies a good standard for judging of the Paulinism of the former. Here Jesus is not merely the Jewish Messiah of the Gospel of Matthew: he is the Redeemer of mankind in general, and, in this sense, the Son of God. In accordance with this his universal mission, the whole representation of his personality which this Gospel gives us is a higher and more comprehensive one than that of Matthew. In all his works, in his teaching, in his miracles, especially in the power he exercises over demons, and in the whole of his revelation of himself, his personality appears to be superhuman. And herein lies the reason of the well-marked advance which this Gospel has made in the view which is taken of the Gospel history, and in the execution of its plan. The conception of the Gospel history which we find here is a long way beyond the views on which the Gospel of Matthew is based, and a long way towards the views of the Gospel of John. The Galilean ministry is very much shortened, while that in Judea and Jerusalem is proportionately extended: the announcement of the death and resurrection of Jesus as the final issue and consummation of his whole earthly activity, appears much earlier in the narrative (ix. 22, 51). In his struggle with his adversaries he takes the offensive, and the struggle is more pronounced and uncompromising. The demonic power whose instruments these adversaries are, interposes at definite crises in the course of the history (iv. 13, x. 18, xxii. 3, 53). By this means, and by repeated declarations, the great truth is clearly set forth, that Judaism is not the true or appropriate field for the accomplishment of the work of Jesus.

But to restrict ourselves here to the main point we have to do with: the features of the Gospel, from which we see that Pauline universalism is the theory which underlies it, are the following. Not only do we not find those utterances of Jesus in the Gospel of Matthew which savour of particularism,[1] but there are several stories and parables which are expressly meant to set forth the universalism of Christianity. The Jews reject the Gospel; it is the Gentiles who frankly and willingly receive it. Though Jesus himself does not proclaim the Gospel in heathen lands, yet he virtually inaugurates the mission to the Gentiles by his travels in Samaria, which, according to Luke's Gospel, he twice entered from Galilee (ix. 52, xvii. 11). The choice of the seventy, moreover, showed that the Gospel was intended not merely for the twelve tribes of Israel, but for the whole of the Gentile races. It is equally indicative of the Pauline character of the Gospel that it knows nothing of the identity which is asserted in the Gospel of Matthew between the teaching of Jesus and the law and the Old Testament. The Gospel of Luke does not contain the utterance, which is so characteristic of the Gospel of Matthew, about the fulfilment of the law and its permanent validity. What the Gospel of Matthew says of the law, that not one tittle of it shall fail, the Gospel of Luke, according to the original reading, applies to the words of Jesus himself (xvi. 17).[2] It even makes Jesus declare that, with

[1] Cf. Köstlin, *op. cit.*, p. 178, *sq.*

[2] The investigations as to the Marcionite Gospel have been taken up again by Schwegler, Theol. Jahrb. 1843, p. 575, *sq.*, Nachaport. Zeit., 1846, i. p. 260, *sq.*, and by Ritschl, Das Evangelium Marcions und das Kanonische Evangelium des Lukas, Tüb. 1846. Thorough discussions of the question have also been contributed by Volkmar in the Theol. Jahrb., 1850, p. 110, *sq.*; and in the work, Das Evangelium Marcions, Leipzig, 1852; and by Hilgenfeld in the Theol. Jahrb., 1853, p. 194, *sq.* The result to which all this has led is, that the Marcionite Gospel contained not only alterations which Marcion introduced designedly, but also, and certainly, readings which there is every reason to think more original than those of our canonical text. I think there is good reason for adding to these passages that which I have mentioned in the text, xvi. 17, and accordingly read with Hilgenfeld, p. 231, *sq.*, Die Evangelien, p. 201, τῶν λόγων μοῦ. On the Gospel of Marcion see Das Markus-evangelium, p. 191, *sq.*

the appearance of John the Baptist, the Mosaic law has come to an end, and that, since that time, the law has been superseded by the preaching of the kingdom of God (xvi. 16). Again, this Gospel speaks of the older apostles in a way which can only be explained by supposing that it was desired to place them in an unfavourable light so as to exalt, at their expense, the authority and the apostolic qualifications of the apostle Paul. A very significant instance of this is, that the Gospel of Luke entirely ignores the declaration of Jesus, given in the Gospel of Matthew, which was the principal evidence for the claims of Peter. Here Peter is called blessed on account of the confession he had made; he is declared to be the rock on which the Church of Jesus is to be built, so that the gates of hell shall not prevail against it; and the keys of heaven are given to him, with power to bind and loose. The Gospel of Luke, of course, could not for a moment admit such a primacy of Peter. In the same way Luke omits the power given to the twelve (Matt. xviii. 18) to forgive and retain sins, with the context in which it occurs. And besides this, in many passages it presents the older apostles in a very unfavourable light, so as almost to suggest to the reader, that if Jesus had no more capable disciples than these, the true and proper disciples were still wanting, such an apostle, *i.e.* as Paul.[1] We cannot suppose that the Gospel of

[1] Cf. my Kritische Untersuchungen, p. 435, *sq*. According to Köstlin, the author of the Gospel of Luke had no intention to lower the authority of the twelve; he only wished to bring out as strongly as possible the exalted nature of the Christian revelation, and for this purpose he dwelt so frequently upon their incapacity to understand Jesus. The claim which he opposes is the claim put forward by the twelve of being the only persons commissioned to preach Jesus. But what purpose do the new set of preachers of the Gospel serve, if those who were there before were quite fit for the office, and the new ones were merely so many more of the same kind? Köstlin even thinks (p. 267) that the introduction of the seventy points to a Gospel of Peter as the source of our Gospel of Luke. The writing in which the seventy originally appeared, he is of opinion, must have been one which sought to assign the Jewish and the non-Jewish mission to different disciples, in order to secure the whole services of the twelve for the people of Israel, and at the same time to show that care had been taken for the instruction of the Gentile world. But when we consider that, after the idea of the mission to the Gentiles had entered the minds of the Jewish Christians (even Peter had not entertained the idea at first, Gal. ii. 7), they set to work to make Peter an

Luke rests on a purer historical tradition than that of Matthew, or that, where such considerable differences occur between it and the other two Gospels, it gives the more true and faithful presentation of the Gospel history. When, therefore, we find that history treated from this peculiar point of view even in its reports of the words and acts of Jesus, we must conclude that this was done in order to provide a historical justification for Pauline universalism. The Gospel of Luke thus testifies to the vigorous self-consciousness with which the Pauline spirit lived on in his faithful adherents after the death of the apostle himself. It makes no secret of that which so much care was afterwards taken to conceal, of the personal relation to the older apostles which was implied in Paulinism, of which it was a necessary assumption that, as Paulinism was higher than Judaism, so the older apostles stood at a lower stage than Paul. The markedly Paulinising tendency of this Gospel has

apostle of the Gentiles, we cannot consider it likely that it was a Petrine Gospel in which the seventy were first introduced into the evangelical tradition. But from whatever source the Gospel of Luke derived its seventy disciples, the antithesis to the twelve which the 10th chapter presents is perfectly clear, and it is impossible to ignore the Pauline interest on which it is based. This conclusion is not weakened by what is pointed out by Köstlin, that the evident distinction here paid to the seventy makes it the more striking that so very little is related about them, and that when they came back, x. 20, they receive from Jesus a somewhat severe exhortation to humility. Notwithstanding this admonition, how could they be exalted more highly than when they are told that their names are written in heaven (comp. Rev. xxi. 12)? The very fact that nothing more is said about them, when we regard it in the light of what is the only possible meaning of the words of Jesus, x. 20, viz., that the important point concerning them is not the result of their activity which is open to the eye here, but what Heaven sees to be connected with their names, clearly shows them to be the representatives of an idea which has still to be brought to light in them, which, accordingly, was to be realised in Paulinism as opposed to Judaism. In dealing with passages like this, where the antitheses are pointedly expressed, it is by no means in the interests of the criticism of the Gospels to labour to remove the antitheses, and show them to be softer than they are, especially if this be done with a view to getting a show of support for a new hypothesis about the possible sources of a Gospel. On the contrary, these are the passages, in the light of which the passages where the tendency is less evident are to be explained. With regard to Luke viii. 54, I cannot but think it an arbitrary proceeding to except the apostles from the πάντες whom Jesus orders to leave the room. Who is left to be the πάντες, if, as we are told in ver. 51, there was no one there but the three apostles and the parents of the damsel? Köstlin, op. cit., p. 196.

given it great importance, for whenever the Pauline spirit manifested itself afterwards with special power, it turned to this Gospel to find there its own purest expression. So much had it the reputation of being the Gospel of the apostle Paul, that Church fathers like Eusebius (iii. 4) thought that when Paul spoke in his Epistles of his Gospel, as at 2 Tim. ii. 7, he must be referring to the Gospel of Luke.

No one placed it higher than *Marcion* did. In the early history of Paulinism he is, next to the author of the Gospel of Luke, the most characteristic representative and champion of the pure Pauline principle.[1] Marcion is by no means a mutilator and falsifier of the Gospel of Luke in the sense in which the Fathers so regarded him. In many passages there can be no doubt that his text is the genuine and original one. Even in cases where he has undeniably permitted himself to abbreviate or to change in the interests of his Paulinism and of his Gnostic system, it is a mistaken judgment which is generally passed on his procedure. He must be judged according to the analogy of the relations in which the authors of our canonical Gospels stand to one another. Each successive evangelist takes the body of the Gospel history, which he supposes to be a thing continuing in the Church unchanged, puts it under a new point of view, and clothes it in a new form of representation. Still there can be no question that the negative, antithetical, critical tendency of Marcion's Gospel bears witness to a distinct and vigorous Paulinism. His aim was to excise from the Gospel, as far as possible, everything that bore the stamp of Judaism, and to exhibit the whole breadth of the contrast between the Gospel and

---

[1] This is not to be understood in the sense which Ritschl, Entstehung, etc., 2d ed., 311, imputes to me, as if Paulinism had developed into Marcionitism, and the pure root-principle of Paul had been preserved in this heresy. This is clear, and Ritschl might have spared himself the further remark, that Monotheism and the recognition of the unity of the Old and New Testaments, which is connected with the idea of the promise, are such inseparable elements of the purely Pauline view as to make Marcion's agreement with Paul, even though intended by him, more superficial and apparent than real. It is notorious that Marcion was not only a Paulinist, but a Gnostic, but this does not hinder his antinomism from being genuinely Pauline, and he is entitled to a place in the history of Paulinism.

the law and the Old Testament. The work which accompanied his Gospel under the title "Antithesis" had a similar object, which indeed is plainly indicated in its name. It consisted of a juxtaposition of sentences of the Old Testament and sentences of the Gospel of Luke, in such a way as to place at once before the reader's eye the contrast between the law and the Gospel, and was intended as an introduction to his Gospel, to indicate the point of view from which the latter should be read.[1] It was not without good reason that he placed the Epistle to the Galatians first in his collection of the Pauline Epistles, not from chronological reasons, though they would have justified the arrangement, but as the principalis adversus Judaismum Epistola.[2] He held Paul to be distinctively and even exclusively the true apostle, and had none of the scruples which were felt in some degree by other Gnostics in bringing up again the strife at Antioch as the most trenchant argument against the Judaism of the older apostles. The Marcionites were wont to quote this scene as showing that in separating the law and the Gospel Marcion had not set up a new principle, but had simply gone back to the pure and original Gospel.[3] His Gnostic dualism necessarily led him to a much more pronounced antithesis to the Old Testament than that of the apostle Paul. His position with regard to the Old Testament did not permit him to resort to allegorical interpretation, since the purpose which it served was to connect the old and the new together, and to reconcile antitheses. Even the apostle Paul made use of allegory for this purpose, which makes it the more remarkable that Marcion rejected it on principle.[4] But while his Paulinism led him to insist on the breadth and reality of the distinction between the law and the Gospel, it was inconsistent

---

[1] Cf. Tertullian adv. Marc. iv. 1 ; Ut fidem instrueret (Marcion evangelio), dotem quandam commentatus est illi (antitheses praestruendo iv. 6) opus ex contrarietatum oppositionibus antitheses cognominatum et ad separationem legis et evangelii coactum. Cf. my work, Die Christliche Gnosis, Tübingen, 1835, p. 249, sq.

[2] Tertull. adv. Marc. v. 2.

[3] Tertull. adv. Marc. i. 20: Ajunt, Marcionem non tam innovasse regulam, separatione legis et evangelii, quam retro adulteratam recurasse.

[4] Orig. Comment. in Matth. xv. 3. Μαρκίων φίσκων μὴ δεῖν ἀλληγορεῖν τὴν γραφήν.

with his ideas to admit distinctions which would introduce division within the sphere of the Gospel itself. We can only regard it as another instance of Marcion's logical application of Pauline universalism, as it led him back to the common evangelical consciousness, which was before all divisions, that he refused in any way to countenance that separation of catechumens from believers, that outward distinction of ranks and classes, in which the foundations of an ecclesiastical constitution moulded after the spirit of the Jewish hierarchy were already beginning to appear.[1] All these features of Marcionitism taken together show it to have been that phenomenon in the early Church in which Paulinism developed its anti-Judaic tendency with the greatest energy. Marcion seems from all accounts to have exercised a remarkable influence upon the Christian Church of the second century. His adherents were widely diffused, and some of them formed Churches of their own not in Rome and Italy alone, but even in the East, and even so late as in the fourth and fifth centuries.[2] All this is to be attributed to the Pauline element which Marcionitism contained. In proportion as Judaism asserted itself, it was necessary for Paulinism to gather itself together and collect itself in the depths of its own self-consciousness. The expression, however, which it found in Marcionitism was extreme, and it was here brought into association with Gnostic heresy. The inevitable result was that it lost with Marcionitism the position of a great opposition which it had occupied, and forfeited more and more of its importance.

With regard to the opponents against whom Paulinism had to contend after the death of the apostle Paul, one of the earliest writings of the New Testament Canon gives certain indications from which further conclusions may be drawn. Who are the Balaamites or Nicolaitanes whom the Apocalypse attacks so vigorously in its letters to the seven Churches of Asia Minor, and especially in those to the Churches of Pergamos and Thyatira? Besides fornication, they are charged with eating meat offered to

[1] Jerome in his Commentary on Galatians, vi. 6. Cf. Tert. de Praeser. Haer., c. 41.
[2] Die Christl. Gnosis, p. 297, sq.

idols, Rev. ii. 14-20. Now the question of the lawfulness for Christians of eating such meat had first arisen when members of the Church of Corinth propounded it to the apostle Paul. He had discussed it in its various aspects, and had applied to the question the standard of Christian freedom, and of the enlightened views of a Pauline Christian. His decision on the merits of the question was against the use of such meat, but he allowed of exceptions in certain cases, in which a thing which was in itself inconsistent with Christianity might yet not be regarded as a sin, in consideration of the views or circumstances of the individual. It is extremely probable that many Pauline Christians were led by their more liberal views (the question put to the apostle by the Christians of Corinth shows what the tendency was, 1 Cor. viii. 1, *sq.*) to go further than Paul contemplated, and observed no very strict rule on the point in their intercourse with Gentiles. Thus, in the eyes of Jewish Christians who regarded the apostle Paul with hostility, the eating of meat offered to idols might come to be a distinctive mark of that lax Pauline Christianity which was on such good terms with heathenism. If this was the case, we might see in the above-named passages of the Apocalypse a hostile reference to Pauline Christians generally, without their alleged abuse of their Christian freedom being laid to the door of the apostle himself. But there can be little doubt that the writer had the apostle Paul himself before his eye as the originator of the doctrine out of which this spurious Christianity had sprung, and that he regarded him as a teacher whose apostolical authority was by no means made out. The Judaistic character of the Apocalypse might of itself lead us to this conclusion, but direct evidence is not wanting. In the passage xxi. 14 the author speaks of the twelve apostles, and of their names, corresponding in number to the twelve tribes of Israel, which are written on the twelve foundations of the heavenly Jerusalem; and the context is such as necessarily to exclude the apostle Paul from the number of the apostles. And to whom can the author be referring but to the apostle of the Gentiles and his apostolical assistants, when he commends the Church of Ephesus, ii. 2, because it could not bear those who said they were apostles, and were not, but tried them and found them false apostles? When we consider the locality to which this passage applies, we see that it gives us important evidence as to the Judaistic reaction against Pauline Christianity. Ephesus, as well as Corinth, had been the residence of the apostle for a considerable time. Here a wide door had been opened to him for his apostolic labours (1 Cor. xvi. 9), and it might have been thought that nowhere was Pauline Christianity established more firmly than in the Churches of Asia Minor, in the midst of which the apostle had lived so long. But at the close of his residence there he had already begun to complain of the many adversaries by whom he was opposed (*in loc. cit*). There were no doubt Judaistic partisans of the same sort as those at Corinth, and here they had found a still more favourable field for their operations. Not long after the apostle Paul left the sphere of his labours at Ephesus, we meet the apostle John at the same place. The Apocalypse was written, according to its own statement, at or near Ephesus. The tradition of the Church was that he lived here for a long series of years, and presided over the Churches far and near, who looked up to him with the deepest reverence, until he died in an advanced old age. Tradition traced to his teaching those ecclesiastical usages which were peculiar to the Church of Asia Minor. Now when we consider all that we know about the apostle John, the position of antagonism to Paul which he had formerly held as one of the pillar-apostles at Jerusalem, and what the Apocalypse tells us of the character of its writer, and when we take into account that he took up his residence in a quarter where Paul had been before him, can we think it improbable that he came to Ephesus with a view to exercising an influence over the whole district of which it was the centre, and upholding the principles of the Christianity of Jerusalem against the encroachments of the Christianity of Paul? If he hated everything that savoured of heathenism, he would naturally try the Paulinising Churches of the district by this standard; he would ask first of all how far they were tainted with heathen views or practices. The words of praise or blame which he metes out to them in proportion as they are warm and active, or lukewarm and indifferent in their zeal for pure and genuine Christianity, have but a vague and general meaning, till we see their point and application in the circumstances we have mentioned. Nothing can show more distinctly the wide difference there is between Pauline views and the Johannine views of the Apocalypse, than the conception which the Apocalyptic writer entertains of the whole Gentile world. Heathenism and Judaism are far as the poles asunder in his eyes; heathenism is simply the kingdom of Antichrist, the Gentiles exist only to share the fate of Antichrist! The apostle Paul places side by side with the positive enactment of the Mosaic law, as possessed of equal importance and validity, that law of nature, which is derived from man's natural knowledge of God, and from the moral consciousness whose voice speaks in the conscience. In the one God he sees the God of the Gentiles as well as of the Jews. The Apocalyptic writer, on the contrary, recognises no such religious instinct or susceptibility as might lead the Gentiles to Christianity: with him each successive plague God sends upon them only makes them more hostile to him, and more blasphemous.[1] With Paul the fulness of the Gentiles enters into the kingdom of God before Israel is converted and receives the fulfilment of the promises. But in the scheme of the Apocalypse all possibility of a historical development is cut off; the catastrophe of the world is to take place in the immediate future, and Judaism is then to celebrate its triumph upon the ruins of the heathen world. After such a proof of Jewish particularism, can we think it strange that John, the writer of the Apocalypse, should, as superintendent of the Churches of Asia Minor, have made war upon Pauline Christianity?

In any case the Christianity which now prevailed in that part of Asia Minor was no longer Pauline, but exclusively Johannine. The Church writers of the period after this belong for the most part to this district; and they either do not mention the name of

[1] Rev. ix. 20; xvi. 9, 11, 21.

the apostle Paul at all, or they speak of him in a hostile sense. *Papias*, who took so much interest in the immediate successors of the apostles, nevertheless does not mention in the celebrated passage where he speaks of these men,[1] either the apostle Paul or any one of his circle. Even in Justin's writings, in many passages of which we should so naturally expect to hear of the apostle Paul, the name never occurs. There can be no doubt that the apostle's writings were widely known when Justin wrote; the Apocalypse of John was well known to him, and he has by no means neglected to speak of it. His strange silence about the apostle Paul and his Epistles certainly suggests to us very forcibly that he meant to ignore them. The first reference to the apostle Paul which we find after this does not testify to a friendly feeling towards him. Hegesippus, a Jewish Christian writer, who lived about the middle of the second century, while not mentioning the apostle's name, refers to the words used by him in 1 Cor. ii. 9, and says they are untrue, and in conflict with divine Scripture, opposing to them the words of Jesus, Matt. xiii. 16. Here he gives utterance to a view regarding the apostolic qualifications of the apostle Paul, which compels us to number him among the apostle's most pronounced opponents. According to the words of Christ in the passage cited, those only are to be called blessed who have seen with their eyes and heard with their ears. This cannot be said of Paul, and accordingly he cannot have been called to be an apostle.[2] What we know in other ways of the character of this representative of the Jewish Christian party fully bears out this view. Between the years 150-160, he visited foreign Churches as the envoy of that party, and conversed with a number of bishops, among whom those at Corinth and Rome are specially mentioned. From this journey he brought back the satisfactory report that the doctrine prevailed everywhere, according to what was declared by the law, the prophets, and the Lord.[3] From this we may conclude, that even in such a Church as that of Corinth the Jewish Christian or Petrine party had gained a decided ascendency over

---

[1] Euseb. Eccl. Hist. iii. 39.   [2] Cf. Paul, etc., i. 225.
[3] Euseb. Eccl. Hist. iv. 22.

the Pauline. In another passage of the same work, all our knowledge of which is derived from the fragments preserved in Eusebius, Hegesippus seems to have spoken of the apostolic age as the time when the Church was still a pure and uncorrupted virgin, and to have dated the entrance of impious error from the time when, after the extinction of the sacred choir of the apostles, the generation of those who had been privileged to hear their divine wisdom with their own ears had passed away.[1]

But when we look into this passage we see that it by no means excludes the possibility of there having been even during the lifetime of the apostles such a false teacher as the apostle Paul was in the eyes of these Jewish Christians. What it declares to have ensued upon the death of the apostles was the open appearance of false teachers, with unveiled head, in the Gnosis falsely so called, which opposed the preaching of the truth. But Hegesippus also says that, even during the lifetime of the apostles, there were men who sought indeed to remain in dark concealment, but still were aiming at the perversion of the sound canon of saving doctrine. This seems to be meant for Paul more than any one else. He was not one of those who had heard the heavenly wisdom with his own ears: and little as his mode of action resembled a heresy, which is seeking for concealment, Hegesippus may have applied these terms to it, both because it vanished as it were in darkness before the brightly shining sun of the holy choir of the apostles, and because it did not appear in its true light, as he conceived, till it produced its heretical Gnostic development. The hints of Hegesippus cover a scarcely mistakable personal reference to the apostle Paul. But what he had hinted, others plainly expressed in so many words; we learn that the Ebionites considered him an apostate and false teacher, rejected all his Epistles, and slandered his memory.[2] The open and outspoken hatred with which the Ebionites regarded him is the extreme point reached by that Jewish Christian opposition to him of which we see the beginnings

---

[1] Euseb. iii. 32.
[2] Irenaeus adv. Haer. i. 26. Eusebius, Eccl. Hist. iii. 27. Epiphanius Haer., 30. 25.

in his own Epistles. The Ebionites are generally regarded as mere heretics, but their connection with the original Jewish Christianity is unmistakable. Thus their view of the apostle Paul is no mere isolated phenomenon.

An important source for our further knowledge of these relations is the pseudo-Clementine writings, the Homilies and Recognitions.[1] In these works we become acquainted with the doctrine and spirit of a party which flourished at and after the middle of the second century, and even then presented the most outspoken opposition to Pauline Christianity. The apostle Paul is not mentioned by name, but the reference to him is unmistakable, and the careful reticence of the work on this point only makes its polemical tendency the more marked. In the Epistle which is prefixed to the Homilies, in which Peter sends his sermons to James the bishop of Jerusalem, and recommends him not to communicate them to the Gentiles, but only to the members of the people who adhere firmly to the doctrine of the unity of God, after the mysterious manner of delivery which Moses had followed with regard to the seventy who afterwards sat in his seat, Peter continues: "If this is not done, our doctrine of truth will be divided into a multitude of opinions. I know this not only as a prophet, but because I already see the beginning of the evil. For some of the Gentiles have rejected the lawful preaching which was delivered by me, and have received the lawless and worthless

[1] The relation of these writings to each other and to an older work, a monument of the Petrine party, the Κήρυγμα Πέτρου, has lately been the subject of very thorough and elaborate discussion, in which, however, the results of different scholars travel widely apart. See Hilgenfeld, Die Clementinischen Recognitionen und Homilien nach ihrem Ursprung und Inhalt, Jena 1848. After him Ritschl took up the subject in his Entstehung der altkatholischen kirche, 1st ed. 153, sq. Lastly Uhlhorn, die Homilien und Recognitionen des Clemens Romanus nach ihrem Ursprung und Inhalt, Göttingen, 1854. Hilgenfeld, Theol. Jahrb. 1854, p. 483, sqq. Cf. his Apostolische Väter Halle, 1853, p. 287, sq. It is specially noteworthy how, as Hilgenfeld has pointed out, the Roman Clemens is introduced at a later stage, on the basis of the original pseudo-Clementine writing. We have here the remarkable fact that this Clemens represents in his own person the progress of that Judaism of the earliest writing, which is so narrow and so exclusive towards all Gentile Christians (Ep. Petri ad Jac. c. 1. Contest. Jac. c. 1.) to a more advanced stage.

doctrine of the enemy. And even in my lifetime some have attempted to pervert my words by cunning interpretations to the abolition of the law, as if I myself held such opinions, and did not teach sincerely or honestly; which be far from me. To do this is nothing else than to act against the law of God, which was given by Moses, and attested by our Lord when he said of its permanent duration: 'Heaven and earth shall pass away, but one jot or one tittle shall not pass away from the law.' But those who profess to set forth, I know not how, my thoughts, and think they can interpret the meaning of the discourses they have heard from me better than I can myself, say to those who have been instructed by me, that my doctrine and opinion is so and so, a thing which never entered into my mind. If they venture to tell such lies against me while I am still living, how much more will they do so when I am gone?" Who can this enemy have been, whose lawless doctrine is being accepted among the heathen, but the apostle Paul?

It is a curious phenomenon, moreover, that in the Homilies and the Recognitions, Paul appears in the character of Simon Magus, and as a Samaritan. Peter obviously refers to the same person as above, when he says that Simon went to the Gentiles before him, and that he followed and came after him as light comes after darkness, knowledge after ignorance, healing after sickness. As the true Prophet said, it was necessary that the false Gospel should come first, by a false teacher, and that afterwards, after the destruction of the holy place, the true Gospel should be sent forth secretly, for the refutation of future heresies.[1] Still plainer is the reference to the apostle Paul, when we find the apostle Peter arguing with Simon Magus as follows: "Even though our Jesus appeared to thee in a vision, made himself known to thee, and talked with thee, he was wroth with thee as an adversary, and therefore spoke to thee through visions and dreams, or it may be by outward revelations. But can any man be commissioned to the office of a teacher by a vision? And if thou sayest it is possible, why did the teacher go about constantly for a whole year with men

---

[1] Hom. ii. 17.

who were not dreaming but awake? And how can we believe that he revealed himself to thee? How can he have appeared to thee, who hast opinions which are contrary to his doctrine? If thou really didst become an apostle by his appearing to thee and instructing thee for one hour, then expound his sayings, preach his doctrine, love his apostles, and dispute not with me who was with him! For thou hast striven against me as an adversary, against me, the strong rock, the foundation of the Church! If thou wert not an adversary, thou wouldst not vilify and abuse me and my preaching, so that men will not believe me when I say what I heard from the Lord himself when I was with him; while it is clear that I who am condemned am worthy of praise. If thou callest me worthy of condemnation, thou accusest God who revealed Christ to me, and attackest him who called me blessed on account of this revelation."[1] Here we meet the same charges which the Jewish Christians had brought against Paul from the very first. The great cause of offence is here as it always was, Paul's doctrine of the law. It is said to be a lawless doctrine; it does not bind the Gentiles to observe the law; it asserts that it is possible to be saved without the law. But he who opposes the true apostles by teaching anything so false cannot be a genuine apostle. Thus the attack is directed against the apostle's person. Not only is his apostolic authority expressly denied; but the evidence to which alone he appealed in support of his claim is declared to be radically worthless. It is impossible not to see a pointed reference to the apostle Paul in this sweeping denial of the value of revelations such as he asserted that he had received, conveyed in visions, ecstasies, and dreams, and in the doctrine advanced on the other side, that immediate personal intercourse with Jesus during the whole period of his public ministry is the only way of entrance into the apostolic office, the only criterion of apostolic authority. We see here how hard the Jewish Christians found it to forgive the apostle Paul his conflict with the apostle Peter: for the scene at Antioch is called up again, and the expression turned over which the former had applied to the latter on that occasion.

[1] Hom. xvii. 19.

But how are we to explain this identification of Simon Magus with the apostle Paul? The simplest explanation seems to be that the narrative, Acts viii. 9, of the encounter of the two apostles Peter and John with Simon Magus, received a new application to the apostle Paul. Such a transference would be a very striking proof of the bitter hatred of the apostle which animated the Jewish Christian party, from which the Homilies proceed; though it would not tell us at what time this hatred arose, nor how widely it was diffused among the Jewish Christians. But when we take into consideration the well-known character of the Acts as a historical work, and the likelihood that it was written at a comparatively late period, we are led to ask if the identification may not be accounted for in another way. Instead of the story of Simon having been transferred to Paul, may not the converse have taken place, in which case the magician of the Acts is not the original with whom the apostle was afterwards identified, but we have to look for the source and occasion of the whole legend in the apostle's own history. The historical existence of the Magus must on independent grounds be deemed very doubtful; and a careful consideration of the facts shows him to be nothing but a caricature of the apostle Paul. This theory at once explains to us as nothing else does, both the greatness and the motives of the hatred with which the Jewish Christians pursued the apostle from the very first. All the distinctive features of the Simon of the Acts, and of the legend as afterwards elaborated, answer to definite facts of the apostle's history; and thus not only afford us a glimpse of the process by which the legend first arose, but also furnish us with evidence as to the early times to which the hatred expressed in it is traceable, and the care that was taken to turn everything to account that could serve to give it point.

What the opponents of the apostle considered to be his first and most grievous offence was, as we might have expected, his assertion that the Lord himself had appeared to him, and called him, directly and in a peculiar manner, to be an apostle. This statement appeared to them to be entirely unreasonable and subjective; and at the best, they could only deem it to be a self-delusion, unattested by any objective criterion of truth. It is obviously this charge against the apostle that is represented in the ecstatic, visionary, and fantastic character which is attributed to the Magus. The reference is the same when the Magus is made to express the opinion, that communication by words can produce only an imperfect conviction, because one does not know whether the man who is before one's eyes may not be lying. But a vision, as soon as it is seen, affords the conviction to him who sees it, that it is something divine. In answer to this, the apostle Peter declares, that personal intercourse and continuous instruction by doctrine and example are the true criterion that what is communicated is divine, and asserts the direct opposite of Simon's view, namely, that he who puts his faith in a vision, or an apparition, or a dream, has no certainty, and knows not in whom he is putting his faith. "For it may be that a wicked demon or a deceiving spirit makes that to appear which is not, and if the man asks who it is that has appeared to him, the spirit can answer whatever he pleases. He remains as long as he pleases, and vanishes like a flash of lightning without giving the questioner the information he desires. In a dream one cannot even ask what one wishes to know, since the sleeper has no power over his own mind. It cannot therefore be concluded from a man's seeing visions, dreams, and apparitions, that he is a good man. To receive communications from without by visions and dreams is not the character of revelation at all, but a proof of the divine anger, as it is written in the law (Numbers xii. 6); or else, when a man sees a vision, he must consider that it proceeds from an evil demon."—(Hom. xvii. 13, sq.) What had the apostle Paul to urge against all this but the assurance of his own self-consciousness?

But the apostle contended that by the supernatural appearance which had been vouchsafed to him he had not only been converted to faith in Christ, but had also been called to be an apostle. This is a further coincidence between the Magus and the apostle, and indeed the chief one. What the apostle affirmed that he was, the

Magus wished to become. His proposal to the two apostles was simply that they should bestow on him the apostolic office. He desired to have the power of communicating the Holy Ghost, in the same way as the apostles did so, according to the narrative of the Acts, where the communication of the Holy Ghost always follows on the laying on of the apostles' hands. We might have thought that no one could be less suspected than the apostle Paul of having taken this road to the attainment of the apostolic dignity. But what is not possible to the malice of such adversaries as his were? The notion is that he felt his pretensions to be baseless, and as he was determined to be an apostle at any price, tried to obtain the dignity through the older apostles. The facts out of which this charge arose must have been the two conferences which, according to the apostle's own narrative, he held with the older apostles at Jerusalem (Gal. i. 18, and ii. 1), as if his object in coming to Jerusalem had been to smuggle himself into the apostolic college. But this was not enough. The great crime of the Magus, with which the general voice of the Church has aptly identified his name, as the father of simony, was that he sought to procure for himself from the apostles by money and purchase the gift of the Holy Ghost and the spiritual function connected with it, of imparting the Holy Ghost by the laying on of hands. This Paul was represented to have done. At this point the whole of the cunning web of hateful charges which the apostle's Judaistic opponents had from the first been concocting and disseminating lies clearly revealed to us. The narrative of the Acts does not enable us to form any clear idea of these effects of the apostolic imposition of hands with which the Magus was so much struck, and which led him to seek to obtain the same power. But the history of the apostle gives us the key by which the whole fiction may be explained. The only occasion on which a question of money entered into his relations with the older apostles was when he was leaving them, and promised that he would try to do what he could for the support of the poor of Jerusalem in the Gentile Christian Churches in which he was to labour. When he wrote his

Epistle to the Galatians he was already able to say that he had not neglected this: and his Epistles to the Corinthians contain most interesting evidence of his exertions in the cause. Now is it not clear that when, at the expense of much labour and with the kindest intentions, the apostle had collected this subsidy for the Church at Jerusalem from the Churches of Galatia, Macedonia, and Achaia, his opponents put the construction upon his efforts that his object was simply to purchase with this money the favour of the older apostles, and thus to attain at last what he had hitherto sought after in vain, his recognition as an apostle on the same level with the others? Thus we find the figure of Simon Magus, characteristic and striking as it is, to be nothing but a picture of the apostle, distorted in the true spirit of Judaism by his opponents' hatred. There can be no doubt that it was the same spirit which attached the name of Simon Magus to the person of the apostle. He was said to be from Samaria, and to be addicted to magic; this is to be understood in the same sense as a passage in John's Gospel (viii. 48), where, when the hostility of the Jews against Jesus has reached its climax of bitterness, the worst they can find to say of him is that he is a Samaritan, and has a devil. There was no stronger way of saying that Pauline Christianity was heathenish and hostile to the law, than to say that it came from Samaria. The Ebionites regarded the apostle as a Gentile.[1] The Samaritans were not, it is true, actually heathens, they were only half-heathens; but this made the strict and orthodox Jews hate them all the more, seeing in them, as they continually did, not only what was false and perverted in heathenism, but the falsification and defacement of divine truth by heathen errors. Now it is said of Simon Magus in the Homilies, ii. 22, that he denied Jerusalem and set up Mount Gerizim instead. And Hegesippus speaks of the Marcionites, Carpocratians, Valentinians, Basilidians and Saturnilians, as having come forth from the seven Jewish heresies, to

---

[1] According to Epiphanius, Haer. xxx. 16, they affirmed of him that he was not a Jew by birth, but a Greek or a heathen; that he was born of heathen parents, and became a proselyte to Judaism afterwards.

which the Samaritans also belonged, with Simon Magus at their head, to be false Christs, false prophets, false apostles, and to break up the unity of the Church into sects by their mischievous doctrines.¹ Heathenism was held to be essentially demonic; and where ecstasies and visions played so great a part as in the case of the apostle Paul, it was natural to trace the operation of demonic magic. Now as the undivine puts on the form of magic in order to encounter the divine, so when the magician attempted to get himself made an apostle by impure means, this was the false Simon in contrast with the true, with that Simon Peter who stood at the head of the apostles. But the latter at once saw through his arts, and exposed his hypocrisy publicly and incontestably; just as Paul was said to have exposed Peter at Antioch.

When the fundamental conception of the Magus had thus arisen, it received manifold accretions. Simon became the great father of heretics; to the fantastic imagination of the early writers of the Church he in his own person represented the highest conceptions and views of heathen Gnosticism. In a short time no one had any idea who this Simon Magus had originally been; yet it was not without some reason, it was a theory not at variance with the nature of the case, which used the legend of the Magus to represent Paulinism and Gnosticism as nearly related to each other.² The wanderings of the Magus come to an end in Rome,

---

¹ Euseb., Eccl. Hist. iv. 22.

² The evidence for the assertion that the Simon Magus of the Clementine Homilies is not only Marcion but the apostle Paul has already been set forth by me in my essay on the Christ-party in the Corinthian Church, Tüb. Zeitschr. für Theol. 1831, iv. 136, sq. For the further criticism of the Simon-legend I may refer to Hilgenfeld, die Clem. Recogn. und Hom. p. 319, and to Zeller's Acts, T. T. F. L., i. 245, sq. Zeller not only gives a critical analysis of the unhistorical narrative in the Acts, but has also strikingly summed up the meaning of the legend in the following words: "If in Acts viii. 18, sq., we substitute the name of Paul for that of Simon, we have a narrative which says in an historical form what, according to 2 Cor. xi. 4, sq., xii. 11, sq.; 1 Cor. ix. 1, sq., the anti-Pauline Judaists affirmed as a general truth." But it was Volkmar who first completed the identification by recognising in the magician's offer of money the apostle's subsidy from the western Churches. Cf. Theol. Jahrb. 1856, p. 279, sq.: The Simon Magus of the Acts and the origin of simony. Zeller remarks very correctly,

and he himself is represented as having there met with strange adventures which proved to be the close of his career. The reflection is a faint one; but here also there is a reflection of the history of the apostle of the Gentiles.

p. 266, that "the author, still aware of the meaning of the legend, wished to forestall any application of it to his apostle even by the position in which he placed it" (prior to the conversion of Paul). Here we have another and a very striking proof of the peculiar way in which the author of the Acts made his materials subserve his apologetic designs. He adheres to what is historical, but he places it in a new light, and it receives another form under his hands. He could not ignore the Simon-legend: if he had passed over it in silence, that would have been to leave it in its original meaning, without saying anything against it. He therefore prefers to mention it; but he gives it such a turn as to make it impossible to think of any reference to the apostle Paul. Originally he was Simon; but Simon is now quite a different person, and has nothing to do with Paul. The author of the Acts treated the notorious dispute between the two apostles at Antioch in a similar way. This was a tender spot which it was desirable to avoid. But he did not merely wish to preserve silence on the subject; he wished to draw off attention from it altogether, and so he substituted for it another incident to suggest that something of the sort had happened at the place, but that it was far from being so important as was generally supposed, as Peter had had nothing to do with it: namely, the dispute between Paul and Barnabas, Acts xv. 38. Cf. Gal. ii 13. This, he suggests, was what happened, not the other; he knows of a παροξυσμὸς of apostles at Antioch, and his historical sense does not permit him to ignore it altogether; and yet he does ignore the occurrence as it actually was, and throws a veil of darkness over it.

In this connection it is impossible to avoid thinking of the apostle's journey to Jerusalem, Acts xi. 29, sq. On chronological and other grounds it is impossible to assume that the apostle was at Jerusalem during the period in which the Acts places this journey, that is between Gal. i. 18 and ii. 1. On that occasion he is said to have brought a subsidy from the Christians at Antioch to their brethren at Jerusalem. But why does the author of the Acts speak of this subsidy, and so studiously ignore the much more important one which the apostle prepared for his last journey to Jerusalem, and which there can be no doubt that he did carry there? For what other reason than that the latter was the origin of the hateful calumny that was raised against the apostle, which it was now thought desirable to forget? Thus a subsidy was mentioned, because such a thing was notoriously a feature of the apostle's history; and yet it appeared without any of its evil associations; the latter might be forgotten along with the former.

II.—THE RECONCILIATION.

When we survey the series of phenomena which have now been set forth, we are led to ask how it was that the tendencies which we have seen to be so divergent came at last to make terms with each other, and to be embraced in a reconciling unity. Some process of this sort there must have been: otherwise we could not understand how a Catholic Church, a Church which cut off from itself everything extreme, and which united opposites within itself, ever came to exist at all. This result cannot have been reached without a greater or less relaxation, on one side as well as on the other, from the strictness of the antithesis. So much is generally allowed: but a number of questions remain behind, which are by no means settled. How was the process accomplished, on which of the two sides have we to look for the moving principle which led to the reconciliation, what was the attitude of the other party, and in what way are we to group and to classify the different phenomena which form the materials we have here to consider: such are the various elements of the problem to which many scholars who are interested in a deeper investigation of primitive Christianity have recently devoted a large amount of laborious study in various directions. Nor have objections been raised only by those who habitually confront modern criticism with a stiff and lifeless assertion of traditional and obsolete views. Even among those who see that the only hope of obtaining new light upon the obscure relations of this period lies in a keener and more searching criticism, there is still a considerable difference of opinion. Schwegler was the first to make the attempt to construct a new and continuous account of the post-apostolic age on the basis of the new critical theory, and he did so with great ingenuity and acuteness.[1] Ritschl came forward as a thoroughgoing opponent of Schwegler's views.[2] To Schwegler's statement of the question, as being to trace the gradual development of Ebionitism into Catholicism, he brought forward the objection that no clear definition was given either of Ebionitism or of Paulinism. He declared that Schwegler "placed Jewish Christianity so low and Paulinism so high as to make it incomprehensible how the belief they had in common could hold the two tendencies together, even outwardly. The mental process by which the religion of the law passed with Paul into the religion of liberty, and the confined and unhappy consciousness was changed dialectically into the assurance of reconciliation, all this has a merely outward connection with the history of Jesus of Nazareth. And thus it is a mere accident that the history of Paulinism and that of Jewish Christianity run together. And this view of the original relation between the two tendencies of early Christianity is fully supported by the very external construction which is given as the historical account of their reconciliation. No inward impulse is recognised, such as would tend to produce communion: and the only account that can be given of the gradual softening of the antithesis is, that unity was seen to be outwardly desirable, and that the literary spokesmen of the parties abandoned one antagonistic element after another, in order to attain it." After this criticism of Schwegler's views, Ritschl of course claims for his own the merit of greater depth and a more correct grasp of the inner connection

[1] Das nach-apostolische Zeitalter in den Hauptmomenten seiner Entwicklung. Tübingen, 1846.

[2] Die Entstehung der alt-katholischen kirche. Bonn, 1850. At the same time with Ritschl Köstlin published an essay on the history of primitive Christianity in the Theol. Jahrb. He adopts Planck's Essay on Judaism and Primitive Christianity, Theol. Jahrb. 1847, p. 258, sq., and enters into a new investigation of the historical process and the character of the first two centuries with special reference to Schwegler's account of the period. In this essay he declares himself unable to agree with Ritschl in those results on which the latter lays the greatest stress in his controversy with Schwegler, viz., the assertion that Jewish Christianity contained no element of Christian development. This he says is merely the abstract antithesis to Schwegler's view.

of the development. On closer examination, however, it becomes apparent that if we disregard minor differences the two views are not so far apart from each other as might at first appear. Ritschl as well as Schwegler proceeds on the assumption that the development of post-apostolic Christianity is in the main to be referred to the Pauline principle. With Schwegler the reconciliation came to pass by the gradual softening down of the two principles as they acted on each other, and the growth of an inward relation between them. With Ritschl a change takes place in Paulinism which leads to the same result. "The doctrine of the apostle Paul," Ritschl asserts, "presents certain aspects which rendered it inevitable that this principle should be developed in a one-sided way. We must of course take into account the decline of the original religious energy of Christianity among the Christians of the second century; but making all due allowance for this we cannot but conclude that the one-sided development of the Pauline principle was due to a one-sidedness in the expression originally given to it by its author. The confusion of opinion as to the post-apostolic development of the Christian idea is traceable in great part to the fact that no account has been taken of the certainty that the Pauline tendency would pass beyond the form in which its author had given it its original dogmatic expression, and would assume a very different and less dogmatic character. The purer motive which led to this change is to be found in the need which was felt to develop the Pauline principle so as to have it in a form in which it might be a clear, direct, and generally applicable rule of life. With this two outward motives co-operated; one negative, namely, the difficulty and unpopularity of the Pauline dialectic; the other positive, namely, the influence of the evangelical tradition or of the doctrine of Jesus, which had exerted no influence on the formation of the Pauline system."[1] "The change through which Paulinism lost its original form consisted in this, that faith ceased to be subjective faith in the atoning death of Christ apart from the law; it was faith in a wider sense, in its relation to God; to it was added the observ-

[1] Ritschl, *op. cit.*, 23, 280, *sq.*

ance of the divine will, or of the law of Christ, as a means of justification, redemption, and salvation in a legal sense: and in spite of the original Pauline formula, this factor came largely to preponderate over faith. Thus we no longer hear of redemption through the death of Christ in Paul's sense: we hear of love, of the disposition for good works, as the means of obtaining the forgiveness of sins." Now this is essentially the same as the formula πίστις καὶ ἀγάπη which Schwegler regards as the term of the development of Paulinism and the basis of the reconciliation of the two parties. But, according to Ritschl, Paulinism is so radically one-sided that the direct and generally applicable rule of life which came in place of it could not have proceeded out of it by inner development, but only *per saltum*. Thus we find with him the same outward relation of the elements of the two tendencies which he blames in Schwegler. Again, Ritschl asserts that the Pauline system was formed quite independently of the teaching of Jesus; and we scarcely see what right he has to condemn Schwegler for having "given a reading of Paulinism according to which it is not derived from the inner spirit of the life of Jesus, or, in fact, from any idea whatever that the influence of Jesus had brought before the world."[1] Nor can Ritschl's assertion be sustained, that the evangelical tradition or the doctrine of Jesus influenced the later modification of Paulinism of which he speaks through the Gospel of Luke. He himself assumes,[2] that the representation of the Gospel history given in Luke is merely the reflection of original Paulinism. The more closely Ritschl's account of the history is analysed, the more does it appear to resolve itself into antitheses which are without any thread of connection to explain their development. On the one side stands Jewish Christianity with the assertion, Christianity is the old law. On the other side stands Paulinism with the contrary assertion, Christianity is subjective faith in Christ without the law. In Jewish Christianity it is said there was no inner power of development; the motive principle is to be found in Paulinism. But neither can the latter develop itself by a

[1] Page 20. [2] Page 300.

natural process; it is too hard and one-sided to produce out of itself a direct and generally applicable rule of life. Paulinism is, it is true, the tendency which stands higher: but we must not shut our eyes to what can be said for Jewish Christianity. "For the assumption that Paulinism is perfect in the orthodox sense, and that there is no gap in the system, is one we cannot adopt, were it only out of respect for the Christianity of those apostles who remained Jewish."[1] Thus neither of the two tendencies is absolutely true; each has its justification as against the other. Now Ritschl asserts that "Jesus neither intended to declare, nor actually did declare any opposition to Mosaism in essential points, and his doctrine was, in virtue of this very feature, the immediate basis of Jewish Christianity as differing in principle from Paulinism."[2] If that be so, then Ritschl gives us little help towards understanding how the dogma and the wide-branching organism of the Catholic Church can have arisen out of the thought that Jesus was the Messiah, a thought which could appeal to none but Jewish minds. Nor, when we come to the point, can we surmount the doubt whether Jesus or Paul was the true author of Christianity.[3] We are told that in the view of Christianity as a law, in the conception of the new law in which those who are universally allowed to be the representatives of the early Catholic Church, Irenaeus, Tertullian, Clemens of Alexandria, and Origen agree with Justin Martyr, there is exhibited to us the relation of the Catholic Church to the apostolic types of doctrine, the Jewish Christian and the Pauline; and the result is said to be that this side of Catholicism is based, not on Jewish Christianity, as from its direct opposition to Pauline principles we might have expected, but on the Pauline tendency.[4] But if the altered form of the latter was due simply to the external motive which we have mentioned, and did not arise out of the essence of Paulinism itself, then we cannot say that the development into Catholicism was based mainly on the Pauline tendency; it may equally well have arisen on the basis of Jewish Christianity. What is said to be the characteristic of Catholic Christianity, viz.,

[1] Page 23. [2] Page 300. [3] Page 19. [4] Page 327.

the co-ordinateness of faith and practical activity or the doing of works, stands in a very natural connection with the character of the Old Testament religion. And finally, Ritschl's account of early Christianity takes no notice of the personal relations between the apostles Peter and Paul. But it was on this ground that the antithesis of the two tendencies first appeared, and came to the sharpest and directest expression which it ever had; and it was on this ground that an accommodation was arrived at, which serves as the clearest landmark we can have to show the complete transition of the divergent tendencies into that unity where all antitheses and extremes were at last atoned.[1]

In what we have said of Ritschl's work we have briefly indicated the principal points with which we have now to deal, and without due attention to which our discussion would fail to accomplish its object, which is to follow the historical development of the different antitheses as they act and re-act upon each other.

[1] In the second edition (Bonn, 1857), Ritschl's work has been entirely recast. This edition appears as a recantation of the first. The author announces that he has now reached a position so far removed from that of the Tubingen school as to make him an opponent of their whole system on essential points (Preface, p. 5). But the difference between him and that school is not so radical and thorough as he asserts; nor can the entire recast of the work be deemed a step in advance. His new position merely produces a larger array than formerly of contradictions and inconsistencies in his conception and delineation of early Christianity. The new view of the relation of Jesus to the law is the direct opposite of his former view, and this is an improvement; but the great defect of the original work remains unchanged; namely, the entire externality with which the antitheses confront each other, and their want of any inner and vital development. There is no fundamental difference, it is said, between the original apostles and Paul: and yet there does remain between them the fundamental difference of Jewish particularism and Pauline universalism. So little is there any living principle of historical movement, that Jewish Christianity and Paulinism are actually declared to be equally incapable of any further development, p. 271, sq., 282. On this and on other works bearing on this question which have recently appeared, compare my work: Die Tübinger Schule und ihre Stellung zur Gegenwart, Tübingen, 1859. It was occasioned by Uhlhorn's essay in the Jahrb. für deutsche Theologie, 1858, p. 280, sqq.; Die älteste kirchengeschichte und die Darstellung der Tübinger Schule. See also Hilgenfeld in the Zeitschr. für wissensch. Theol. 1858. Das Christenthum und seine neuesten Bearbeitungen von Lechler und Ritschl. He says very correctly, p. 381, that with Ritschl as with Lechler the development of Gentile Christianity and Jewish Christianity into Catholicism appears to be the work of blind chance.

The point of departure lies in the antitheses already pointed out: the result is that they are accommodated to each other, and disappear. In the interval between these two extremes, there must be steps of reconciliation; and from the nature of the case nothing is more probable than that the movement towards unity proceeded, not from one side only, but from both, of course in different ways. We should expect to find that both parties, feeling more or less distinctly that they belonged together, act upon each other in the living process of development, each party modifying the other, and being modified by it in turn. Without such a process, the result, as it lies before us in history, the appearance of a Christian Catholic Church, could never have come to pass at all. But would this process have been possible if the two parties, Gentile Christians and Jewish Christians, had continued to present to each other an attitude of unyielding and repellent opposition, if Jewish Christianity in its various forms had been incapable of further development, and if, on the side of Paulinism, what bridged over the gulf between Catholic and Apostolic Christianity had been simply the incapacity of the Gentile Christians to understand Paul? Can this have been what led them to Catholic Christianity, that the fundamental conceptions of the apostles as to the new basis of the religious relation which God hath provided in Christ were only intelligible by the help of the Old Testament, and that they could not reproduce them to themselves in a correct and living way? It is a complete mistake, and will altogether prevent us from seeing these relations as they were, if we suppose that the point at issue between the two opposing parties was one of difference in doctrine; that the question was whether the relation between the Jewish doctrine of the law and the Pauline doctrine of faith should be formulated in this way or in that. It is in vain to seek for the principle of the movement within the sphere of abstract ideas, as if union would ensue when they came to regard each other with indifference. From such a combination no new or vigorous life could possibly proceed. The principle of the movement is to be sought in the concrete centre where questions were arising which pressed for an answer: where Christianity, set in the midst of the great forces of the age, had still to struggle for a place among them and assert its own right to exist, and had, at the same time, to create the forms within which its historical development was to proceed.

When Paulinism and Jewish Christianity first came to stand in open opposition to each other, we find the motive power in those Judaists who met the apostle Paul with an uncompromising resistance at every point of his sphere of labour. There is no stronger proof of the capacity for development which was inherent in Judaism, than the undeniable fact that it found no difficulty in giving up even those positions which it had defended with the greatest zeal, as soon as it became apparent that such a course would help it to a more effective assertion of its preponderance over Paulinism. This is the only possible explanation of the fact that baptism all at once appears in the place of circumcision. At first the Jewish Christians of Jerusalem asserted in absolute terms the necessity of circumcision, and demanded that the Gentiles also should submit to that rite, and we have no reason to assume that the older apostles did not originally share this view. In the Epistle to the Galatians the apostle's Jewish Christian opponents are still insisting on circumcision as the absolute condition without which there can be no salvation. But after this where do we hear of the Jewish Christian party as a whole continuing to make this demand, as a matter of principle? Even the pseudo-Clementine writings do not mention circumcision as an essential article of Judaism. Only here and there is there a hint of the importance which had been attached to it formerly, as in the directions given in the Contestatio about the writings sent by Peter to James, that they should only be communicated to a good and pious believer who was prepared to teach, and circumcised. From this we may justly infer that the Jewish Christians themselves gave up the necessity of circumcision, a fact which can only be explained by supposing that, as they saw large and increasing numbers of Gentiles converted without submitting to circumcision, they came to feel it to be simply impossible to insist upon a point which the history of Gentile Christianity had practically settled. How they reconciled this with their view of the necessity of the observance of the law, we need not now inquire; in any case, we cannot but regard it as a concession made by them to Pauline universalism. And it seems to be closely connected with this, that, as circumcision ceases to be mentioned, baptism now becomes invested with a religious significance similar to that of circumcision. It was, of course, necessary to have some form or other for the admission of Gentiles to the Messianic community, and what form could be more suitable for the purpose than baptism? There can be no doubt that its general introduction and its higher religious significance are very closely connected with the conversion of the Gentiles. Even the apostle Paul seems to indicate as much, when, writing at a time at which circumcision was made an indispensable condition of salvation, he declares baptism to be the condition of communion with Christ (Gal. iii. 27). "Whoever," he says, "has been baptized into Christ, has put on Christ, and there is no longer any difference between Jew and Gentile." Thus, as circumcision makes a Jew, so baptism makes a Christian. Again in Matt. xxviii. 19, the commandment of baptism which there can be no doubt belongs to the last recension of the Gospel, stands in the closest connection with the injunction to convert all nations. From the nature of the case, baptism would originally bear this meaning only for the Gentiles; but we see from the pseudo-Clementine Homilies how Jewish Christians came to look upon it in the same light. That work only calls baptism the means ordained by God for the putting off of heathenism ($ἀφελληνισθῆναι$), but at the same time regards it as the necessary condition on which alone man can attain the forgiveness of his sins and future blessedness.[1] Thus circumcision was given up by the Jewish Christians as soon as there came to be another form of attaining the assurance of salvation which they could allow to be equally significant. In the case of the Gentile Christians, baptism was naturally and at once regarded as a substitute for circumcision. Jewish Christians

---

[1] Hom. xiii. 9, 11, 13.

were Jews by birth, and did not need any such substitute, but the number of born Jews who adopted Christianity was constantly decreasing, and so baptism came more and more to be the universal form of making the Christian confession, and to be considered the characteristic mark of the Christian, as circumcision was of the Jewish religion.[1] We see then that it was on the question of circumcision that the absolute power of Judaism first gave way. It is true that there still continued to be Jewish Christians, who not only continued to regard the law as absolutely binding on themselves, but even declined all fellowship with Gentile Christians who did not observe the law as they did. But this was the more rigid type, and there was another class of Jewish Christians, holding less extreme opinions, who made no such demand on Gentile Christians, and who nevertheless recognised them as Christian brethren.[2] Yet even this class of Jewish Christians could not altogether release the Gentile Christians from the observance of the law. The obligation of the law must not be cast off altogether; and so those ordinances, at least, were to remain in force, which the author of the Acts gives as the decrees of his alleged apostolic council. It has long been shown,[3] that the apostles cannot have drawn up these

---

[1] According to the Recognitions baptism came in the place of the sacrifice, which had now been discontinued (i. 39). Ut tempus adesse coepit, quo id, quod deesse Moysis institutis diximus, impleretur, et propheta quem praeciunerat, appareret, qui eos primo per misericordiam Dei moneret cessare a sacrificiis, et ne forte putarent, cessantibus hostiis remissionem sibi non fieri, baptisma eis per aquam statuit. In this view baptism acquired religious significance for the Jewish Christian also, who from his Jewish birth required no compensation for the loss of circumcision. This view is, there can be no doubt, of Essenic-Ebionitic origin. The religious washings of the Essenes, to which they attributed power to purify and to release from sin, rested on their rejection of the Mosaic sacrificial worship: which explains in a very natural way how, among the Elkesaites, the baptism which procured the forgiveness of sins was capable of repetition. Cf. Ritschl Zeitschr. für Hist. Theol. 1853, p. 582, sq.; altkath. Kirche, 2d ed., p. 188; Hilgenfeld, Zeitschr. für wissensch. Theol., 1858, p. 422, sq. The fact that baptism is here connected with sacrifice (see on the passage of the Recognitions Uhlhorn, op. cit., 251; Ritschl, altkath. Kirche, 2d ed., 239) is in any case perfectly consistent with the assumption that baptism was what actually came in the place of circumcision.

[2] Cf. Justin Dial. c. Jud. Tryph. c. 47.

[3] See my "Paul, etc.," i. 131. Zeller's Acts, ii. 27, sqq.

decrees as we now have them; and that what they contain is that minimum of the demands of the law, which the Jewish Christians required from the Gentile Christians, when experience had shown what was practicable, and might be asked. The conditions are the same as those on which the Israelites admitted proselytes of the gate into their communion. (Leviticus xvii. 8, 16; xviii. 26.)[1] This shows us how the Jewish Christians adhered to the standpoint of the law in this matter, and recognised no other standard for their relations towards the Gentile Christians than that provided in the law for the regulation of the intercourse of Jews with Gentiles. But, on the other hand, they had now conceded the very utmost that could be conceded to Gentile Christians by Jewish Christianity. If the Gentile Christians would only observe these provisions, there was no further obstacle to prevent that free intercourse of Jewish and Gentile Christians, which the question of circumcision had formerly threatened to render quite impossible. As soon as they could look upon the Gentile Christians as proselytes of the gate, the Jewish Christians felt that their objections to them were removed. And this is an instance of how all that Jewish Christianity required, in order to enter into friendly relations with Paulinism, was frequently nothing more than a way of putting the case, so as not to jar upon the religious susceptibilities of the Jewish Christian. In fact, when there had come to be a new Christian world outside of Judaism, and quite independent of it, when this had become a matter of fact, which could not be questioned or undone, the Jewish Christians would gladly have laid claim to the whole of Pauline universalism, had its originator only been Peter instead of Paul. Indeed Pauline universalism was actually taken from Paul and given to Peter. This is the only possible reading of the fact, that in the pseudo-Clementine writings Peter is the apostle of the Gentiles, whose mission it is, "to travel to the nations who say that there are many gods, and to preach and teach them that there is only one God, who has made heaven and earth, and all that in them is, that by loving Him they might be

---

[1] Cf. Ritschl, *op. cit.* 117, *sq.*, 2d. ed., 129, *sq.*

saved."[1] The same circle in which Paul travelled as a missionary among the nations is in the pseudo-Clementine Homilies described by the apostle Peter: he also, as an apostle to the Gentiles, must go on from city to city, from land to land, and can finish his career nowhere but at Rome.[2] It is true that in his mission to the Gentiles Peter is here represented as undoing the mischief wrought by an adversary: he follows on the steps of Simon Magus, to confute his false doctrine, and convert the nations from it to the doctrine of the true prophet: he is merely labouring to repair the ravages which the false apostle has made before him. This, however, is only the external form to cover the claim which the Jewish Christians put forth on behalf of their apostle to the work and merit of the apostle of the Gentiles. They are perfectly willing to accept the facts such as they had now come to be: they are well aware that the time is now past when a demand could be made on the Gentiles which would render it impossible, or even difficult, for them to enter into the Messianic kingdom. The conversion of the Gentiles is an accomplished fact, and it is useless to dispute it; it must be accepted, since it has so come about. But it could not be allowed that this was due to the labours of an apostle not recognised by the authority of the Jewish Christian apostles. It was desirable to show that the condition had been complied with which those opponents of the apostle, with whom we are acquainted from his own Epistles, had at the very outset declared in their doctrine and their acts to be indispensable before the conversion of the Gentiles could be held to have been lawfully accomplished. To accomplish this end, and at the same time to set aside the true apostle of the Gentiles, and bring him into utter oblivion, so that not even his name should go down to posterity, he is supplanted by another, a man who could not fail to be the object of universal hatred and detestation. For the name of Paul there is substituted

[1] Hom. iii. 59. Cf. Recogn. iii. 56; vii. 7; x. 16.

[2] Cf. the Epistle of Clement to James, c. 1, where it is said of Peter that he τῆς δύσεως τὸ σκοτεινότερον τοῦ κόσμου μέρος ὡς πάντων ἱκανώτερος ἐφώτισα· κελευσθεὶς καὶ κατορθῶσαι δυνηθεὶς—μέχρις ἐνταῦθα τῇ Ῥώμῃ γενόμενος θεοβουλήτῳ διδασκαλίᾳ σώζων ἀνθρώπους, αὐτὸς τοῦ νῦν βίου βιαίως τὸ ζῆν μετήλλαξεν.

that of a false teacher; and the victory obtained over this false teacher secures to the legitimate apostle the credit of what the illegitimate and false apostle was formerly supposed to have done. The bitter and deadly hatred with which the pseudo-Clementine Homilies reproduced and exaggerated the old odious charges against the apostle Paul testifies unmistakably to a desire to extinguish his name from the memory of men. In no other way can we explain why such charges should be dwelt on at a period when to the greatest part of the Christian world the whole dispute had become a thing of the past. And this is the more remarkable, when we consider the character and position of Clement, the important personage of these writings. He is of Gentile birth, and the first-fruits of all the Gentiles converted by the apostle Peter;[1] and as such he is the natural mediator between Jewish and Gentile Christians. But he is also thoroughly versed in Hellenic culture;[2] it is in this way that the religious interest has been awakened in him which leads him to Christianity, and brings him into the closest relations with the apostle Peter. Thus he represents that more spiritual Christianity which took up into itself all the better elements it found in Paganism. Nay, even in the historical narrative in which these writings are framed we find Christianity presented to us as the religion which brings about the union of everything that is noble in human nature, where the separated and those who have wandered on the most widely different paths, meet again, find themselves to be members of one and the same family, and in virtue of their common human nature akin to one another; so that they at once attain peace of soul, and the most perfect assurance with regard to all the dispensations of life.[3] How does all this agree with the irreconcilable antipathy manifested in these writings towards the apostle Paul?[4]

[1] Ep. Clem. ad Jac. c. 3.
[2] Hom. i. 3; iv. 7. Κλήμης—πάσης ἑλληνικῆς παιδείας ἐξηκησμένος.
[3] Cf. Die Christliche Gnosis, p. 372, sq. Hilgenfeld, die apost. Väter, p. 297, sq.
[4] From the account we have given of the origin of the legend of Simon, it is evident that this keen antipathy to the apostle Paul is not to be accounted for by saying that it is a curious feature of these writings, and peculiar to them. In

In any case the circumstance proves the energy of Jewish Christianity. It left no expedient untried; it would use any means in order to maintain its claim of superiority against Paulinism, and not suffer the supremacy over the Gentile world to pass to other hands. And in fact, were we to disregard this episode altogether, and to judge by the historical results alone, we could not estimate too highly the influence of Jewish Christianity on the formation of the Christian Church. It is indeed in the renewal of its youth, when it developed into Jewish Christianity, that Judaism appears before us in the full splendour of its historical significance. For whence were all those theocratic institutions and aristocratic forms derived, in which the Catholic Church found ready to her hand the elements of her future organisation, and which contained in themselves all the conditions of a power that should conquer the world, whence but from Judaism? The true centre and living pillar of Catholicism, the organising and animating principle of the whole body corporate, is the episcopate. Now the early idea of the episcopate was, that the bishop was to be to the individual community of Christians, concretely and visibly, what the Jewish Messianic idea in its Christian development represented Christ as being for the Church general in his heavenly dignity. And thus in the first beginnings of the episcopal constitution we see before us the whole papal hierarchy of the middle ages. Here is the boundless capacity for development which belonged to Jewish Christianity, the impulse inherent in Judaism towards a theocratic empire of the world. This impulse displays the same energy inwardly in the tenacity with which it adheres to its own peculiar principle, and outwardly in its vigorous expansion and assertion of its place as a great power in the world. It was Paulinism that conquered the

marked contrast with their exclusiveness and one-sidedness towards the apostle Paul are the breadth and liberality with which the Homilies insist on the practical side of Christianity as the most important. Indeed, the universalism of Christianity is here flattened out into a doctrine, according to which there is no difference between Jewish and Gentile Christians, or even between Jew and Gentile, if only they do what is commanded them, and do not hate him whom they do not know. Hom. viii. 4; xi. 16. Die Chr. Gnosis, p. 363, sq.

soil for Catholic Christianity: it was the Pauline mission to the Gentiles which added to the original congregation of the sealed the great multitude of those who came from all nations, and kindreds, and people, and tongues.[1] But it was Jewish Christianity which supplied the forms of organisation and erected the hierarchical edifice upon this basis.

But great as the influence of Jewish Christianity was in this direction, Paulinism was able to assert on its side the right it had won, and even the superiority of its principle. When Paulinism rebutted the aristocratic claims of Jewish particularism, and destroyed the very root from which these claims sprang, it made the principle of Christian universalism an integral element of the general Christian consciousness. It thus secured for itself, for the whole future of the Church, the power to step forward again and again with all its original keenness and decision, whenever hierarchical Catholicism should again overgrow evangelical Christianity, and offend the original Christian consciousness in its most vital element. In every case of this sort men were driven back to those simple and fundamental truths by which the apostle Paul, taking his stand upon the moral consciousness itself, had shown that there was no difference between Jew and Gentile before God. In the transition to the Catholic Church Paulinism, as has been justly said,[2] developed into a universal rule of life, in which the doctrine of justification receded more and more into the background, while faith began to go hand in hand with works. This, however, is not to be regarded as a renunciation of the Pauline principle; it is not a declension or a reaction, if we understand rightly the relation in which the apostle himself placed faith and works to each other.[3] Paulinism only presents its sharp doctrine of justification by faith in its most incisive mode of statement when it has to contend with Jewish Christianity for the ground of its existence, and for its

[1] Rev. vii. 9.—Here in a genuinely aristocratic and hierarchical spirit the Jews are arranged according to the twelve tribes of Israel, and each has his own number and place: the Gentiles are merely the great uncounted multitude.

[2] P. 101.

[3] Cf. my Abhandlung über den Römerbrief, p. 184: Works and Faith.

warrant on grounds of principle. It was the energy with which the apostle fought this battle which alone enabled Paulinism to assert itself against the still overwhelming power of Jewish Christianity. But as soon as this end had been attained, Paulinism was quite at liberty to concede to works their proper place by the side of faith. The apostle had himself recognised the moral value of works, and had spoken not of a mere abstract faith, but of a faith working through love. The mistake was only that Paulinism did not at once come forward to assert its doctrine of justification as outspokenly as before, whenever Jewish Christianity began to threaten new encroachments in any direction. Even in the post-apostolic age such a case had arisen, when the Church was proceeding to assume its hierarchical constitution.

We have now indicated the principle, in the light of which we have to conceive the inner relations of those elements of Christianity during this period of its historical development, elements which certainly differ from each other essentially, and yet are essentially connected. Our further task is now to place under this point of view those canonical writings which stand nearest to the apostolic age, and to inquire what relation they bear to the one side or the other of this process of reconciliation; whether their conciliatory tendency bears a more Pauline or a more Judaistic character; and whether the ideas and views which they contain are such as refer to special and subordinate parts of the great question, or such as look away from particulars, and seek to establish on broader grounds the necessity of a reconciliation in which all differences should be united and harmonised.

Among the writings which we have here to consider, the Epistle to the Hebrews is undoubtedly entitled to the first place, both in point of chronology, and from its subject-matter.

A great part of the early Church reckoned this work among the Pauline Epistles, and this testimony makes it exceedingly probable that the Epistle, though not composed by the apostle himself, is yet a product of Paulinism. The author himself seems anxious to create this impression; his express mention of the brother Timothy

(xiii. 23) must be intended to mark his Epistle as one proceeding from the apostle Paul's immediate circle. The author's style of thought, however, is that of one holding firmly to the standpoint of the ancient chosen people; and when we consider the spirit and the tendency of the Epistle, we cannot doubt that it is a product not of Paulinism, but of Jewish Christianity. This statement, however, requires to be modified, inasmuch as it is not the old, harsh, and exclusive Jewish Christianity, to which this Epistle owes its origin, but a Jewish Christianity more free and spiritual, which is broad enough to have Paulinism itself as a pre-supposition. Though we nowhere find in the Epistle the specifically Pauline ideas and doctrinal formulas, yet it contains nothing antagonistic to them. It does not expressly identify itself with Pauline universalism, but neither does it do so with Jewish particularism; on the contrary, it is quite at one with the apostle Paul in the view that Judaism belongs to a very subordinate, imperfect, and transitory stage of religious development, and is to be succeeded by a higher and more perfect dispensation which will last for ever. Thus the antitheses here are, generally speaking, the same as those in which the apostle Paul feels himself placed. There is this remarkable difference, however, that the author of the Epistle to the Hebrews at once proceeds to give a mode of reconciling the antitheses, in which he seems to take up a higher position than Paul. This is not altogether the case: what he does is simply to find in Judaism itself the broader conception in the light of which the antitheses may be reconciled. This conception is in a word the priesthood. Christ is essentially a priest, Judaism has also its priesthood; and thus everything that either distinguishes Judaism from Christianity, or unites them together, may be referred to the nature of the priesthood. This view at once blunts the edge of the antithesis which has to be adjusted. It is no longer an antithesis of things directly opposite and excluding each other, such as that of faith and the works of the law, but one which, notwithstanding the deep significance that lies in it, yet admits of being approached as a relative opposition and one of degree. The two members of the antithesis are merely the perfect and the imperfect priesthood: Judaism is essentially the same as Christianity: it contains imperfectly and defectively that which arrives at perfection in Christianity.

But the author of the Epistle to the Hebrews does not stop here. He has something to place above both the imperfect and the perfect priesthood, which embraces both the members of the antithesis in a higher unity. This is the priesthood of Melchisedek. The priesthood of Melchisedek stands above the Levitical priesthood, and the difference between the priesthood of Christ and the Levitical priesthood is simply that Christ is a priest after the order of Melchisedek.[1] In thus reverting to an Old Testament standpoint which lies beyond Levitical and Mosaic Judaism, the author of the Epistle to the Hebrews seems merely to be following the example of the apostle Paul. Paul placed the faith of Abraham above the law and the righteousness of the law, and saw in the faith which Christians now had the fulfilment of the early promise given to Abraham. But here there is a great difference between the two writers. The author of the Epistle to the Hebrews places the priesthood of Melchisedek, the Levitical priesthood, and that of Christ all in one line: here it is evident that continuity is a part of the idea which runs through his scheme. The apostle Paul, on the contrary, interposes the law between the promise given to Abraham on the one side, and its fulfilment in Christ on the other, and it is hard to see why the law should come in in this way. It appears to be there for no end but to keep the promise and the fulfilment apart. The apostle himself speaks of it as a thing quite adventitious. He says that the law was given because of transgressions, that sin might have its full course (Gal. iii. 19), and this appears to amount to declaring a complete rupture with the Judaism of the law. From the point of view of the Epistle to the Hebrews, there is no opening for any such idea. It is completely excluded by the notion of the priesthood: a notion which was quite outside the apostle Paul's circle of ideas. To the apostle

[1] Heb. iv. 14; v. 6; vi. 20; vii. 1.

Judaism is essentially law, and what he sees in the law is chiefly its negative relation to Christianity. What the author of the Epistle to the Hebrews advances against the law, for he does call it fleshly, weak, and unprofitable, because it brings nothing to perfection (vii. 16, *sq.*), acquires quite another meaning from the fact that the idea of the priesthood underlies all that he says. He himself marks very happily the difference of his point of view from that of the apostle Paul, when he says, vii. 12, that "the priesthood being changed, there is made of necessity a change also of the law." The priesthood is thus in his eyes the primary element, the starting-point in considering the whole subject: the law is a secondary thing, and the latter must adjust itself to the former. The idea of the priesthood has so high and absolute a significance for him, that it determines his whole view of the world and conception of Christianity.

But we shall fail to see the full and solid significance which this idea had for our author, if we do not regard it as discovering to us that relation of type and antitype which is one great condition of his thought. The priest after the order of Melchisedek and his identity with Christ are the principal instance of type and antitype, but everything belonging to the sphere of the Old Testament religion has an ideal, typical, symbolical meaning with reference to Christianity. In the typical, however, we have again to distinguish between the archetype and the copy. Actual Judaism is merely the copy, the shadow, the reflection, of an archetypal religion standing above it, from which such primary types as the high priest Melchisedek project into it. What Christianity is in its true essence, what distinguishes it from Judaism, is ideally and essentially present in those archetypes. Thus Judaism, the actual, legal, Levitical Judaism, standing as it does between the Old Testament religion, which is ideal Christianity, and historical Christianity, can only be regarded as the declension from the idea, as the shadow of the idea, the provisional and untrue form of the true religion which is still concealed; the form through which the idea has to move before it can attain to its true historical realisation, its consummation in Christianity. Thus the whole history of the world and of religion is the process of the idea of religion, which, moving through Judaism and Christianity as its steps, in Christianity is filled with its concrete contents. In the apostle's view of the world, Adam and Christ, or the first and second Adam, possess in "the man from heaven" (1 Cor. xv. 47) an archetypal unity in a region above the antithesis. This unity bears some analogy to that found in Melchisedek. Other antitheses through which the process moves in the apostle's view are those of sin and grace, death and life. From the standpoint of the Epistle to the Hebrews, this process is represented as that of the archetype, realising itself by means of its type or copy. The distinction between the two views may thus be said to be that the tendency of the one is ethical, and that of the other metaphysical. In seeking to comprehend the relation between Judaism and Christianity from the standpoint of a higher and more comprehensive view of the world, Paul and the author of this Epistle are entirely at one; but in all the principal points they take up they follow different paths. A matter which to the apostle Paul's mind has the profoundest inward and subjective importance, and reaches down to the very depths of the moral consciousness, is to the author of this Epistle a purely theoretical question, which he is able to sum up in the reflection that it is a contradiction of the objective view of the world which he has set forth to prefer the imperfect to the perfect, the mere shadow to the substance of the thing itself. With all the moral conceptions which belong to the Pauline anthropology, the power of sin which renders the fulfilment of the law impossible, the power of the flesh over the spirit, and the consequent universality of sin, the author of the Epistle to the Hebrews is entirely unacquainted. The death of Christ is indeed a sacrifice for atonement, but Christ is not the one who has died for all, inasmuch as all died in him. With the apostle there are no other sacrifices of atonement for sins; he even reckons the sacrifices of the Old Testament among the works of the law. The Epistle to the Hebrews, on the contrary, thinks it all-important to compare the sacrificial institutions of the Old Testament with the sacrificial death of Christ, with a view to show that although Judaism did in its own way contain every essential element of religion, yet Christianity possesses the same in a much better and more perfect way. The symbolism being carried out in this spirit, the two worships are brought so near each other that though the difference in quality cannot from the nature of the case be mistaken, yet in each instance it nearly disappears and leaves the quantitative difference in the foreground.[1] This effort to prove an analogy and show that the one *cultus* contained already all that is in the other, has of course the result of generalising and flattening out the specific Pauline ideas. This is most notably the case with the conception of faith, when we find that the same saving faith existed under the old covenant as under the new, xi. 1, *sq.*, and that the contents of faith are simply that God is, and that he is a rewarder of them that seek him, xi. 6. 26.

Thus the relation of type and antitype, on the basis of the genuinely Jewish idea of the priesthood, is the determining principle of the view of the world set forth in this Epistle. A further and most important point in his peculiar conception of Christianity is that the relation of type and antitype is equivalent to the relation of the present and the future world. It is a part of the fundamental conception of the Epistle, that in the present world of time there is nothing true or lasting, that only in the future world does everything come to perfection. But as only that can be perfected which has in itself the principle of perfection, everything may ultimately be reduced to the antithesis of the heavenly and the earthly. The heavenly is the perfect, the self-existent, the true, archetypal being, ix. 11, 24, x. 1; and since the type is now in possession in place of the archetype, and the present world is but the reflection of the archetypal, it is only in the future world

---

[1] Hence the constantly recurring comparatives, Christianity is an ἐπεισαγωγὴ κρείττονος ἐλπίδος, a κρείττων διαθήκη, vii. 19, 22. Christ has a διαφορωτέρα λειτουργία, etc., viii. 6, he came διὰ τῆς μείζονος καὶ τελειοτέρας σκηνῆς, ix. 11, his sacrifices are κρείττονες, ix. 23, etc.

that all things can attain to reality. Christianity also has no reality but there: it is identical with the future world (ii. 5, vi. 5), and so far is the author of the Epistle from allowing it to obtain any firm footing on the quaking ground of this transitory world of time, xii. 27, that he even transfers the act of the atonement from the present world to the future, and represents Jesus as having died here merely in order to have the blood which he requires in order to enter heaven as the great high priest. This is not Paulinism: but it is Alexandrinism. The Alexandrine idealism obviously governs the whole style of thought of the Epistle. All the antitheses to which this view of the world gives rise are at the same time statements of the relation between Judaism and Christianity. They are related as archetype and type, as the heavenly and the earthly, as the absolute and the finite, or, since the absolute itself must enter into the finite, and can only be through the mediation of the finite, that which it is to be—as the present and the future world. From the standpoint of Alexandrine idealism, the temporal earthly world is only a vanishing momentum of the essential ideal world. Such accordingly is the relation of Judaism and Christianity to each other. Judaism being the religious constitution of this actual finite world, is advancing towards the dissolution which is appointed for it: it is from its very nature that which is decaying and waxing old and ready to vanish away, viii. 13. Christianity exists in the present world only in so far as it reaches over from the ideal and future world into this one, and manifests itself to subjective perception in the powers of the world to come, vi. 5. In the death of Christ the two worlds are separated, but as Judaism still subsists, and Christianity with its true being has not yet come, the present world is a mixed state of Judaism and Christianity. In each of them the other also is seen, but only figuratively, in a more or less dim reflection, such as is characteristic of the whole of the symbolical, allegorical way of looking at things which is common to the author of our Epistle with Alexandrine Judaism.

It is this feature of the Epistle which enables us to define its relation to Pauline universalism. That doctrine is not directly excluded, in fact it is rather presupposed, though it is nowhere explicitly indorsed. But if the Epistle had undertaken to define the place of heathenism in its theory of the world, it must necessarily have placed it in the same negative and preparatory relation to Christianity as Judaism. And if Judaism itself, notwithstanding its close relation to Christianity, is yet but a shadow of the true substance of things, how little could have been said in a positive way of heathenism! This accordingly is another instance of the Jewish Christian character of the Epistle, that it says nothing of heathenism, and tacitly comprehends it in Judaism. On the other hand, however, all the defectiveness and unsubstantiality of Judaism had not prevented it from serving in this transitory order of things to prepare the way for the ideal and essential which should come after it : and why should not this be true of heathenism as well ? Thus, in the transcendental view of the world which the Epistle takes, Judaism and heathenism are comprehended in one.

The universal principle of Christianity which breaks through Jewish particularism is also to be recognised in the Christology of the Epistle. Christ, the priest after the order of Melchisedek, is also the Son of God, who is exalted above all, and comprehends all things by his power.[1]

[1] Cf. on the Epistle to the Hebrews Köstlin in the Theol. Jahrb. 1853, p. 410, sq., 1854, p. 366, sq., 463, sq. Köstlin has demonstrated the Alexandrine origin and character of the Epistle with great thoroughness. In one point, however, I cannot agree with him, viz. : that he pronounces the Epistle to be a simple polemic against Jewish Christianity which adhered closely to the ritual law, and says that it has a mediating tendency only in so far as it takes the trouble to give a detailed proof of the transitory nature of the law and of the dissolution of the old covenant from the Old Testament records themselves. Köstlin also declares that he finds in the Epistle no trace of any attempt to bring about an approximation between Jewish Christianity and Paulinism. Now the Epistle cannot be said to be a direct attempt at mediation ; its Alexandrinism, however, is neither Judaism nor Paulinism, but stands between the two, and limits both of them, and thus places itself above them. It assumes the character of mediation unconsciously in the same way in which Alexandrinism in general has a tendency to mediation in favour of Judaism. Ritschl continues to maintain that the premisses to the leading idea of the Epistle can be traced to the original apostles (op. cit., 2d ed., p. 169, sq.), but in this particular also his view appears to be a very one-sided and contracted one. Compare against it Hilgenfeld, Zeitschrift für wissensch. Theol. 1858, p. 104, sq.

The Epistles to the Ephesians and Colossians, which stand in the series of the Pauline Epistles, are to be considered from the same point of view; only with this difference, that as the Epistle to the Hebrews represents the standpoint of Jewish Christianity, these Epistles take up their position on the side of Paulinism. They also are striving after a conception of Christianity, in which the difference between Jewish and Gentile Christians shall retire before the concrete vision of a unity standing above the antithesis, and so fade imperceptibly into a vanishing momentum of the common Christian consciousness. Universal reconciliation, reunion of the severed and divided, is the dominant idea which runs through the contents of both the Epistles, and in which everything centres. This idea reaches its highest expression in the Christology of the Epistles. All things in heaven and earth are to be made one in Christ. This is the decree formed by God from eternity, which is fulfilled and realised in Christ at the time appointed for that end (Eph. i. 10). Especially is this the object of his death upon the cross. God purposed to reconcile all things in him and in reference to him, *i.e.* so that everything has its final cause in him, and so in the blood of his cross God has made peace through him for all things that are in earth and in heaven (Col. i. 20). This is brought about in various ways. The two Epistles regard the death of Christ as a contest with a power which is hostile to God. The lofty and all-embracing view which is taken of the person and the work of Christ intensifies the idea of the contest. The death of Christ is the defeat of the hostile principalities and powers: he has disarmed them and led them in triumph, Eph. ii. 2, iii. 10, vi. 12; Col. ii. 15. Thus the ἄρχοντες τοῦ αἰῶνος τούτου of whom the apostle spoke in a vague and indefinite way, 1 Cor. ii. 8, have developed into a supersensuous power, and the conflict with and victory over these principalities and powers is an act which affects both the visible and the invisible world.

We have a nearer approach to the Pauline doctrine when we find the removal of the law spoken of as specially belonging to the atoning work of Christ. God nailed the law, the book of the reckoning against man, to the cross, in order thus to take it away out of the world, Col. ii. 14, and by this men are reconciled to God. The means of the atonement was the fleshly body of Christ, which was slain. In the death of Christ the fleshly body, the seat of sin, was taken off us and borne away. The consequence of this atonement is that we stand before God in the consciousness of freedom from the law, and of the forgiveness of the debt of sin, holy and unblameable, and not subject to condemnation, Col. i. 20, *sq*., ii. 11. One special feature of the universal process of reconciliation which is accomplished in the death of Christ is the union of Jews and Gentiles in one and the same religious communion. This indeed must be regarded as the practical end which these Epistles have in view. The death of Christ is an arrangement made by God for the purpose of removing the wall of partition between Gentiles and Jews, of making peace between them, and thereby reconciling them both together to God. The absolute privilege of Judaism is taken away from it by the removal of the Mosaic law. In this way all national distinctions and divisions are removed, as well as every other cause of separation which arises out of the different relations of life; and in Christianity a new man appears, who is not indeed quite disengaged as yet from the old man, but has to put off the old man more and more by practical conduct, Col. iii. 9; Eph. ii. 10, 15, iv. 22. The two parties, Gentiles and Jews, being thus united in one body, are reconciled with God, and have access to the Father in the same Spirit, Eph. ii. 16-18. As the distinction between Gentiles and Jews disappears in the unity of the new man, so Christianity stands above Paganism and Judaism as the absolute religion, according to the description of the absolute superiority of Christianity in the Epistle to the Ephesians, iii. 5, *sq*., as the mystery preordained before the beginning of the world, which extends infinitely beyond all other things, which was hid in God from eternity, which had never before been made known to men, but had at last been declared by Christ and revealed through the Spirit to his apostles and prophets.

If Christianity is the absolute religion, then Paganism and Judaism must stand in the same negative relation towards it. Yet we hear of a certain identification of Judaism with Christianity. The Epistle to the Colossians, like the Epistle to the Hebrews, regards the Old Testament as a shadow of something else, ii. 17. If the ordinances of the Old Testament religion are but a shadow of things to come, while the reality is to be found in Christianity alone (τὸ σῶμα τοῦ Χριστοῦ), it is only a small measure of truth and reality that is conceded to the Old Testament religion. Yet the relation of type and antitype being there, that religion, weak and imperfect as it is, has so much connection with Christianity as the type must have. And in this sense the Epistle to the Colossians seeks to demonstrate analogies between Judaism and Christianity. Judaism has lost, it is true, that absolute claim which it used to put forward in its commandment of circumcision, but Christianity has a circumcision of its own to replace that one, not a fleshly one indeed, or made with men's hands, but a spiritual one, consisting in the putting off of the fleshly body; the circumcision of Christ which takes place in baptism, and in which Christ quickens those who are dead in uncircumcision of the flesh, by this, that they renounce all sensual lusts and desires, and are dedicated to a morally holy life, ii. 11, *sq.* This statement at once involves that Judaism and Christianity are drawn near each other, and regarded as essentially one. This is done still more unmistakably in Eph. ii. 11, *sq.* Here it is said of the Gentiles that they being called uncircumcised by the so-called circumcision in the flesh, had been during the whole period of paganism without Christ, aliens from the commonwealth of Israel, strangers to the covenants of promise, without hope and without God in the world; but that now they who sometime were afar off have been brought near in the blood of Christ. But all that is said here is that the Gentiles have received a share in that which the Jews had possessed before, and thus Christianity is not the absolute religion in which Judaism and Paganism are alike absorbed, but Judaism itself is the substantial contents of Christianity, and there is only this change, that through the death of Christ Judaism has been extended to the Gentiles in the universalism of Christianity. From this point of view the Gentiles hold no higher position than that of having come in afterwards and been admitted to participation; but on the other hand it is stated with the greatest emphasis that they have now been introduced to the full enjoyment of the same rights of citizenship; they are no longer strangers and aliens, but fellow-citizens of the saints and of the household of God. The author of the Epistle to the Ephesians can find no words strong enough to set forth this equalising of the Gentiles with the Jews; he says of the ἔθνη that they are συγκληρόνομα καὶ σύσσωμα καὶ συμμέτοχα τῆς ἐπαγγελίας ἐν τῷ Χριστῷ διὰ τοῦ εὐαγγελίου, ii. 19, iii. 6. Thus, though it cannot be denied that the Jewish Christians had the priority of possession, yet they have no longer any advantage over the Gentile Christians: the relation of the two parties to each other is a very different one from that laid down by the author of the Apocalypse, who is unwilling to regard the Gentiles as excluded from the Messianic community, but is unable to conceive of their admission on any other footing than that of being brought under the legal title of the old twelve tribes of Israel. Only in this way could they in his view be taken up into the number of the qualified members of the Church of God : Rev. vii. 4.

The fundamental conception of the two Epistles is the body of Christ, in which the two parts are to become one body (Eph. ii. 16); the σῶμα Χριστοῦ, as the Christian Church in which Jews and Gentiles are united in one and the same community. Feeling as they do the power of the antitheses which hold Jews and Gentiles asunder, and the necessity of removing them, if there is to be a Christian Church at all, the writers insist with the greatest earnestness and emphasis on the unity of the Church. Unity is the very nature and essence of the Church; this unity is provided by Christianity with all the momenta which belong to it; there is one body, one Spirit, one Lord, one faith, one baptism, etc. (Eph. iv. 4). This unity was founded by the death of Christ : in him the enmity, the wall of partition, everything positive by which the two were divided, is put an end to (Eph. ii. 14, sq.). Starting from this point the writer rises higher, to where the ground of all unity is to be found. The power of the death of Christ to unite and to found a universal communion can only be understood when it is considered that Christ is the central point of the whole universe, sustaining all and holding all together. The Christian consciousness, as it contemplates the Church in the process of self-constitution, and is filled, in this contemplation, with the absolute contents of Christianity, feels more and more the impulse to regard this absolute as an existence above the world and time. The Christology of the two Epistles is therefore intimately connected with that need which arises out of the circumstances of the immediate present, of union in the idea of the one Church which absorbs into itself all distinctions and antitheses. When we place ourselves within the mode of view of these Epistles, we find that the consciousness to which they give utterance is a genuinely catholic one. Comparing them on the one side with the Epistle to the Hebrews, and on the other with the pseudo-Clementine Homilies, we have three different interpretations of Christianity, in all of which the same impulse towards unity is seeking to find its highest expression and its dogmatic starting-point. In the Epistle to the Hebrews Christ is the high priest, in the pseudo-Clementine Homilies the prophet of the truth, and in the Ephesian and Colossian Epistles the central being of the whole universe; but in each of these forms the Christian consciousness beholds the principle of the same unity, the idea of which was to be realised in the antitheses of the different contending parties.

Another point in which the catholicising tendency of the two Epistles to the Ephesians and the Colossians is distinctly to be recognised is, that in them works, the practical realisation of the moral, take up a very independent position over against faith. It is true that the Epistle to the Philippians, which belongs to the same category with the two of which we have been speaking, appears to lay great and studied emphasis on the Pauline doctrine of justification by faith as opposed to justification by the law (iii. 9), but this is done in a purely external way. We fail to see that profound interest at work which Paul had, to establish it as a general truth that faith and not works was the principle of justification. In the Ephesian and Colossian Epistles we only hear of forgiveness of sins, redemption, atonement: it is ascribed to faith that we are saved by grace (Eph. ii. 8); but along with faith great stress is laid upon works, which are even included in God's foreordination (Eph. ii. 10). In the transcendent Christology of these Epistles everything that bears upon the salvation of man lies beyond the sphere of temporal existence, and is connected with the eternal decree of God which is realised in time. And in this view man's salvation and all that belongs to it can only be regarded as a free gift of the grace of God. Grace is the principle which creates man anew by faith in Christ. For man must become something new by Christianity: the old man is to be put off, and the new man put on, who, as compared with the former, is another man (Col. iii. 9; Eph. iv. 21, *sq.*). Yet there is but renewed in man the image according to which he was originally created by God. As the apostle Paul sets most value upon faith as the principle which brings about union with Christ, these Epistles fix their attention chiefly on that moral perfection of man which proceeds from faith, and the history of which process moves through the same antithesis of death and life which is represented in Christ (Col. iii. 1, *sq.*).[1]

The numerous echoes of Gnosticism and its peculiar doctrines which are to be found in the three Epistles to the Ephesians, Colossians, and Philippians are sufficient, had we no other ground to go upon, to fix the position of these works in the post-apostolic age. Still more directly and indubitably do the Pastoral Epistles carry us to the period of the Gnostic heresy. These Epistles occupy, like the others, a well-marked place in the series of the efforts after unity which proceeded from the Pauline side. They belong to a period in the history of the development of the nascent Church, when danger had begun to threaten from the heretics, and

[1] Cf. my Paul, T. T. F. L. ii. 1-44: Schwegler das nachap. Zeitalter, ii. 325, *sq.*

it was felt necessary to resist them. This could not but make it appear very desirable to confirm the unity of the Church, to draw the different members of the ecclesiastical community closer together, and to obtain an organisation which should extend to all the relations of the Church's life. The tendency of these Epistles is the same as that of the pseudo-Ignatian Epistles and of the pseudo-Clementine writings. Now the efforts which were made to give the Church a firm constitution resting on definite principles, appear to have proceeded originally from the Jewish Christian party, and thus the Pastoral Epistles are evidence of the readiness with which these advances were taken up on the Pauline side, and of the willingness of Paulinists to co-operate for the end proposed. They place in the mouth of their apostle Paul a series of pastoral instructions which he cannot possibly have thought of, but the inculcation of which was now in the interest of Paulinism as well as of Jewish Christianity.[1]

The equally pseudonymous Epistles, that of James and the first of Peter, are to be placed somewhat earlier than the Pastoral Epistles. Our discussion of them must be confined to the question how the two members of the antithesis which is now being adjusted are here related to each other, and in what direction we can recognise in them a more definite formation of Catholic Christianity.

It is impossible to deny that the Epistle of James presupposes the Pauline doctrine of justification. And if this be so, its tendency is distinctly anti-Pauline, though it may not be aimed directly against the apostle himself. The Epistle contends against a one-sided conception of the Pauline doctrine, which was dangerous to practical Christianity. The expressions in which this is done go straight to the principle; against the Pauline formula of justification there is set up another formula, according to which, in the relation of faith and works, works are as distinctly the real and substantial element as faith is with Paul.[2] On the other side,

[1] Cf. my work: Die sogen. Pastoralbriefe des Apostels Paulus, 1835.

[2] The chief point of the difference lies in the notion of πίστις. In contrast to the ideality of the Pauline faith the author of the Epistle of James occupies the

however, the author is not unacquainted with the Pauline idea of making the law an inward thing. Not only does he speak of the commandment of love as a royal law; he also speaks of a law of liberty. The law can only have become such a law of liberty for him by his standing over against the outwardness of the law and knowing himself inwardly free from it, as the apostle Paul was from his standpoint. The same endeavour after inwardness is to be seen in the fact that he places the principle of salvation, not indeed in faith, as Paul does, but in the word of truth as a principle of regeneration immanent in man. For the λόγος ἀληθείας can only be a λόγος ἔμφυτος, a living impulse of fruitful activity implanted in man, on the supposition that there is an inner consciousness of truth which answers to the outward revelation. The Epistle proceeded from the endeavour to counteract an impractical tendency which was declining into doctrinal formalism, and to produce such an impression upon the Christian consciousness, now settling into the form it was to wear, as was in the interest of Jewish Christianity. Accordingly the author of the Epistle, who has to represent Jewish Christianity, is the highest authority on the Jewish Christian side. James, known to us in other ways, writes to the twelve tribes in the dispersion, *i.e.* to the Jewish Christians who lived among Gentile Christians, and thus figures here as elsewhere, as the head of the mother-church at Jerusalem. The author by no means intends his Epistle to be a mere polemic against the Pauline doctrine of justification; he places before himself the general task of giving, from the standpoint of his more liberal and spiritualised Jewish Christianity, a comprehensive view of the whole field of the Christian life as it manifests itself in its essentially practical nature, in suffering and in action. He aims at delineating the Christian as he ought to be, as a perfect man in the perfection of

standpoint of genuine Jewish realism, and considers a faith without works to be as good as nothing, a dead and lifeless thing (ii. 17, 26), which, in fact, has not arrived at existence at all, since in its pure ideality it can give no empirical proof of its reality (ii. 18). Faith, even when existing in itself, only comes to its full reality in works. In any case, it does no more than co-operate with δικαιοῦσθαι ἐξ ἔργων (ii. 22).

the Christian life, which can only be properly conceived as a perfect work. This shows us how well the writer was aware of his position in the age, and of the significance of his Jewish Christian standpoint. His contention was perfectly justified from his side, and yet was free from any personal polemic, and in the doctrine of works and of the practical behaviour of the Christian which he thus upheld, he made a by no means unimportant contribution to the formation of catholic Christianity which was now going on. Whatever is opposed to one-sided tendencies, and seeks to adjust one thing with another, and to place the contraries in their proper position of equilibrium, is essentially and at once in the spirit of catholic Christianity; and it would be doing an injustice to the Epistle in this respect to ascribe to it a harsh anti-Pauline tendency.

The characteristics of the Epistle of James, then, are, that it expressly takes up a Jewish Christian standpoint, and that the author writes to the Christian Churches of the Diaspora, while on the other hand the Epistle bears unmistakable traces of the influence of Paulinism, and of the need that was felt to come to an understanding with it. In other ways also the Epistle betrays the circumstances of a later age. All this applies to another Epistle also which is closely allied with that of James, the First of Peter. A comparison of the supposed doctrine of Peter with that of Paul shows a very striking affinity between the two. This is not denied by such scholars as believe both in the authenticity of the Epistle and in the existence of a peculiar and independent Petrine doctrine, and the only explanation they can give is, that the apostle Paul read and used the Epistle of Peter. But those who are convinced that the Epistle carries them to the time of Trajan's measures against the Christians, and to a time when the legend of the apostle Peter's residence at Rome had already become current, have an equal right to adopt the opposite interpretation. They will see in the parallels of this Epistle with that to the Romans and that to the Ephesians an accommodation to Pauline ideas, which proves, if nothing more, how strong an inclination there was upon the Jewish Christian side to look favourably upon a system which adopted such ideas as the Pauline doctrine of the death of Christ, 1 Pet. iv. 1, and turned them to the uses of practical Christianity. The aim and tendency of the Epistle are clearly disclosed by the author himself when at the close (v. 12), he names Silvanus, the well-known companion of the apostle Paul, as the bearer of his Epistle, calls him a faithful brother, and says that the object of his writing is to give his readers a confirmatory testimony of the truth of their Christian faith, and to show that whether they be Jewish or Gentile Christians, if they only are agreed and stand fast in what he has expounded to them as the true contents of the Christian faith, they are to be regarded as orthodox Christians. In the Petrine Epistle also the practical interest predominates, and the circumstances of the time are seen to be establishing the conviction that the essence of Christianity consisted above all in the righteousness of a good conversation; so that the differences of the first age of the Church are more and more left out of sight.[1]

In spite, however, of all these advances on one side and the other to an approximation and a compromise, there was still, as the close of the Petrine Epistle reminds us, one great obstacle which it was necessary to remove if the work of unification was not to fall to pieces again for the want of a sufficiently secured foundation.

How could Jewish and Gentile Christians draw closer to each other and join in one and the same religious and ecclesiastical community, how could the Christian Church which arose out of

[1] Cf. on the Epistle of James, the time to which it is to be assigned, and its contents and character, my Paul, ii. 297 ; and on the First Epistle of Peter, my Dissertation in the Theol. Jahrb. 1856, p. 193, sq., where I have stated at length my opinion on Weiss's work on the Petrine doctrine : Berlin, 1855. It is difficult to understand how any one can continue to defend the alleged apostolic authorship of writings which bear the marks of pseudonymity so plainly on their face, by such random and loose assertions as are to be found only too often in the pages of Ritschl and Weiss. One would say that an apologetic like this was bent on blocking up the way to a sound and living conception of the history of the earliest age of the Christian Church. It is not worth while to discuss vague hypotheses which have no support in history and no coherence in themselves. Cf. Hilgenfeld, op. cit. p. 405, sq.

their union regard itself as a Church built on the foundation of the apostles, if it could not get rid of the consciousness that the two apostles who had stood at the head of the two great parties had held such antagonistic views and principles, and if it was impossible to think of these apostles without remembering the conflict which had arisen between them, and which had never been reconciled? It is evident that any agreement which Jewish and Gentile Christians might desire to form could only be regarded as well founded, if the relation now actually subsisting between them could be regarded as one which the two apostles had themselves contemplated, and could be traced to their mutual agreement. This is the point where the Acts of the Apostles not only finds its place as a literary product, but also plays its part as an independent factor of the history in the development of these relations. It has been shown incontrovertibly by recent investigations,[1] that the Acts is not to be regarded as a purely historical work, but only as a presentation of the history following a certain definite tendency. The true aim of the work, then, must have been to carry back the solution of the questions which were then the object of universal interest to the point of the discussion of the apostle Paul's position relatively to the older apostles. If Paulinism appears in this work in a form greatly modified from the original,—and looking at the work from the point of view we have indicated we cannot but judge this to be the case,—it yet very decidedly asserts its Pauline character in two particulars. It holds fast as the essence, the principle of Paulinism, the universal scope of Christianity, the right of a Gentile Christianity, free from the law, by the side of Jewish Christianity. It carries this universalism through all the stages of the history which it deals with, beginning with the words which it puts in the mouth of the Lord before his ascension (i. 8), when the disciples ask him about the restoration of the kingdom of Israel, and he answers them by directing them to preach the Gospel in Jerusalem and in the whole of Judæa and

---

[1] Cf. Schneckenburger, über den Zweck der Apostelgeschichte, 1841. My Paul, i. p. 4, *sq.*, and Zeller, Acts, vol. ii. p. 139, *sq.*, 173, *sq.*

Samaria, and to the uttermost parts of the earth, and ending with the declaration which closes the missionary activity of the apostle Paul when he says to the Jews that the message of salvation is sent to the Gentiles, and that they will hear it (xxviii. 18). As decidedly does it insist on the conditions without recognising which it was impossible for Christianity to fulfil its universal mission. It leaves it open to the Jewish Christians to be subject to the law as much as before, but it absolves the Gentile Christians from the law, and merely imposes upon them the obligation to abstain from those habits which were most offensive to the Jewish Christians, and stood most in the way of a brotherly union, xv. 28, *sq.*

We must take up our position at this central point of the Acts, its Paulinism, in order to appreciate aright the aim and character of the work. In the two points we have mentioned it compromises nothing of the Pauline principles. In everything relating to the person of the apostle Paul, however, it is lax and full of concessions. If we compare the account which the Acts gives us of his character and conduct with the picture which he gives us of himself in his own writings, we find a very remarkable contrast between the Paul of the Acts and the Paul of the Pauline writings. According to the Acts he made concessions to the Jewish Christians which, according to his own clear and distinct enunciation of his principles, it is impossible that he should have made. On the other side we find the same phenomenon. The Acts presents Peter to us in a light in which we can no longer recognise him as one of the chief representatives of the Jewish Christianity of Jerusalem. We are thus obliged to think that the immediate object for which the Acts was written was to draw a parallel between the two apostles, in which Peter should appear in a Pauline, and Paul in a Petrine character. Even in respect of the deeds and the fortunes of the two men we find a remarkable agreement. There is no kind of miracle ascribed to Peter in the first part of the work which does not find its counterpart in the second. It is even more striking to observe how in the doctrine of their discourses, and in their mode of action as apostles, they not only agree with each other, but appear to have actually changed parts. In the discourses of the apostle Paul we find him setting forth monotheism as against pagan polytheism, preaching the resurrection and the Messiahship of Jesus, and exhorting to repentance and good works; while only in one place, and there but faintly, do we hear a word of the peculiar Pauline doctrine of the law and of justification, xiii. 38, *sq.* The older apostles, on the other hand, Peter and even James, deliver themselves in a much more Pauline spirit. There is no difference before God, says Peter, xv. 9, between Jew and Gentile, for even the Gentiles, the unclean, are purified by faith: he calls the law, xv. 10, a yoke which neither they nor their fathers were able to bear; he declares that Jews as well as Gentiles can only be saved through the grace of Christ, and that in fact God accepts in every nation, without respect of persons, every one that fears him and works righteousness, xv. 11, x. 34. Even James makes a confession of Pauline universalism, xv. 17. It is the same with the rest of the conduct of these two apostles. Before Paul appears at all, Peter is made to baptize the first Gentile, Cornelius, with the consent of the Church at Jerusalem, while Paul performs the rite of circumcision on Timothy, the Gentile Christian, out of regard for his Jewish fellow-countrymen, and in general conducts himself as an Israelite pious in the law. Even amidst the most pressing business of his apostolic office, he does not neglect to make the customary journey to Jerusalem: he undertakes a vow and becomes a Nazarite, with the express object of refuting the calumny that he taught people to abandon the law; he has so high a respect for the theocratic privileges of his people, that from first to last he always preaches first to the Jews, and only turns to the Gentiles when compelled by their unbelief, and constrained by divine commands to do so. The two apostles are even made parallel with each other in respect to their call: Peter as well as Paul has a vision in which he is charged with the apostolate to the Gentiles.

The only possible explanation of all this is, that the facts of the case were deliberately altered in accordance with a certain tendency.

This, however, cannot have been done for a merely apologetic object, referring only to the person of the apostle Paul. We cannot doubt that the tendency of the Acts is conciliatory or irenical. The work aims not merely at a personal vindication of the apostle Paul from the charges and prejudices of the Judaists, but also at opening up a way for them to be reconciled with Pauline Christianity. With this end not only were Paul and his cause to be recommended to Jewish Christians, but such a conception of Christianity and such a representation of the character and of the doctrine of Paul were to be made current upon the Pauline side, as should remove or at least conceal the most offensive aspects of Paulinism, and render it more fit for that union with Jewish Christianity to which the author aspired. The Acts is thus the attempt at conciliation, the overture of peace, of a member of the Pauline party, who desired to purchase the recognition of Gentile Christianity on the part of the Jewish Christians by concessions made to Judaism by his side, and sought to influence both parties in this direction. It thus gives us a very clear idea of the efforts made at that time with a view to a catholic Christianity. But for all his deliberate and systematic arrangements for this end, the author could not fail to be aware what the real point was on which the attainment of his object ultimately depended. A union of the two parties could only be attained practically in so far as their knowledge of the persons of the two apostles enabled them to feel that the union was possible. This is the real point of the delineation of the Acts, pervaded as the whole work is by its tendency. In this respect it deserves to be specially noticed how carefully it refrains even from touching the irritating element which was present in the history of its apostle. How striking it is to find that it passes over the conflict at Antioch, of which the Clementines had so lively a remembrance, in complete silence; that it does not even mention Titus, the companion of the apostle, who, according to Gal. ii. 1, caused such great offence to the Christians of Jerusalem; and that, instead of these two scenes, it mentions the strife with Barnabas, as if this much less important incident had been all that was wrong at that time! It looks as if the writer felt it necessary to make up in some way for his silence about the refusal to circumcise Titus, when, in place of that incident, he gives the circumcision of Timothy, with regard to which the apostle was so ready and willing to meet the wishes of the Jews. In these particulars is there not a distinct attempt to throw a veil over the past in order to bury it for the future in the night of oblivion? And how careful the Acts is, on the other side, to bring the apostle in contact with the older apostles on every opportunity; thus suggesting, of course, that a truly brotherly relation had subsisted between him and them. What the Acts desired people to believe did actually come to be believed, and the belief never afterwards wavered. This proves how well the author of the Acts understood the age he lived in, and how accurate an estimate he formed of what it was necessary for the general good of the Church to keep a hold of.[1]

[1] The considerations which made the author of the Acts think it essential in his labours with a view to unity to go back to the personal history of the apostles, were also at work in the production of a number of those Epistles which bear apostolic names, but which we are obliged to pronounce pseudonymous. Nothing could pass into the general consciousness that did not rest on apostolic authority; and thus it was necessary, even with what was addressed to the special circumstances of the later age, to go back to an apostolic name, or even to place it in the mouth of the apostle to whose party the writer belonged, in the shape of an Epistle which he was said to have written. Thus, when we have satisfied ourselves that many of the writings of that age are tendency-writings, their pseudonymous character becomes perfectly natural. Pseudonymity, *i.e.* the use of a name long familiar to the public and representing a particular tendency, is the means by which a writer obtains the ear of his age with a view to exerting an influence upon others. In an age which moved in such strong antitheses, we are not surprised to find such a number of tendency-writings. It is important to bear this in mind in seeking to arrive at a correct appreciation of the extensive pseudonymous literature which is a characteristic feature of that age; and we shall thus escape from the mistake, possible indeed only to men of prejudiced minds and with a limited knowledge of antiquity, that pseudonymity and literary deception are equivalent terms. On this question cf. Schwegler, Nachap. Zeitalter i. p. 79, *sq.;* my Paul, ii. 110; Theol. Jahrb., 1844, p. 548; Ritschl, Entstehg. d. alt-kath. Kirche, 1st ed., p. 193, *sq.* The most comprehensive and thorough discussion of the question is that by Köstlin in his Dissertation on the pseudonymous literature of the primitive Church, a contribution to the history of the formation of the canon: Theol. Jahrb., 1851, p. 149, *sq.* No other New Testament book allows of so convincing a demonstration of the tendency under which it was written, as the Acts of the Apostles.

The works of the apostolic Fathers form a group by themselves after the canonical writings. The idea that these writings are separated from the whole body of the canonical books by as wide a gulf as that which divides from each other two wholly different periods of Church history, is only possible to those who hold the most extravagant view of the inspiration of the whole canonical collection. Several of the canonical works belong to the post-apostolic age, and at a first view the only thing to indicate to us that we are passing from one class of writings to another, is that the pseudonymous titles are not from the circle of the apostles, but from that of their disciples. The latest investigations[1] have placed it finally beyond question that pseudonymity prevails here as well as in the canon, and that the names of Barnabas, Clement, Ignatius, do not indicate the real origin, but only the character and tendency of these works. Here again, then, the chief question comes to be as to the relation in which the two factors of the historical movement, Paulinism and Jewish Christianity, stand to each other in these writings, and in how far we can trace in the growth of that relation the development of these two factors into catholic Christianity. In this respect also the line of division between these writings and the canonical ones is not clearly marked, but fluctuating; yet the former certainly take up their position on the one side of the antithesis or on the other in a more decided manner than the character of canonical writings permitted. Yet this does not dispose of the question as to their position, nor prevent it from being still a matter of controversy. Thus Schwegler has taken up a view of them which brings out chiefly the Ebionitic element which they contain, and allows Pauline elements only in so far as they may be credited with the object of a capitulation between the two parties. Ritschl, on the other hand, has been carried so far by his disagreement with Schwegler's conception of the post-apostolic age, as to reckon even the Shepherd of Hermas and Justin Martyr as adherents of the Pauline tendency.

---

[1] Cf. Hilgenfeld, die apostolischen väter, Untersuchungen über Inhalt und Ursprung der unter ihrem Namen erhaltenen Schriften: Halle, 1853.

The Epistle of Barnabas and the pseudo-Ignatian Epistles stand most distinctly upon the Jewish Christian side. The Epistle of Barnabas holds the typical allegorical view of the relation of Judaism to Christianity which we find in the Epistle to the Hebrews, with the distinction that it looks at that relation not in the objective but entirely in the subjective aspect. The two are related to each other as type and substance, but the important point is to have the consciousness of this relation. Christianity is not so much Judaism completed and come to its full reality, as Judaism unveiled and made manifest. That which lay concealed in Judaism under types and allegories, but from the beginning had reference solely to Christianity, is now disclosed to the consciousness, and known in its true significance as that which it really is. Christianity then is essentially this knowledge: it is a Gnosis in that sense of the word in which it denotes a knowledge arrived at through allegorical interpretation. From the objective point of view of the Epistle to the Hebrews the idea which is realised in Christianity is at least discernible in Judaism as in a shadowy reflection: according to the subjective view of the Epistle of Barnabas Judaism and Christianity are related to each other simply as not knowing and knowing. Moses spoke so entirely in the spirit, and the meaning of his ceremonial law is so entirely allegorical, that the law virtually did not exist for the Jews at all, since they were ignorant of this sense, and so entirely misunderstood it. Moses, it is true, gave the covenant to the Fathers, but by reason of their sins they were not worthy to receive it, and Moses accordingly broke the tables of the law. We are now the heirs of the Jews, and as such we have received the covenant of Jesus; for Jesus was appointed to deliver us from darkness, and to institute us into the covenant by his word (cap. 14). Circumcision cannot have been meant to have that carnal significance which the Jews attribute to it, for it is practised by other nations as well, by the Syrians, the Arabians, the Egyptians, and by all the priests of the idols. It was only with a spiritual reference to Jesus that Abraham introduced circumcision (cap. 9). All this at once falls away as soon as it is understood in its true meaning, and so Christianity is a new law, which imposes no yoke of compulsion, but asks man to present himself as a sacrifice to God (cap. 2). In fact the writer comes so near the Gnostic degradation of Judaism as to explain the failure of the exhortations of the prophets to raise the Jews out of their carnal mind to more spiritual conceptions, by saying that the people was bewitched by an evil angel (cap. 9). Here then we find an utterance of the feeling that there was something new in Christianity, something that Christianity had revealed for the first time; and this is spoken of in a way which, to say the least, strongly reminds us of Paulinism.[1]

In this antagonism to Judaism the pseudo-Ignatian Epistles stand next that of Barnabas. The author of these Epistles expressly acknowledges the apostle Paul as his model, and applies this name to Christianity itself in contrasting its newness and autonomy with Judaism. As disciples of Christ, the author of these Epistles reminds his readers, they must live according to Christianity (κατὰ Χριστιανισμὸν); he who is called with another name than this, does not belong to God. It is a contradiction to call Jesus the Christ, and yet to adhere to Judaism, for Christianity did not believe in Judaism, but Judaism in Christianity. What truth there was in Judaism belonged not to Judaism but to Christianity: the prophets of the Old Testament and the Jews before Christ

---

[1] The Epistle is founded upon the basis of Paulinism, but its true character is Alexandrine, as is that of the Epistle to the Hebrews. Cf. Hilgenfeld, die apost. väter, p. 37, sq.; and Zeitschr., für wissensch. Theol., 1858, p. 569, sq. In the first edition of the Entstehung d. alt-kath. Kirche, p. 276, Ritschl characterised the standpoint of the Epistle as an evolution of the Pauline principle; but in his second edition, p. 570, he no longer recognises the Pauline standpoint of the author, but holds that his view bears all the marks of Gentile Christianity at the time when it was becoming catholic. Against this view Hilgenfeld justly observes (Zeitschr. p. 570) that what is said of the original apostles is enough to demonstrate the pure Paulinism of the author. Who but a Paulinist could have not merely placed the twelve apostles in the closest connection with the twelve tribes of the Jews, but also represented them in the most unfavourable light as having been beyond conception sinful (cap. v.)? As for the date of the Epistle, I see nothing in the remarks which Hilgenfeld has made upon the other side, to induce me to change the view I have expressed in my Lehrbuch der Dogmengesch., 2d. ed., p. 80.

who hoped for his coming were even then not Jews but Christians. So decided is the author of these Epistles in his anti-Jewish spirit, and so anxious is he to remove everything Jewish from the Christian society, and to create a fixed outward distinction between the two, that he can allow no name to be applied to the Church but Χριστιανοί, Χριστιανισμός.[1] In spite, however, of this complete breach with everything Jewish, he was working towards the foundation of a catholic Church under forms which involved that the Gentile Christians should attach themselves to the Jewish Christians. We shall have to return to this feature of the Epistles at a later part of this work.

In the first Epistle of Clemens Romanus to the Corinthians and in the Epistle of Polycarp there are clear indications of Paulinism. It is remarkable how Clement not only names the two apostles, Peter and Paul, together, but even represents the fame of the latter as outshining that of the former (cap. 5). And in the Epistle of Polycarp there is an eulogium upon Paul which would leave no doubt as to the Pauline character of those writings, even had we nothing else to judge by. He is called the blessed and glorious Paul, whose wisdom no other can equal, who by his own presence founded the Philippians accurately and firmly in the word of truth, and in his absence also wrote Epistles to them, which can build up those who read them in the faith which is the mother of all. It cannot, however, be denied that faith as the means of justification in the Pauline sense is very evenly balanced by an emphatic exhortation to good works and to love. The two tendencies resolve themselves into a neutral form of Christianity in which faith and works stand side by side without any attempt to bring them together.[2] The Ignatian Epistles go so far as to place love above faith. The first Epistle of Clement does not forget to insist upon the other side; it asserts that we are not justified by ourselves, nor by our wisdom, intelligence or piety, or by works

---

[1] Cf. my Dissertation über den Ursprung des Episcopate, p. 179, sq.; Schwegler, Nachapost. Zeit. ii. 163, sq.

[2] Cf. Köstlin, op. cit. p. 247, sq. The characteristics of the Epistle which Köstlin dwells on most are the interest it shows for the law and for the Old Testament revelation.

which we have accomplished in holiness of heart; but it has equally emphatic exhortations not to be weary in well-doing, nor to let love be wanting, but to work out every good work with zeal and cheerfulness, and to follow the divine will in the work of righteousness. The Epistle of Polycarp places edification in faith, which as the mother of all is preceded by love and followed by hope.[1]

The Shepherd of Hermas, which belongs to the same class of writings, is unquestionably a product and a monument of Jewish Christianity. The strict monotheistic Judaism of this work appears in the proposition which it puts prominently forward as being the fundamental article of the commands communicated to Hermas by the Shepherd, and as the whole substance of faith, namely, that there is one God who has created all things. The requirement which naturally follows from this is to follow the will of God. Attention has been drawn to the facts that the Shepherd of Hermas does not declare the law of Christ to be identical with Mosaic law, and that it contains no reference to the specific Jewish Christian duties, neither to circumcision for the Jews nor to the laws of the proselytes for Christians of Gentile birth; and it has been argued that a work marked by such omissions must have proceeded from a circle of Chris-

---

[1] Cf. Schwegler, *op. cit.*, p. 129, 157, 168. As against Ritschl and Lipsius (de Clementis Romani Ep. ad. Cor. priore diquisitio, Lips., 1855), Hilgenfeld, *loc. cit.* p. 572, *sq.*, considers Clemens Romanus to be a thorough Paulinist, only he says it cannot be overlooked that this Paulinism is an advance towards a milder and more conciliatory attitude towards Jewish Christianity than we find in the Epistle of Barnabas. In following the inner development of Paulinism we here come to a more conciliatory spirit, and find a view of the apostolic decree prevailing which was entirely unknown to the apostolic age. There is also satisfactory proof of the existence of a similar conciliatory disposition on the part of the Jewish Christians of Rome, in the Gospel of Mark, also Roman, and belonging to the same period. On internal grounds Hilgenfeld thinks there is every probability that in Christian Rome, which even at that period was able to assert a certain degree of independence of the Jewish Christian mother-Church at Jerusalem, and was predestined to be the new centre of the catholic Church, the two original opposing elements of Christianity first came into a certain equilibrium with each other. I agree with this view. We see from the Epistle of Barnabas that the Epistle of Clemens Romanus cannot be placed at a very early period (cf. p. 139). The exact determination of its date depends on the result yet to be arrived at from the investigations set on foot by Hitzig and Volkmar on the book of Judith, as the earliest citation of that work occurs in the Epistle of Clement.

tianity which occupied an independent position with regard to Judaism, i.e. from the Pauline circle.¹ But all that these facts prove is that Jewish Christianity had by this time advanced to a much more liberal spirit. The fundamental idea of the work is, as in the Apocalypse, the number of the twelve tribes. To the twelve peoples of the Church of God the believing Gentiles have been added, so as to make good the gaps which had been produced by the unbelief of the Jews. The people of God who before the earthly appearance of Christ stood under his immediate superintendence and guidance was the Jewish people, and so when Christ blots out the sins of the people and gives it a new law which leads to life, it is the Jewish people that is meant, the old people of God, not a new people from among the Gentiles. So the number of the twelve tribes corresponds to the number of the twelve apostles; yet while this number is retained as it is in the Apocalypse, Paul is not included in it, but stands, as in that work, among the subordinate teachers and preachers of the Son of God. The author's mode of view is strongly marked with the stamp of legalism. Everything depends on the observance of the divine commandments and the meritoriousness of works. Faith itself stands at the head of the commandments. In two points the Shepherd cannot deny the universalism of Christianity. The law communicated by Christ is with him the preaching of the Son of God to the ends of the earth; and the righteous men of the Old Testament do not enter into the kingdom of God until they have been baptized by the apostles and evangelists in the under world.²

These writings contain in greater or less degree the elements out of which catholic Christianity arose. Of the period of transition we have no more faithful representative than Justin Martyr. He stands equally near to the apostolic Fathers, on the one hand, and to the catholic doctors of the Church, on the other. Like the author of the Epistle of Barnabas, he sees in Christianity a new

---

¹ Ritschl, op. cit., 1st ed., p. 297, sq.; 2d ed., p. 288, sq.

² For evidence to support these statements see Hilgenfeld, Zeitschr. für wissensch., Theologie, p. 423, sq.; and die apost. väter, p. 161, sq.

law; and he further agrees with that writer in the reason he assigns
for this, that the Jews misunderstood the ceremonial laws and
religious institutions which constitute the true essence of Judaism,
by interpreting them in a carnal way, so that the true understanding
of them has only been reached in Christianity.¹ Circumcision
had not that carnal significance which the Jews assigned to it.
The true meaning of it is to be found in that spiritual circumcision in which the foreskin of the heart is taken away. Even the
patriarchs had this spiritual circumcision, and Christians now
receive it in baptism, in which as sinners they receive forgiveness
of sins through the mercy of God.² And everything of this kind,
such as the Sabbaths and festivals, the prohibitions with regard to
food, the sacrifices, and the temple-worship, had only a spiritual
meaning, which had reference to Christianity. The intention of
all these institutions was merely transitory, they were given merely
on account of the hardness of the people's hearts, and were simply
to serve to keep the thought of God, in this external way at least,
close to the people's minds. That they had no inner religious value
of their own is clearly apparent from the fact that at the time of
the patriarchs they did not exist: the patriarchs obtained the
favour of God without them, as for instance Abraham, as every
one is aware, obtained from God the testimony that he was
righteous, not on account of his circumcision, but on account of
his faith. And since God is always the same, and was no other
at the time of Moses than at the time of Enoch, the scope of all
these institutions of the Jewish religion must have been limited
to a particular period.³

[1] Dial. cum Jud. Tryph. c. 14.   [2] *Op. cit.* chap. 43.
[3] Justin distinguishes three elements in the Old Testament—a moral, a typical,
and a directly positive element. No one, he says (Dial. cap. 44), can receive
anything of the blessings bestowed through Christ, except those who in their disposition are like the faith of Abraham, and know all mysteries, λέγω δὲ ὅτι
τὶς μὲν ἐντολὴ εἰς θεοσέβειαν καὶ δικαιοπραξίαν διετέτακτο, τὶς δὲ ἐντολὴ καὶ πρᾶξις
ὁμοίως εἴρητο, ἢ εἰς μυστήριον τοῦ Χριστοῦ ἢ διὰ τὸ σκληροκάρδιον τοῦ λαοῦ ὑμῶν.
The moral contents of the Old Testament Justin calls τὰ φύσει καλὰ καὶ εὐσεβῆ
καὶ δίκαια, or τὰ καθόλου καὶ φύσει καὶ αἰώνια καλά, cap. 45: this is the chief
substance of the religion of the patriarchs, and from this the πρὸς σκληροκαρδίαν
τοῦ λαοῦ διαταχθέντα are distinguished, as the purely positive element.

Of circumcision Justin has but a low estimate: he declares it to be the sign by which the Jews were to be made recognisable among all other nations, as those who deserved to suffer all that was inflicted on them at the hands of others. What we see in this instance is characteristic of Justin. To his way of thinking, things and institutions, which had a religious significance in Judaism, were all turned into prophecies, types, and allegories, the true nature of which could only be discerned from the standpoint of Christianity. Thus his religious consciousness assumed an attitude of repulsion towards Judaism, but this by no means prevented it from turning towards the Old Testament. It was only by means of the Old Testament, in the contemplation of its prophetical and allegorical meaning, that he could reach the deeper, richer contents of his Christian consciousness. With all its affinity to Paulinism, his attitude towards the Old Testament is essentially different from the Pauline one : it is, as in the case of the Epistle to the Hebrews, rather Alexandrine than Pauline. The stress laid upon the typical, symbolical, allegorical, interpretation of the Old Testament (and this is the great characteristic of Alexandrine Judaism) tends to preserve the position of the Old Testament as the absolute source of truth. Thus, while Judaism is very greatly lowered in comparison with Christianity, and the difference between the two brought out in all its breadth, yet from this point of view it is felt to be all-important to maintain the identity of Christianity with the religion of the Old Testament. Paulinism finds the absolute contents of Christianity immediately in itself, in the spiritual consciousness which is awakened by faith, and for this consciousness everything connected with the Old Testament has only a very secondary importance. The other view loses itself so completely in the Old Testament way of thinking as to consider that there is no way of arriving at the truth of Christianity but through the Old Testament. Everything Christian was in the Old Testament before. The newness of Christianity is merely the newness of the consciousness which has arisen as to the contents of the Old Testament. The absolute antagonism which Paulinism set up between law and gospel thus became more and more relative and subjective. Still, so long as the view that historical Judaism was only meant for a certain period was not supported in a more thorough way than it is by Justin, it remained wavering and unfixed. The idea by which the relation of Christianity to the Old Testament revelation was more definitely fixed, and which arose principally out of this, namely, the idea of the Logos, is certainly to be found in Justin, but this also is a mere point of connection. This want of fixedness in his idea of the Christian consciousness is what makes Justin's position as a whole so wavering and uncertain. This appears notably in his judgment on the Jewish Christians of his time. Considering his low estimate of Judaism we should expect a severer verdict upon those Christians who were nearer Judaism than Christianity. But with regard to those who, while they believe in Christ, at the same time observe the Mosaic law, Justin is not disposed to deny to them the hope of salvation, provided only they do not seek to bind Gentile Christians to observe it. He has no censure to express except for those Jewish Christians who declined to have any sort of association with Gentile Christians. But as for those whose opinion was weak, and who thought it necessary to add to hope on Christ and the observance of the commands of eternal and natural righteousness all the ordinances given by Moses on account of the hardness of the people's hearts, while, however, living together with Christians without demanding from them that they should be circumcised and keep the Sabbaths and other such things, he has no hesitation in acknowledging them as true brethren of the Christian community.[1] This view shows a liberal way of thinking in the direction of Judaism; but in the other direction Justin repels with the greatest strictness whatever does not harmonise with his opinion, so that our commendation of his liberalism is somewhat modified. The freer Pauline view of the use of meat offered to idols is so little to his taste, that he declares it to be no less abominable than heathenism, and will hold

[1] *Op. cit.* cap. 47.

no kind of communion with those who allow themselves the use of such meat.¹ This judgment is not directed against Pauline Christians, but only against Gnostics, yet it is expressed in broad and general terms; and if we compare it with the judgment he passes on Jewish Christians, we can see that with Justin, when all is considered, the scale dips rather on the side of Jewish than on that of Pauline Christianity. In other respects, Justin presents us with the same type of doctrine which is now to be regarded as the most prevalent expression of the Christian consciousness. On the one hand, Christ has taken upon himself, according to the will of God, the curse to which all men had made themselves liable by the transgression of the law, and has cleansed by his blood those who believe in him; but the condition of forgiveness of sins is not faith in the Pauline sense, but repentance, change of mind, observance of the divine commandments. Justin insists emphatically on this last point; man is to put forth in action his own moral power.² Christ is thus less the Redeemer than the Teacher and Lawgiver, as Justin expressly calls him.³ After all this it is superfluous to discuss the question whether Justin belongs to the Jewish Christian or to the Pauline tendency, whether his dogmatic standpoint is to be termed Ebionitism or Paulinism. He cannot be placed distinctly either on one side or on the other; his general position is too undefined and uncertain to allow of a definite place being assigned to him. He marks himself off from the Jewish Christians, and declares that his agreement with them is more outward than inward; but a much more striking thing than this is, that he nowhere gives any express recognition of Pauline Christianity. It is said to be beyond a doubt that he borrowed his view of the faith of Abraham from the Epistle to the Romans, and wished, by laying stress on the righteousness that is by faith, to represent himself as a Paulinist.⁴ If this be so, it is certainly remarkable that he never once mentions even the name of the apostle Paul, a fact which can scarcely be explained from his

---

¹ *Op. cit.* cap. 35. ² Ritschl, 1st ed., p. 310, *sq.*; 2d ed., p. 304.
³ Ὁ καινὸς νομοθέτης. Dial. cap. 18. ⁴ Ritschl, p. 309; 2d ed., p. 303.

consideration for the Jews. If he be a Paulinist in fact, he does not wish to be one in name. What we have in him, though not expressly and openly declared, is just Catholic Christianity with its adjustment of those differences and party tendencies which had hitherto stood opposed to each other. The phenomenon we have before us here is entirely analogous to that which we have to deal with in the question as to Justin's Gospels. It may be beyond a doubt that Justin was acquainted with one of our Gospels or another, but he has named none of them. The thing is there, but there is no expression or name for it as yet, and as long as this is wanting, the fixity and definiteness which the conception of Catholic Christianity requires are still in the future. What we have in Justin is the transition to Catholic Christianity.[1]

We have now to see how this transition was accomplished. Looking back to the commencement from which we started, we see

[1] In the second edition of his work, p. 310, Ritschl calls in question the position which I have assigned to Justin. With Justin, so Ritschl asserts, we have to recognise the predominant influence of Pauline ideas, though in a broken form, because this doctor is the first to bring to completeness the Pauline idea of the new law. With regard to Justin's Paulinism, I have to add the following remarks:—Justin distinguishes only two classes of Christians (Dial. cum Tryph., cap. 35 and 80 ; cf. Theol. Jahrb., 1857, p. 219, sq.): first, true orthodox Christians, disciples of the true, pure doctrine of Jesus, who believe in a resurrection of the flesh and a millennial reign ; and second, those who confess Jesus and call themselves Christians, but eat flesh offered to idols, and assert that this does not compromise their Christianity, i.e. Gnostics ; Justin afterwards calls them by this name. Now, in which of these two classes did he include the Pauline Christians? On this point it is asserted that Justin's judgment on the use of meat offered to idols cannot have been directed against Paul or against a party of Paul, because Paul himself rejected this license, and directly forbade participation in heathen sacrificial meals (1 Cor. x. 20, 21). But is not this a very one-sided interpretation of the passage in which Paul deals with the question (1 Cor. viii.-x.) ? The apostle not only forbade the use of meat offered to idols, but also permitted it, and declared it to be a thing indifferent both in itself and for the man who practised it. He certainly expressed himself in such a way as to justify an appeal to his authority on this side. On this question Paulinism and Gnosticism approach each other very nearly. And a Christian like Justin, who was filled with the idea of the demonic nature of heathenism, might easily come to doubt how he ought to regard Paulinism. This explains in a very natural way his silence on the subject, without requiring us to infer anything more about Justin than that his opinion was still wavering and undecided.

that what determined the course of the development was not only the opposition of two radically different tendencies, but also the division of the two apostles who stood at the head of them. The two tendencies have now gradually approached each other; the original sharpness of the antithesis has been softened down; from both sides there is an effort to find a middle position in which the antitheses may be as far as possible united. But it was still uncertain how the apostles, whom their strife divided from each other, came to be reconciled and to adjust their differences. And till the assurance could be had that the founders of the Church held out to one another the hand of peace, and mutually recognised each other as brethren, there could be no firm foundation for the union of the two parties, nor any guarantee for the continuance of the ecclesiastical unity which had now been brought about. It was impossible to remain in doubt upon this point. And the fact that every doubt that might still be entertained upon this question disappeared just at the time when the Catholic Church came fully into existence in her chief representatives, is the clearest proof that this was the point in which the final completion of the Church was arrived at. In Irenaeus we find the first declaration of what by his time had come to be a standing fact, that the Roman Church, the greatest and the oldest, and the universally known, had been founded and ordered by the two most glorious apostles;[1] and Tertullian speaks of the Church, cui totam doctrinam apostoli cum sanguine suo profuderunt, ubi Petrus passioni dominicae adaequatur, ubi Paulus Johannis exitu coronatur.[2] From this time forward we find that with Irenaeus and Tertullian, with Clement of Alexandria and Origen, and with all the Church Fathers of the period, whose entire agreement in doctrine and tradition, and in all the principles of the work of the Church, shows that the Catholic Church was now actually existing, every recollection of a dispute or of a difference of opinion between the two apostles has completely vanished, and the authority of the one is as firmly established as that of the other. During this period the canon of the New Testament writings, which

[1] Adv. Haer. iii. 3. [2] De Praescr. Haer. c. 36.

was the essential basis of the Catholic Church now constituting itself, was gradually being settled. And the writings of the apostle Paul are those of whose canonical character there is the least doubt. This equalisation of the two apostles is no longer merely an object to be kept in view and worked out, as it was for the author of the Acts. What he aimed at is now actually attained, and has passed into the general belief of the Church. Indeed the idea of the Church, which was now coming to be realised, necessarily presupposed their equality. In the Roman Church itself it was held as a historical tradition that the two apostles had suffered martyrdom at Rome together, and at the time of the Roman Presbyter Caius, at the beginning of the third century, the places were pointed out where they had died as martyrs and were buried.[1] If this were a matter of pure historical fact, we should simply have to accept it as a piece of history. But the story, whether we consider its matter or its form, is opposed to all historical probability; indeed, there are good grounds to doubt whether Peter ever was at Rome at all; so that the historical interest of the story lies precisely in its unhistorical character. A tradition so entirely devoid of historical foundation must have been designed to serve some particular interest.[2] After what has been said, there is no need to discuss further what that interest was. It was felt desirable to bring the apostles as near as possible to each other—each was to have a part in the merit and the glory of the other; and as they had worked harmoniously together in life, so their death was to testify and seal the brotherly communion of their apostolic career. If we try to pick up the traces of the formation of the story, we shall at once see the efforts which were made to remove the various hindrances which stood in the way of the desired result. The two Petrine Epistles contain some remarkable data for such an investigation. The writer of the second Epistle, which is not only distinctly spurious, but one of the latest books of the canon, makes the apostle Peter, in drawing his Epistle to a close, speak of the apostle Paul as his beloved brother, who, according to the wisdom given unto

[1] Euseb. Eccl. Hist. ii. 25. [2] Cf. Paul, i. 239, sq.

him, has written of the subject now under consideration, namely, the approaching catastrophe, in the same sense,—as also in all his Epistles, when he speaks of these things; in which there are some things hard to be understood, which the unlearned and unstable wrest, as they do also the other Scriptures, to their own destruction (iii. 15, 16).¹ In what a brotherly spirit Paul is recognised here as an apostle, and what pains does his apostolic brother take to remove the prejudice which might still exist in some quarters against his writings, and the misinterpretations they were exposed to! Nay, the Epistles of Paul are here spoken of in the same category with the canonical Scriptures! There are other marks of a mediating tendency to be found in the Epistles; but this direct and pointed testimonial to the apostle Paul's apostolic authority is quite sufficient to prove the specific object which the writer had in view. He is merely giving utterance to a sentiment which the great majority of Christians must long have felt, that there was no reason for refusing to the apostle that recognition to which his writings and all that was remembered of his apostolic activity gave him the justest claim.² Even in the first Epistle of Peter we may discern this tendency: and the probability that this is so rises in direct proportion to the improbability of the apostolic origin of that Epistle. Peter cannot possibly have written an Epistle which the

---

¹ It is doubtful whether in 2 Pet. iii. 16 we ought to read ἐν οἷς or ἐν αἷς. But even if we read ἐν οἷς, the expression which follows, ὡς καὶ τὰς λοιπὰς γραφάς, shows that the things to which the relative refers must be these things as they are spoken of in the Epistles of the apostle Paul; so that δυσνόητα refers exclusively to those Epistles. What was the writer thinking of when he spoke of δυσνόητα? Probably of Gal. ii. 11, sq., as well as of other passages.

² Fellow-apostle of Peter is now the highest official predicate which is given to Paul from the Petrine side. Thus, for example, in the Apostolic Constitutions, 6, 8, where Peter says of Clement the 'Ρωμαίων ἐπίσκοπός τε καὶ πολίτης, that he was μαθητευθεὶς καὶ Παύλῳ (the disciple not only of Peter but also of Paul), τῷ συναποστόλῳ ἡμῶν καὶ συνεργῷ ἐν τῷ εὐαγγελίῳ. At the beginning of the Epistle, the Gentile Christians are addressed by the author, speaking in the name of the Jewish Christians, as those whose faith had the same value and rested on the same foundation as that of the others. The Jewish Christian author, however, who writes in Peter's name, and puts forth this recognition as his parting declaration (i. 13, sq.), still lets Peter's superiority appear as an eye-witness of the glory of Christ: Paul is only extolled for his σοφία, iii. 15.

general opinion of scholars declares to be so Paulinising and so strikingly dependent upon the Epistles of the apostle Paul. This writing can only be regarded as an additional evidence of the general desire to obtain positive demonstrations of the agreement of the two apostles. This is the motive of the explicit statement at the close of the Epistle (v. 12), that it is written by the faithful brother Silvanus. It is quite in the style of such pretended apostolic Epistles to betray the tendency in which they are written by weaving in such minor incidents, and using the names of well-known assistants of the apostles. In this way Peter writes this Epistle by Silvanus, the well-known companion of the apostle Paul; while, on the other side, the Petrine Clemens is associated with Paul (Phil. iv. 3), and the same Mark whom Peter here calls his son also appears in Paul's company (Col. iv. 10). These companions and assistants seem to be meant as a kind of go-between from the one apostle to the other. How could there be any doubt as to the good understanding which prevailed between the apostles, if their friends and companions were equally intimate with one of them as with the other? The Babylon from which the apostle dates his Epistle can only mean Rome; and we are led to suppose that the interest-making for unity which gave birth to these Epistles existed mainly in the Roman Church. It was in this Church that the apostle Paul placed his hope of a better understanding, and many works which were intended to promote the same end, the Acts of the Apostles for one, were probably composed at Rome. In no other church were there such powerful motives to seek such a reconciliation as here, where the high claims of the two great apostles confronted each other; the weight of historical recollection enforcing those of the apostle Paul, while those of Peter derived equal weight from the respect with which he was early invested as the supposed head of the Roman Church. It also consists with the character of the Roman Church, where the Jewish Christian element preponderated from the first, that, with all the efforts that were made to equalise the two apostles, the apostle Peter still retains a certain precedence. In the fifteenth chapter of the Romans, which there can be no doubt was added to the Epistle by a later hand, we find a carefully designed division of territory. On the one side, on the east, the apostle Paul only comes as far as Illyria; and on the other, the western side, he at once turns his eye to Spain; so that he appears in Rome only as one passing through (15-24). The only satisfactory explanation of this is that the writer designed to draw a geographical line, as it were, between the two apostolic fields, and reserved to another apostle what lay between Illyria and Spain, namely, Rome and Italy and the neighbouring Gaul.[1] Peter must be in every way the special apostle of the Roman Church; but, if this is conceded by the other side, the bond of brotherly unity between the two apostles is drawn the closer.[2] In no other Church was the consciousness of Catholicity developed so early, or carried out so consistently, as in the Church of Rome. And to that Church the great merit is due of having first made good this essential condition of Catholicism.

[1] Cf. Theol. Jahrb., 1849, p. 493, sq.

[2] The two apostles act together in instituting the first bishops at Antioch and at Rome: Apost. Const. vii. 46. It is clear that it is only for the sake of an equal adjustment that Linus is placed between Peter and Clemens. The true successor of Peter at Rome is Clemens. Cf. the Ep. Clem. adv. Jac. ii. 19; Tert. de Praescr. Haer. c. 32; Hieron. ad Jovin. i. 7, de viris illustr. cap. 15. According to an acute surmise of Volkmar, Theol. Jahrb., 1856, p. 309, sq.; 1857, p. 147, sq., the key to the elucidation of the enigmatical passage, Phil. iv. 2, is to be found in the relation of the two apostles and their parties.

III.—JOHANNINE CHRISTIANITY.

From the sphere in which that great antithesis was developed which found its final adjustment in the co-ordination of the names of the two apostles, Peter and Paul, in the unity of the Catholic Church, historical thought turns to another side, on which the idea of the Catholic Church approached its realisation in a different way. How was it, we have now to ask, with the third pillar-apostle? Peter is now connected in fraternal union with the apostle Paul, and James belongs to the Church of Jerusalem alone. We have still to consider the apostle John and the circle of phenomena which culminate in the Johannine Gospel. We have already seen how he stands opposed to the apostle Paul in various relations, as one of the pillar-apostles, as the successor of the apostle in his sphere of labour at Ephesus, and as the author of the Apocalypse. Where we now are, however, it is the Johannine Gospel which forces itself on our attention as a new *nodus* of development.[1] It is here that the well-known critical questions regarding this Gospel, its apostolic origin and its relation to the Apocalypse, appear in their great historical significance. The appearance of such a Gospel as this would be inexplicable at any other point of the historical development, but that which we have now reached, namely, the

---

[1] Cf. my Krit. Unters. über die Kanon. Evang., 1847, p. 77, *sqq.*; Köstlin, Theol. Jahrb., 1850, p. 277, *sq.*; 1851, p. 183, *sq.*; Hilgenfeld, die Evangelien nach ihrer Entstehung und geschichtlichen Bedeutung, 1854, p. 229, *sq.*; my essay: die Johanneische Frage und ihre neuesten Beantwortungen (by Luthardt, Delitzsch, Brückner, Hase) Theol. Jahrb. 1854, p. 196, *sq.*; Hase, die Tübinger Schule, Sendschreiben an Dr. Baur, Leipzig, 1855, 1, *sq.*; my answer to this Sendschreiben, Tübingen, 1855, 8, *sq.*; Hilgenfeld, das Urchristenthum in den Hauptwendepunkten seines Entwicklungsganges, Jena, 1855, p. 6, *sq.*; my essay, zur Johanneischen Frage, über Justin den Martyrer Theol. Jahrb. 1857, p. 209, and Die Tübinger Schule und ihre Stellung zur Gegenwart, Tübingen, 1859, p. 83, *sq*.

transition to the Catholic Church, marked in the Roman Church by the legend of the two apostles, Peter and Paul. The more closely we trace the progress of the historical development, the more must we be persuaded of the great difference, and in fact opposition, that exists between the Apocalypse and the Gospel, and feel that even the long life attributed to the apostle John is insufficient to bridge over the gulf between them. The argument for a Johannine authorship admits, by what is said of the long life of the apostle, that from the contents and the character of the Gospel itself, it cannot have entered into the progress of the historical development at an earlier period. But should not this argument lead a step further? What reason is there for assuming the early existence of the Gospel, when there is not the slightest historical trace of it for so long after? It would be an equally grave mistake, however, on the other side, to let the difference and opposedness of the two works blind us to the close connection which exists between them. That connection is entirely independent of the question of authorship. It is impossible to assume that the author of the Gospel was one and the same person with the author of the Apocalypse, but it is equally impossible to ignore the fact, that the evangelist conceived himself in the place of the Apocalyptic writer, and meant to use the weight of John's name for the purposes of his Gospel, since as apostle, as the author of the Apocalypse, and as the head who had presided for so many years over the Churches, John had become the highest authority for the Church of Asia Minor. Indeed there is more than a merely outward appeal to a venerable name; inner points of connection are not wanting between the Apocalypse and the Gospel; and we cannot but admire the breadth of true feeling and the delicate art with which the evangelist has seized those elements which led from the standpoint of the Apocalypse to the freer and higher standpoint of the Gospel, so as to spiritualise the Apocalypse into the Gospel. It is only from the standpoint of the Gospel that the attitude which its author took up towards the Apocalypse can be rightly apprehended. The author of the Gospel felt his standpoint to be a new and peculiar one, and essentially distinct, both from the Pauline and the Jewish Christian; but this very fact forced upon him the necessity of giving a genuinely apostolic expression to the new form of the Christian consciousness. The names of Peter and Paul were already in current use to denote certain tendencies of the contemporary Christian world, and what name could suit the purpose of this writer better than that of the apostle John? Not only did this name possess the highest authority in the district in which the Johannine Gospel is generally assumed to have come into existence, but the apostle John was held in Asia Minor to be the author of the Apocalypse, a work presenting many points of connection for a higher conception of Christianity. If this is the only account that we can give of the connection of the name of the apostle with this Gospel, then the name denotes a new and peculiar form of the Christian consciousness, distinct from the two other tendencies, the Jewish Christian and the Pauline. We have now to consider in what its difference from these two tendencies consists.

The most characteristic difference lies in the idea of the Logos, in which the evangelist expresses most distinctly and immediately the absolute contents of his Christian consciousness. But this idea is only the unity of the different relations and antitheses amidst which the evangelist finds himself placed. His mode of view completely transcends the two other tendencies, and comprehends them, and with them Judaism and heathenism, in a higher, universally human unity. It is in his view of Judaism that the evangelist is furthest removed from the Apocalyptic writer. With the latter the name Jerusalem is of the first importance; the whole absolute significance of Christianity is bound up in that name. With the evangelist, on the contrary, the hour has already come when men are to worship the Father neither on Mount Gerizim nor at Jerusalem, but the true worshippers of God are those, and those only, who worship him in spirit and in truth (iv. 21). Heathenism and Judaism are thus alike negatively related to Christianity, as the one true and absolute religion. Judaism has, it is true, the advantage over heathenism, that in worshipping

God it knows what it worships, *i.e.* it is directed to the true object of the religious consciousness (iv. 22): in the knowledge of the one true God it has eternal life (xvii. 3). Thus the Messianic salvation can only come from the Jews (iv. 22), and there is, moreover, in the Scriptures of the Old Testament a progressive prophecy, and pointing forward to the Redeemer of the world (v. 46, vi. 45, viii. 56, xii. 41, etc.). But heathenism has also a certain share in the light of the Logos, which from the beginning shines in darkness, and gives light to all men (i. 9). If, as the evangelist emphatically asserts, Jesus was to die, not only for the Jewish people, but also that by his death he might gather together in one the children of God that were scattered abroad (xi. 52), there must have been such scattered children of God in the Gentile world too. The greater the unbelief of the Jews, the more does the evangelist, in the true Pauline spirit, see what was unfulfilled with the Jews fulfilled in the Gentile world. He attributes to the latter a much greater receptiveness for the Word of God and for faith in Jesus, and in several passages (cf. ch. iv.; xii. 20) he expressly recognises the superiority of the Gentiles over the Jews in this respect. The one fold of the one shepherd points to the same idea. If the fold is not made up of Jews alone, but other sheep were to come to it, then the negative attitude of the Jews in their unbelief of the Gospel will leave the Gentiles to form the greater proportion of the fold. In fact, the unbelief of the Jews, which is worked out in all its phases, is one side of the great theme of the Gospel. That they did not believe in Jesus, in spite of all the manifestations of his glory, this is the result with which the evangelist brings his account of Jesus' public ministry to a close (xii. 37). An unbelief like this, increasing in all its forms from stage to stage, could only result in a catastrophe such as the death of Jesus was. The death of Jesus is thus the work of the Jews alone: all the grievous guilt of it falls upon them. The fact that this unbelief, in which the whole power of darkness is revealed, is the expression of the character of a whole nation, invests the crisis which follows in the death of Jesus with the deepest significance. In the Johannine representation the Gospel narrative moves in the antithesis of the two principles, light and darkness, and in the death of Jesus these two powers finally join issue, and take up their proper relative position to each other. In the moment of this death, accordingly, the whole period of the Old Testament religious history reaches its conclusion. In order to make the death of Jesus appear in the full significance of such a crisis, the evangelist is careful to introduce all the Old Testament passages which may be taken as referring to the event. All the types and prophecies of the Old Testament which are still awaiting their accomplishment are now at last to be accomplished, in order that the Scriptures may be fulfilled (xix. 24, 28, 36, 37). The leading idea of the evangelist in connection with this scene is expressed in the last word of the dying Jesus, the word τετέλεσται (xix. 30)—" It is finished ; " that is to say, everything is finished that had to happen to Jesus as the Messiah, in order to the fulfilment of the Old Testament (xix. 28). We must place ourselves at the point of view of this great historical contemplation, if we are to understand the evangelist aright in his description of the death of Jesus. What we have to recognise in the moment of the death of Jesus is the turning-point between the two religious economies, the passage from the Jewish consciousness of the Old Testament to the Christian consciousness of the New. The old is run out and has reached its end: the new has come into existence. With his last word on the cross he who was sent by the Father has finally discharged all the claims which Judaism and the Old Testament had a right to make upon him as the promised Messiah, and placed himself in a completely free relation towards them. Judaism and the Old Testament now belong to a period that has run its course. We cannot but regard it as an indication of the late origin of the Gospel, that the author sees Judaism so far behind him, and that the opposition of Judaism to Christianity is with him so entirely a standing and settled historical fact. At the standpoint at which the evangelist stands, everything positive in Judaism, such as the Sabbath and circumcision (vii. 22, sq.) has become completely indifferent. Even of the Mosaic law he speaks in a very significant way as a thing that only concerns the Jews, that only they can call their law (viii. 17; x. 34). The law is given by Moses, but grace and truth have come through Jesus Christ (i. 17). The law is thus superseded by the Gospel; and since its grace and truth have been so decidedly and openly rejected by the unbelief of the Jews, Judaism has condemned itself. So entirely has the consciousness of the evangelist become detached from all connection with Judaism, that he is quite untouched even by that national interest which we find in the apostle Paul, and which, if there was little comfort in the present position of Judaism, yet opened up to it the hope of comfort and reconciliation in the future. Having placed Judaism and heathenism in opposition to each other, and expecting as he does that the glorification of the Son of Man which was wanting in Judaism is to take place in the Gentile world, he has to make the penalty of unbelief fall heavily upon the Jews, as with the writer of the Apocalypse it falls upon the Gentiles. With the apostle Paul the breach of Christianity with Judaism appears in the form of a dialectical process, the discussion is still going on, and the final position of parties is not yet decided; in the Johannine Gospel this breach has come to be an accomplished fact, and here we have to notice a further point in the apostle's view of Judaism, namely, that he defined more accurately than any one had done before the relation of the prophecies and types of the Old Testament to Christianity. This historical Judaism had certainly been greatly lowered and depreciated by previous writers, yet it had always been held that the Old Testament contained the archetypal idea of Christianity; and great stress had been laid on the prophecies, types, and symbols of the Old Testament; it was only through them that one could learn what Christianity really was; it was in contact with them that the truly Christian consciousness emerged. In this way of thinking Judaism and Christianity are so closely interwoven with each other, both in substance and form, that neither can exist without the other; only in the form which is contained in the Old Testament could the contents of Christianity be truly known. The

Johannine Gospel takes an important step in advance. The type is no longer held fast for the sake of what it signifies, and regarded as essentially one with it. On the contrary, so soon as the thing signified by the type has come, so soon as the reality appears of that which was typically present before, the type is declared to be quite extinct and done away, to be a form now quite destitute of meaning.

The weightiest and most significant of all the Old Testament types and symbols is for this evangelist the Paschal lamb. The writer's religious leaning nowhere declares itself so directly and emphatically as in the passage xix. 35-37. The supreme significance of the crisis of the death of Jesus is found in the fact that blood and water flowed from his wounded side. The reason why blood and water flowed from his side was that his side was pierced, and it was pierced because piercing was substituted for the breaking of the bones. With him there might be no breaking of bones, because the word of Scripture about the Paschal lamb was to be fulfilled in him, xix. 36. He himself then is the Paschal lamb. But if he is the Paschal lamb, he must be the true and real one, as distinguished from the merely typical one of Judaism, which has fulfilled its purpose, in accordance with the rule that the type ceases to be what it is as soon as the substance to which it refers has come. The point at which the typical Paschal lamb passed into the real and actual one in the crucified Christ is the turning-point at which Judaism ceased to be what it had hitherto been, its absolute importance came to an end, and Christianity took its place as the true religion. The water and blood which flowed from the side of Jesus as the true Paschal lamb is the symbol of the spiritual life which through the death of Jesus is communicated in all its fulness to mankind. We see how important it was for the evangelist to find in Christ the true and real Paschal lamb from the influence which this idea exercised on his representation of the Gospel history. We find here the only possible explanation of the well-known difference between him and the Synoptics with reference to the day on which Jesus died. If Christ is the real and true Paschal lamb he must have died on the same day, and at the same time when the Paschal lambs of the Jews were killed according to their legal custom: i.e. not on the 15th Nisan, as the synoptic writers report, following no doubt a historical tradition, but on the 14th. If he died as the Paschal lamb on this day it follows further that he cannot have kept the feast of the Passover on this day with his disciples. If he ate a meal with his disciples before he died, it must have been on the preceding day, on the 13th; and so this cannot have been the Passover. This, as every one knows, is also one of the features of the Johannine narrative in which it differs from the Synoptics. Thus Christians have nothing whatever to do with anything relating to the Passover. The whole institution is extinct and done away, by the fact that Christ died himself as the Paschal lamb on the eve of that Passover. By this fact Christianity has now completely disengaged itself from its connection with Judaism. It is true that in this point as in others, Judaism and Christianity are related as type and antitype. But what end is to be served by going back to the type and poring into the images and symbols of the Old Testament when the substance has come, that which is absolutely real, and besides which nothing else has any real significance?

With the idea of Christ as the true and proper Paschal lamb another controversy is connected. It is noteworthy, that the greater the repulsion of the Christian consciousness toward Judaism, the more firmly does it hold to this idea: while on the other hand where it lives in Judaism and regards Judaism and Christianity as essentially one, the feeling on behalf of this idea diminishes: Christ may be held to be the Paschal lamb, but just in the same way as other types and symbols are said to apply to him. The first to call Christ the Paschal lamb of Christians is the apostle Paul. When exhorting the Corinthians, 1 Cor. v. 7, to purify themselves from all leaven that they may be a new lump, he gives as a reason, "For Christ is slain for us, as our Passover." Perhaps it was nothing more than a casual association of ideas that led him to this notion: he wrote the Epistle as it happened, shortly before Easter, and may have meant nothing more by calling Christ the Paschal lamb than he meant by applying the figure of leaven to Christians. Yet he was the first to give utterance to the idea: and from his view of Judaism, the figure cannot have carried the meaning in his mind that Christianity was to be held in Judaism, but that it was to be separated from Judaism. He draws no further conclusions from the idea; the only passage in his writings where we might think there is some reference to his notion of the Paschal lamb is his description of the last supper. In describing the institution of the last supper he gives not the slightest indication that it was the Passover which Jesus and his disciples were celebrating; he speaks simply of the night in which the Lord Jesus was betrayed, 1 Cor. xi. 23. If then the tradition to which he appeals informed him that the meal was a Passover, the fact had no further interest for him. The main point was not the connection of the action of Jesus with the old Jewish festival custom, but only the new act with which Jesus was engaged, the institution of a new covenant. The apostle did not approve of that παρατηρεῖν ἡμέρας καὶ μῆνας καὶ καιροὺς καὶ ἐνιαυτούς (Gal. iv. 9) which was so closely connected with the observance of the Jewish festival customs: he repudiated it as a bondage to the powers of nature which still clung to Judaism, and was unworthy of the true religion. He could not then desire to connect the commemoration of the Lord, which was the object of the Lord's supper, with the annual return of the Jewish Passover. The Pauline author of the third Gospel agrees with the other two Synoptics in describing the last meal of Jesus with his disciples as the Passover: indeed he makes Jesus express a heartfelt desire to eat this Passover with his disciples before he suffered (Luke xxii. 15). But as if he felt this to be a sufficient fulfilling of all righteousness with regard to Judaism and the older apostles, he lays the more emphasis on the other side of the action of Jesus, and makes the institution of the supper (v. 19, 20) follow after the celebration of the Jewish Passover (v. 15-18), in such a way as to indicate that the former has now taken the place of the latter. The institution of the supper is a new act of Jesus, and is quite apart from the Passover. This is the first step of the transition from the synoptic representation to the Johannine, where the Jewish Passover meal is entirely excluded.[1] Thus the Johannine idea of Christ as the true and proper Paschal lamb has points of contact with Paulinism, so that we can scarcely doubt the existence of an inner connection. On the other side, however, the idea is completely strange to the two other Synoptics. Careful as these writers are in other cases to point out the fulfilment in Jesus of Old Testament types and prophecies, they quote no passage of the Old Testament referring to the Paschal lamb. The idea is also strange to the writer of the Apocalypse, and the difference is one which can only be explained from the deeper divergence of the two great tendencies. There may still, it is true, be some difference of opinion as to the sense in which the apocalyptic writer calls Jesus the ἀρνίον ἐσφαγμένον. The view that he meant the expression to designate Jesus as the Paschal lamb, has again found a resolute supporter.[2] But a careful consideration of the data which require to be considered for answering the question must lead to a different result. In no other passage of the Apocalypse is there the slightest allusion to the Paschal lamb: this single expression ἀρνίον ἐσφαγμένον is the only one in which such a reference is possible; and it can be referred equally well to the passage of Isaiah liii. 7. This passage is applied to Jesus in the Acts (viii. 32, 33), and this application of the words of the prophet was common and habitual. Even where Christ is called the Passover he is not termed the Paschal lamb, but the "lamb led to the slaughter" (ὡς πρόβατον ἐπὶ σφαγήν ἀγόμενον) of the prophet. It is therefore unquestionably much more natural to think of the latter in the Apocalypse.[3]

[1] Cf. Hilgenfeld, Kritische Untersuchungen über die Evangelien Justin's, p. 472, sq.; Köstlin: die synoptischen Evangelien, p. 177; Hilgenfeld: die Evangelien (p. 213, sq.)

[2] Ritschl: 1st ed., p. 146, 2d ed., p. 121, sq.

[3] Cf. the passages quoted by Ritschl from the Test. xii. Patr. Test. Benj. c. 3; Justin: Dial. c. iii. 72, and the fragment of Clement of Alexandria in the Chron. pasch. (ed. Bonn. p. 14.) There is little force in the argument that the ὀργή τοῦ ἀρνίου, Rev. ix. 16, would be out of keeping with the Jesaianic picture of the

The predicate ἐσφαγμένον, moreover, is given to the ἀρνίον in the Apocalypse with such emphasis, that it evidently implies more than is included in the idea of the Paschal lamb. The Paschal lamb could not be regarded as a propitiatory sacrifice at all; the slaying of it had no special meaning, and did not require to be mentioned; it was understood. The slaying spoken of here, on the other hand, must be one which can be combined with the full conception of suffering, quietly and self-devotedly endured for the sins of men, which is the leading thought in the passage of the prophet.

The idea, then, that Christ is the real and true Passover lamb is not to be ascribed to the apocalyptic writer, but to the evangelist. If this is so, we are at once placed in a position to observe a difference in which these two writers are very distinctly opposed to each other. In the second half of the second century there was a very active controversy in Asia Minor about the Christian celebration of the Passover. Not only was the Church of Asia Minor divided into two parties on this question, but the majority which represented the Church of Asia Minor found an opponent in the Church of Rome. The controversy reached its height when the bishop Polycrates of Ephesus and the Roman bishop Victor stood against each other on opposite sides of the question. The occasion thus arose which has provided us with our sources of information as to the remoter commencement and occasion of the controversy. The question first came to be discussed when Polycarp, the bishop of Smyrna, came to Rome, about the year 160, for the purpose of conferring with the Roman bishop Anicetus on various ecclesiastical affairs. One of these affairs was the question of Easter. The two bishops found it impossible to agree upon this point; Anicetus could not prevail upon Polycarp to refrain from observing that which he had observed with John the brother of the Lord, and with the other apostles with whom he had associated; nor could

meek and gentle lamb. If meekness and wrath were exclusive of each other, an ὀργὴ τοῦ ἀρνίου could not be spoken of at all. Nor does the passage from Jeremiah, xi. 19, which was doubtless present to the mind of the apocalyptic writer, where the prophet calls himself an ἀρνίον ἄκακον φερόμενον τοῦ θύεσθαι, point to the Paschal lamb.

Polycarp induce Anicetus to observe it; the latter appealing to the consideration that the custom of his predecessors must be maintained. Still they parted in peace, and the peace of the Church in general was not disturbed, although it was divided into two parties (into τηροῦντες and μὴ τηροῦντες).[1] It was otherwise, however, a few years afterwards. About the year 170 a violent controversy broke out at Laodicea, during the very days when the festival was being celebrated. The Church of Asia Minor was now divided in opinion, and controversial pamphlets appeared on both sides of the question. On the one side, Melito, bishop of Sardis, came forward; and on the other, Apollinaris, bishop of Hierapolis, from whose work two fragments are preserved in the Chronicon Paschale. Clemens of Alexandria also wrote, on the occasion of the work of Melito, and therefore, as his opponent, on behalf of the view which Apollinaris supported.[2] This, however, was only the prelude of the controversy which broke out about the year 190, and now no longer confined itself to the Church of Asia Minor. It extended to Churches in other countries as well, and the Church of Asia Minor now found its great opponent in the Church of Rome. Eusebius tells us[3] that many synods were held and many synodical writings composed. The Churches of Asia believed that their tradition bound them to observe the fourteenth day of the month (Nisan) as the festival of the σωτήριον πάσχα, the day on which the Jews were commanded to sacrifice the lamb. Fasting was always to be discontinued on this day, they held, without reference to the day of the week on which it might fall. The other Churches, on the contrary, observed, according to apostolic tradition, the rule which afterwards came to prevail, that fasting was to be discontinued only on the day of the Redeemer's resurrection. On the side of the Roman Church, of which Victor was then bishop, stood Palestine, Pontus, Gaul, Osrhoene, Greece. The Church of Asia Minor, on the other hand, held firmly to its old

---

[1] Cf. the letter which Irenaeus sent to the Roman bishop Victor in the name of the brethren of Gaul—Eusebius, E. H. v. 24, 25.

[2] Euseb. E. H. iv. 26.   [3] E. H. v. 23.

custom. What high importance this custom had for the inhabitants of Asia Minor may be seen from the letter which Polycrates, bishop of Ephesus, sent to the Roman bishop Victor in the name of the Asiatic bishops. He appealed to all the authorities of his Church, to the great princes of the Church who had fallen asleep in Asia, and who would rise again at the day of the coming of the Lord; to the apostle Philip, who fell asleep at Hierapolis, with his two daughters, one of whom rested at Ephesus; to the apostle John, fallen asleep at Ephesus, who lay on the Lord's bosom, and bore the emblem of the high-priestly office, and was a martyr and doctor; to Polycarp in Smyrna, bishop and martyr, and many others,—all of whom observed the fourteenth day of the Passover according to the Gospel. Nor would he, who had grown grey in the service of the Lord, who was versed in all the Holy Scriptures, depart from this day, or suffer himself to be intimidated by threats: greater men than he had said that we ought to obey God rather than men. In spite of this the Roman bishop Victor at once attempted to cut off at one stroke the Churches of Asia Minor and the neighbouring countries from the union and communion of the Church. He stigmatised them as heterodox in epistles in which he excommunicated all the brethren in these districts from the fellowship of the Church. But this act met with the disapproval even of those who, like Irenaeus in Gaul, agreed with the Roman Church upon the merits of the question, and affirmed, as that Church did, that the mystery of the resurrection should only be completed on the Lord's day.

The question as to the actual subject of the controversy has always been considered to be a very difficult one, and has accordingly received only very unsatisfactory answers. Nor is the view which is the only correct one, completely established even now; it has still to be defended against its opponents. It might seem natural to suppose that the party of Asia Minor, as a strictly Judaizing party, kept the Passover just in the Jewish fashion. But this was not the case; and there is nothing in the polemic of their opponents, who could not have passed over such a fact in silence, to suggest that it was so. To the inhabitants of Asia Minor, as well as to other Christians, the Passover was the πάσχα τοῦ σωτῆρος or the σωτήριον πάσχα, i..c. a Christian festival, the Jewish Passover transformed into a Christian festival in consequence of the way in which Jesus had kept it with his disciples before his passion. The characteristic of the Quartodecimans, as they were called, was simply that they adhered to the fourteenth day of the Jewish month Nisan in the same way as the Jews did, for whom that day was the day of the actual Passover, from which the following days were distinguished as the feast of ἄζυμα. This is the meaning of the term τηρεῖν, which is a standing phrase in the history of this controversy. The complete form, as we find it in the Epistle of Polycrates, is τηρεῖν τὴν ἡμέραν τῆς τεσσαρεσκαιδεκάτης τοῦ πάσχα. This, however, does not make it clear what the exact significance of the day was to them. We find further light upon this point in the fact that they considered it necessary to bring the fast to an end on this day, while their opponents desired to carry on the fast which was customary before Easter to the Sunday on which the resurrection of Christ was celebrated. What, then, the day of the resurrection, Sunday, a fixed day, was for the one party, the fourteenth day of the month was for the other, on whatever day of the week that day might fall. But what was the 14th of Nisan to them, that they observed it in this way?

It is a too hasty conclusion to suppose that the contrast must be between the time of the resurrection and the time of the death, and that the whole question was simply at what point of time the boundary-line was to be drawn between the joy of the festival and the mourning of the fast, whether at the fourteenth, though it was earlier, or at Easter Sunday. According to this view, to the Christians of the West the day of the resurrection was the infinitely-important, never-to-be-forgotten day on which the little flock of believers had first been freed from all their fears, and saw the reality of redemption placed in the brightest light before them after the dreadful doubts and darkness of the fatal days preceding. This day removed a crushing weight from the disciples, and was to them the true day of deliverance. For the Christians of the East, again, the day of the crucifixion had the prerogative; this day possessed the deepest significance in their eyes. Up to the point of death the sufferings of the Lord had been a painful and mournful thing, but with the moment of death the Lord's sufferings were at an end, the great work of atonement was completed, the eternal redemption was accomplished, and the glorification of Christ began. This may not have been clear at the moment to the minds of the disciples, but nevertheless it was the case. According to this view, the Western observance is to be characterised as more subjective, personal, individual, as more closely adhering to fixed and stereotyped historical traditions, and seeking to reproduce as closely as possible the whole of the outward features of the original Passion-week. The Eastern standpoint, on the contrary, appears to be more objective, dogmatic, universal, free and plastic; the Eastern observance seems to proceed from an endeavour to express the essence, the inner meaning of the act of salvation, and not merely a historical form of consciousness regarding it. What this observance looks to as the regulating principle in fixing the term of the celebration of the death, is not the outward outline of the first Passion-week, but an ideal consideration of religious history which lay in the events of that week.[1]

This is without any historical foundation, and the whole question is too much removed from solid ground, and taken into the sphere of *a priori* presuppositions and abstractions. It cannot even be affirmed that the fasting could only have a meaning where the thought of the death of Jesus was the leading idea; and that the conclusion of the fast on the 14th must necessarily have involved the assumption that Christ died, and brought about the atonement, not on the 15th of Nisan, but on the 14th, as the Paschal lamb.[2] It is true that the customary fasting before Easter—and there was a difference about

---

[1] Weitzel: die Christliche Passahfeier der drei ersten Jahrhunderte, 1848, pp. 101, 110, 131.

[2] Ritschl: 1st ed., p. 250; 2d ed., p. 269.

this too, since, as Irenaeus says in his Epistle, some fasted one day, others two, others still longer, some forty hours during day and night[1] —could only refer to the sufferings and death of Jesus. But it is an erroneous conclusion to think that because fasting is the sign of mourning, the end of the fasting, the eating which came in place of the fasting, necessarily expressed the opposite mood of mind, and that the eastern Christians therefore kept the day of Jesus' death as their day of rejoicing, instead of the day of the resurrection, which was the day of rejoicing kept by the Christians of the West.[2] Even if the death of Jesus brought up no other idea than that of the accomplishment of the atonement, still the sentiment of grief must have been uppermost, and it would be incomprehensible how the Christians of the East, if they meant their breaking

---

[1] Οἱ δὲ τεσσαράκοντα ὥρας ἡμερινάς τε καὶ νυκτερινὰς συμμετροῦσι τὴν ἡμέραν, Euseb. 5. 24. This can only mean: they make forty hours by day and night equal to the measure of their day: they thought themselves obliged to have a period of fasting of forty hours, but counted these forty hours only as one day. Gieseler (K.-g. i. 1, p. 240) proposes to read τῇ ἡμέρᾳ αὐτῶν, and to interpret the passage thus: they measure out forty hours together with their day; *i.e.* they fast on the day which they keep as the Passover, or the day of the death of Christ, and with the hour of the death they begin a new fast of forty hours to the resurrection. This is clearly wrong; the Christians of Asia Minor left off fasting on the evening of the 14th.

[2] Steitz's observation (Theol. Stud. u. Krit. 1859, p. 728) on this fasting is but one proof more of the wrongness of his whole view of the Easter celebration of Asia Minor. Steitz thinks that if the Church of Asia Minor intended its solemnity to be a commemoration of the Lord's last meeting with his disciples, their fasting on this day is quite incomprehensible. Why should they receive fasting what the disciples received from their Master during or after the meal on that evening? This would no doubt be exceedingly strange; but who asserts that this was the case? The main point of the view which Steitz is contesting is simply that the Easter festival of Asia Minor refers not to the Communion or Eucharist as such, but to Jesus' last meeting with his disciples. It is therefore quite beside the mark to bring in here the Church canon of fasting before the Communion; and it is in the highest degree natural to take this fasting as the expression of the mournful state of mind in which the disciples were on that day, which was the beginning of the time in which *sponsus ablatus est*. This coincides with what Steitz himself says of this fasting, p. 733, only that the object it has in view is not the death of Jesus, but the Lord, still sojourning in the circle of the disciples, but now going to meet his πάθος. Steitz might have saved himself many superfluous words, had he taken the trouble to understand his opponents' views more thoroughly.

off the fast as an expression of joy, could have chosen to do so on the day of the Passion. There must unquestionably have been some particular reason for the practice, and we have to ask what led them to celebrate this particular day, the 14th, not fasting but eating? And if they did not fast but ate on this day, must we not ask if the presumption is well founded that they kept this day as the day of Jesus' death? The answer to this question is not to be sought in the way of ingenious combinations; it lies plainly enough before our eyes in the fragments preserved in the Chronicon Paschale.[1] The reason of the difference is most distinctly expressed in a fragment of Hippolytus, who, speaking as a champion of the Western custom, puts into his opponents' mouth the following words: "What Christ did on that day was the Passover, and he suffered at that time. For this reason I likewise must do as the Lord did." To this Hippolytus answers: It is a mistake if one does not know that at the time the Lord did not eat the legal Passover when he suffered, for he was the Passover spoken of by prophecy, which was fulfilled on the appointed day. In another fragment also Hippolytus says: "As the Lord had already said that he would no more eat the Passover, he ate this meal before the Passover, but the Passover itself he did not eat; for it was not the time for him to eat it." From this it is as clear as possible, that the orientals kept the 14th, not as the day of the death of Jesus, but as the day on which he kept the Passover with his disciples. The question between them and their opponents was that between a doing or a suffering on the part of Jesus, or more distinctly, between $\phi\alpha\gamma\epsilon\hat{\imath}\nu$ and $\pi\alpha\theta\epsilon\hat{\imath}\nu$. If Jesus ate the Passover on the 14th, he cannot have died on that day. His followers cannot therefore commemorate his death on that day; they must feel it incumbent on them to do what he did; not to fast, but to eat a meal in commemoration of the Passover observed by him. This meal naturally formed the conclusion of the fast that was customary before Easter. The western Christians again reasoned in the opposite way. Since

---

[1] Chronicon Paschale, in the Bonn edition of the Corpus Scr. Hist. Byz.; vol. i. 1832, p. 13, sq.

Jesus suffered and died on the 14th, he cannot have eaten the Passover on that day; and so there is no reason for concluding the fast on the day on which the Jewish Passover was held, or to take the 14th of Nisan into account at all in connection with the Christian celebration of Easter.

The fragments of Apollinaris of Hierapolis yield just the same result. He states the position of his opponents, the orientals, exactly as Hippolytus does: they say that the Lord ate the lamb with his disciples on the 14th, and himself suffered on the great day of the feast of unleavened bread. They read Matthew in such a way as to make him say exactly what they take to be the case. But the consequence of this is simply that their view does not agree with the law, and that they make the Gospels appear to be in conflict with the law. This conflict with the law that Apollinaris speaks of must mean that contradiction which the other party declared must arise between the Gospel and the law, if it appeared from the Gospels that Jesus did not die on that day on which as the Paschal lamb he needs must die, to fulfil the directions of the law about the slaying of the Passover. To the Western Christians then the meaning and importance of the controversy were derived from the idea of Christ as the Paschal lamb. This idea is distinctly expressed in the second fragment of Apollinaris, in such a way as to leave no doubt as to the nature of the argument supporting the Western view.[1]

---

[1] *Op. cit.* p. 14. ‛Η ἰδ' τὸ ἀληθινὸν τοῦ Κυρίου πάσχα, ἡ θυσία ἡ μεγάλη, ὁ ἀντὶ τοῦ ἀμνοῦ παῖς Θεοῦ, ὁ δεθεὶς ὁ δήσας τὸν ἰσχυράν; καὶ ὁ ταφεὶς ἐν ἡμέρᾳ τῇ τοῦ πάσχα. The proofs are of this nature. To those drawn from Hippolytus and Apollinaris we have to add that of Clemens of Alexandria. In a fragment which is also preserved in the Chronicon Paschale, *op. cit.* p. 14, he says that in the preceding years the Lord ate the Passover with the Jews, but that on this occasion he announced himself as the Passover on the 13th, and then suffered on the following day (ὁ ἀμνὸς τοῦ Θεοῦ, ὡς πρόβατον ἐπὶ σφαγὴν ἀγόμενος, αὐτὸς ὢν τὸ πάσχα καλλιερηθεὶς ὑπὸ Ἰουδαίων). In all these passages the point at issue is clearly presented to us, and we see also the important bearing which the data of the Paschal controversy have upon the question of the apostolic origin of the 4th Gospel. In order to get rid of this inevitable inference Weitzel asserts, *op. cit.* p. 16, *sq.*, that we have to distinguish between Catholic and heretical Quartodecimans, and that the evidence of Hippolytus and the others only refers to the

What the opponents of the Christians of Asia Minor regarded as fixed before everything else was that Christ was the true and real Passover. From this it necessarily followed for them, since it was necessary that type and antitype, prophecy and fulfilment, should agree as closely as possible, that Christ died on the same

heretical party of them. There is thus an important difference between the Paschal controversy as it was in the year 170, and as it was in 190. In the year 170 Church did not stand against Church, the great representatives of the Church stood against an isolated party, against certain Judaizing Laodiceans, who appeared with their Judaizing Passover ritual in the year 170. But these pretended heretical Quartodecimans are a pure fiction. No proof of their existence can be brought forward; on the contrary, the whole character and history of the contest entirely excludes such a supposition. How clearly does the Epistle of Irenaeus show us that it is one and the same controversy from the very beginning! In this Epistle we find Polycarp and Anicetus at issue about the same alternative, τηρεῖν or μὴ τηρεῖν, as formed the subject of dispute between Polycrates and Victor, as we gather from the Epistle of the former. Had the Quartodecimans in question been a heretical, i.e. a Judaizing party, we should have had some clearer proof of their Judaizing tendency. But the dispute was not about the Passover as such, it was not proposed to keep it with the Jews as a Jewish festival. The dispute was about the action of Jesus in connection with the Passover, whether it was at a Passover that he ate his last meal with his disciples. The 14th was to be kept, not for the sake of the Passover, but in remembrance of Jesus and what he had done. This is the plain meaning of the passages which we have quoted. What was there here that was specifically Judaistic, and that was not to be found with the Catholic Quartodecimans as well? The Church knew nothing of heretical Quartodecimans in the sense here assumed. This may be seen from a passage in the newly discovered Philosophoumena of Origen (vii. 18, ed. Miller, p. 274, sq.), where he speaks of those who keep the Passover on the 14th day of the first month, κατὰ τὴν τοῦ νόμου διαταγήν, and justify the practice by referring to the curse of the Mosaic law, but do not consider the significance of the true Paschal sacrifice in Christ and the words of the apostle Paul, Gal. v. 3. In the same way as Apollinaris and Hippolytus accused their opponents of contentiousness and ignorance, these persons are called φιλόνεικοι τὴν φύσιν, ἰδιῶται τὴν γνῶσιν; but not as Judaistic heretics; on the contrary, the testimony of perfect orthodoxy in other respects is expressly accorded to them: ἐν δὲ τοῖς ἑτέροις οὗτοι συμφωνοῦσι πρὸς πάντα τὰ τῇ ἐκκλησίᾳ ὑπὸ τῶν ἀποστόλων παραδεδομένα.

Cf. on the Paschal controversy my Krit. Unters. über die kanon. Evang. p. 269, 334, sq., 353, sq., and the essays in the Theol. Jahrb. 1847, p. 89, sq.; 1848, p. 264, sq.; Hilgenfeld: der Paschastreit und das Evangelium des Johannes mit Rücksicht auf Weitzel's Darstellung; Theol. Jahrb. 1849, p. 209, sq., and Der Galaterbrief, Leipzig, 1852, p. 84, sq. In spite of its evidently incorrect assumption, Weitzel's view is a very convenient sanction for refusing to accept the results of recent criticism; and it is repeated by Lechler in the work quoted, p. 52, who how-

day on which the Jewish Passover was slain. But if the 14th was only distinguished as the day of the death of Jesus, and if what was meant by Jesus dying as the Passover was that He finally and for ever removed the old, that had reached its fulfilment, by placing in its stead the new, that had now come into being, then there could be no need to retain the 14th as the standing anniversary of the death of Jesus. To the Christian festival-calendar the only possible fixed day was the Sunday of the resurrection. Thus, while for the Easterns the 14th was the day of a standing festival, and everything else had to be arranged with reference to that day, with the Westerns the days of these yearly festivals were fixed on the opposite principle: the day of the death depended on the day of the resurrection, and as the latter was always a Sunday, the former was always a Friday. Though the Roman custom more and more gained the upper hand, yet the difference continued to exist even in later times, and was in fact one of the causes of the Council of Nice, for even at that time there were several ecclesiastical provinces in the

---

ever fails to apprehend correctly the point at issue. In his second, thoroughly revised, edition of 1857, Lechler brings forward only what is quite familiar, and was refuted long ago. For the literature of the question cf. Steitz: die Differenz der Occidentalen und der Kleinasiaten in der Passahfeier, auf's Neue kritisch untersucht und im Zusammenhang mit der gesammten Festordnung der alten Kirche entwickelt, in the Theol. Stud. u. Kritiken, 1856, p. 721. Against this my Dissertation on the Johannine question in the Theol. Jahrb. 1857, p. 242, *sq.*, and Hilgenfeld, p. 523, *sq.* In defence of his view or of Weitzel's hypothesis, Steitz gave certain further observations in the Stud. u. Krit. 1857, p. 741, which I did not neglect to answer; see Zeitschr. für wissensch. Theol., 1858, p. 298, *sq.* The question has been so long the subject of investigations and so thoroughly discussed on both sides that two points may now be regarded as established results against which it is not likely that any new argument of importance will be adduced. These are—(1.) The Passover on the 14th was not consecrated to the Redeemer dying or already dead, but to the Lord now entering into his sufferings (his πάθος), and still sitting in the midst of his disciples. (It was this, as I pointed out when I last wrote on the subject, that filled these last moments with recollections of such infinite tenderness. Hence it was that for the Christians of Asia Minor, everything was wrapped up in that one day, and that they would know nothing of any consideration that would have detached them from the sentiment so intimately connected with that day. Everything was concentrated on the few hours of the Passover held after the fast in memory of Jesus' last supper. Far from being a festival of joy, the æsthetical antithesis to the fast just brought to a conclusion, as some think it must have been, it must have been kept in the solemn

East in which the Passover was kept at the time when the Jews kept it.[1] The Judaism of the Quartodecimans had given offence from the first; and the same anti-Jewish feeling still finds expression in the declaration of the Council of Nice, that it was improper to be guided by the custom of the unbelieving and hostile Jews. All the Christians of the East, who had hitherto been keeping the Passover with the Jews, were in future to celebrate it in conformity with the usage of the Roman Church. Indeed, so strong was the desire to have nothing in common with the Jews in this festival, that when the Easter full moon fell on a Sunday, Easter was to be celebrated not on the day of the full moon, but on the following Sunday.

So lively and universal was the commotion aroused by this question not only in Asia, but among the Christian Churches of the age in general. And this makes it impossible to disregard the attitude of the Gospel of John with regard to the dispute. It takes its stand most decidedly upon the side of the Western tradi-

---

mood appropriate to a supper of farewell, but a mood lifted above mere sorrow by the deepest sentiment of piety.) (2.) The pretended heretical Quartodecimans are utterly unvouched for by any historical evidence; in fact they are simply a makeshift of apologetics. In his "last words," in which he (Steitz) finally wound up his investigation into the Paschal controversy viewed aesthetically and otherwise (der ästhetische Charakter der Eucharistie und des Fastens in der alten Kirche, Theol. Stud. u. Krit. 1859, p. 716 *sq.*), he sums up his result as follows, p. 737 : "There is every reason not to set too high a value on the statements of Polycarp and Polycrates about John. The Church of Asia Minor will have received from the beloved disciple the fact attested by the fourth Gospel, that Christ died on the 14th of Nisan, and perhaps also the usage of celebrating this day as the standing anniversary of his death; but there is no doubt that the manner of celebration belongs to a later age, and was formed by a process of historical development, though probably upon the basis of the fourth Gospel (cf. xvi. 6, 7 ; xix. 30.)" This is a view of history dominated and limited by the "beloved disciple;" and it ends in simply denying the value of historical evidences, such as those of Polycarp and Polycrates, which do not suit the writer's purpose, while the question under discussion is no nearer a solution at the conclusion of the argument than it was at the beginning.

[1] Cf. Athanas. de Syn. 5, where there is special mention of οἱ ἀπὸ τῆς Συρίας καὶ Κιλικίας, καὶ Μεσοποταμίας, as those who ἐχώλευον περὶ τὴν ἑορτὴν καὶ μετὰ τῶν Ἰουδαίων ἐποίουν τὸ πάσχα. Cf. Eusebius, de vita Const. iii. 5. 18. Socr., H. E., i. 9.

tion. It is evidently with deliberate purpose that it arranges its account of the death of Jesus in such a way as to preclude the idea that his last meal was the Passover.

In xiii. 1 it says expressly, that before the feast of the Passover Jesus ate a supper (δεῖπνον, not τὸ δεῖπνον) with his disciples, which, notwithstanding its difference in many respects from the supper of the Synoptics, yet coincides with theirs in being the last he ate. The repeated allusions, again, to the festival as still approaching, as xiii. 29, xviii. 28, seem to be designed to prevent all doubt upon the point that this meal was the same meal eaten by Jesus with his disciples on the night of his arrest, as that which is described by the Synoptics, only with the difference that it was not the Passover. On this point especially, there is such a radical discrepancy between the synoptical and the Johannine narratives, that there is scarcely another exegetical result so firmly established as the utter futility of all attempts to interpret the one account into the other.

And yet this same apostle John is represented as one of the chief witnesses to the genuinely apostolic origin of the tradition of Asia Minor—the apostle to whose authority the venerable Polycrates, bishop of Ephesus, appealed. That bishop calls to witness his grey hairs and all that was holy and worthy of reverence to him, in such a way as to make it as impossible to question the historical trustworthiness of his testimony as it is to impugn the above-mentioned exegetical result. In what other way can this obvious contradiction be overcome than by supposing that the author of the Gospel was a different man from the apostle John, the author of the Apocalypse?[1]

---

[1] According to Gieseler, Lehrb. der K.G., 4th ed., i. 1, p. 241, sq., this contradiction admits of an easy solution. He says: "At the outset the Jewish Passover was kept up in the Christian Churches only with the difference that it was referred to Christ, the true Passover (1 Cor. v. 7). John found this practice existing at Ephesus, and left it unchanged. He corrected it in his Gospel only so far as to preclude the belief on which it may have proceeded that Christ ate the Passover with the Jews on the day before his death: he made it appear distinctly, that Christ was crucified on the 14th of Nisan. But this did not make it necessary to

The historical datum which is given to us in the information we have about the Paschal controversy does but confirm the result which rests on so many other incontrovertible grounds. These all combine to place the origin of the Gospel of John at a later date, and we now conclude, that it can only have arisen within the circle of those movements which were called forth by the Paschal controversy, and must have proceeded from the same interest which caused the Church of Rome to take up more and more an attitude of opposition to the Churches which still adhered to the original Jewish-Christian tradition. There is no doubt that historical tradition was on the side of the Quartodecimans of Asia Minor, and that in this view they were right. We have no reason for doubting the trustworthiness of the testimony to which they appealed in proof of the apostolic origin of their tradition; and the synoptic account of the death of Jesus, which coincides with this tradition in every respect, produces the impression that it is the oldest transmitted record. All the testimony is agreed upon the point that Jesus died on the 15th of Nisan, and kept the Passover on the 14th with his disciples.

The other tradition, according to which Jesus died on the 14th, the day of the Passover, and his last meal was not the Passover, proclaims itself as of a later origin. It is true that in the Church of Rome Anicetus appealed against Polycarp to the tradition of his

change the celebration at Ephesus; on the contrary, the 14th of Nisan was now shown to be the true Passover-day for Christians as well: the fulfilment of the type fell on the same day with the type itself." As if the contradiction did not lie in this very point, that he laid the utmost stress on the 14th, as the day of Christ's death, and yet was so indifferent as to the mode in which the day was celebrated! How could he allow the contradiction of the φαγεῖν and παθεῖν on the same day to remain unremoved? How could he sanction that contradiction by personally taking part in the Passover of Asia Minor, while in his Gospel he did all in his power to oppose it? And what brought him to correct the belief he found existing in Asia Minor, and thereby to run counter to the universal tradition, confirmed by the Synoptics, according to which Christ died on the 15th? One who supposes that the self-contradiction into which the apostle John would thus have been involved can be got rid of in this easy way, must have failed entirely to see how radical a difference was involved in the question of the day of the death of Jesus.

predecessors. But the Epistle of Irenaeus to Victor, the bishop of Rome, shows that the line of bishops of Rome, whom Irenaeus designated as μὴ τηροῦντες (though at the same time they stood in friendly relations to the τηροῦντες), could not be traced further than Anicetus, Pius, Hyginus, Telesphorus, and Xystus. The last of these, Eusebius tells us (E. H. iv. 4), was bishop of Rome during the time of Hadrian from the third to the twelfth year of the reign of that emperor (cir. 120-129). Whatever the causes may have been which combined to give the Church of Rome a more and more anti-Jewish tendency during the course of the second century, there is no doubt that the inner reason was the freer development of the Christian consciousness. The principal expression of this tendency was in connection with the Old Testament typology, the relation between type and antitype coming to be more exactly defined. Justin, though he holds the Passover of the Old Testament to be a type of Christ, yet agreed with the synoptic version with regard to the day of the death of Jesus.[1]

But when it was emphatically maintained against opponents that Jesus did not keep the Jewish Passover, it became necessary to look for grounds to justify this assertion. And the only way to justify it was to define the relation of type and antitype more accurately. The more completely the type and antitype coincide, the less is it possible for the type to retain any importance, when once the full reality of the antitype has taken its place. This became the fundamental and guiding thought upon the subject: we find this thought also in the Gnostic writers of the period, when they attempt to define the exact significance of the types and symbols of the Old Testament.[2] Allegorical interpretation being regarded as

[1] Dial. c. Tryph. c. iii.; cf. c. 40. In the latter passage the manner in which Justin considers the Passover to be a type of Christ is especially deserving of notice. He sees the typical element only in the blood which was put upon the houses, and in the form of the cross, which the lamb presented when it was being roasted. He thus leaves quite unnoticed that sign to which the evangelist, xix. 36, attaches the highest importance. How could he have done so if he had been acquainted with the Gospel of John?

[2] Cf. in particular the Epistle to Flora of the Gnostic Ptolemaeus in Epiphanius, Haer. xxxiii. 5. Πάντα ταῦτα, Ptolemaeus says of the Old Testament types,

the key to the Scriptures, and as the highest knowledge, those who occupied this point of view, and thought it enabled them to gain a deeper insight into the relation of type and antitype, considered themselves to be standing at a higher stage of Christian knowledge than others. This is the point of the charge which we find in the fragments of Apollinaris and Hippolytus, where they speak of the ignorance and contentiousness of their opponents, since being destitute of that true insight into the subject which is possible only to those who know how to distinguish correctly between type and antitype, and to place them in their true relation to each other, they yet obstinately adhere to their alleged tradition, and contend against their opponents with regard to that which the latter believe themselves to understand far better.

In this view of it the Paschal controversy is one of the most important stages in that series of endeavours which the Church put forth in the second century to indicate the positions which had been attained in the freer development of the Christian principle, by purifying and disengaging itself from the elements of Judaism that still adhered to it. The Gospel of John is essentially a product of these movements, and is the purest expression of that higher form of the Christian consciousness which issued out of this process of development. It regards the breach of Christianity with Judaism as an accomplished fact, and the attitude which it takes up to Jewish Christianity is a similar one. Since Christ has been sacrificed as the Passover, the Passover no longer concerns Christians. The Passover is now a purely Jewish festival: for Christians it is abrogated (τὸ πάσχα τῶν Ἰουδαίων, ii. 13, vi. 4, xi. 55). This is part of the general view of this Gospel, according to the language of which even the law is merely the law of the Jews. What led the author of the Gospel to identify himself in this way

among which the Passover is specially named, εἰκόνες καὶ σύμβολα ὄντα τῆς ἀληθείας φανερωθείσης μετετέθη, κατὰ μὲν τὸ φαινόμενον καὶ σωματικῶς ἐκτελεῖσθαι ἀνῃρέθη, κατὰ δὲ τὸ πνευματικὸν ἀνελήφθη, τῶν μὲν ὀνομάτων τῶν αὐτῶν μενόντων, ἐνηλλαγμένων δὲ τῶν πραγμάτων.

with the apostle John can have been nothing but his consciousness that he had reached a higher stage of development, where all particularism was left far behind. John alone—but only John as spiritualised in the sense of this Gospel—is for the author the highest expression of the Christian consciousness. In the Johannine Gospel, then, John is distinguished as the most intimate disciple, as the beloved disciple who was nearest to Jesus—a thing which is quite peculiar to this Gospel. Indeed this is carried so far as to assign to John a position in which Peter himself has need of his mediation, and is designedly represented in a subordinate position to him. This is a most obvious protest against the primacy attributed to the apostle Peter by the Jewish Christians.[1] The John who thus claims a position above Peter himself is not a historical but a merely ideal person. The evangelist's conception of the Spirit tends in the same direction. The Spirit only comes in his fulness after the close of the earthly life of Jesus, and thus stands, as the universal Christian principle, high above the personal authority even of the apostles. In the difference which existed between Paulinism and Judaism on this subject, the Johannine Gospel goes a step beyond even Paulinism.[2]

The same is the case with his doctrinal system. The Jewish-Christian and the Pauline doctrine are here blended together in a higher unity. Faith has the same inwardness in which its value consists with Paul; but its object is not the death of Jesus with its efficacy for the forgiveness of sins, but the whole person of Jesus as the incarnate Logos; or, since Jesus as one sent cannot be thought

[1] Cf. my Krit. Untersuch. p. 320, sq., 377, sq.
[2] The Spirit is sent forth to operate unrestrictedly after the glorification of Jesus, and represents the person of Jesus himself. He who believes on him, the Jesus of John says, out of him flow rivers of living water (vii. 38). It is the sphere of pure spirituality into which this Gospel transports us. As Paul by his vocation broke in upon the old apostolic circle, so the bearers and possessors of the apostolic spirit are now said to be the believing disciples in general: cf. xvii. 20, sq. According to the Johannine view, therefore, it is by no means an essential condition with regard to the origin of such a Gospel as that of John, that its author should be an apostle.

of apart from his intimate oneness with him who sends him, the object of faith is God himself. The relation of Jesus, as the Son to the Father, is the absolute type for the whole relation of man to God. What the Son is absolutely, those who believe on him are to become through his mediation. In the same relation in which the Son stands to the Father believers also stand not only to the Son, but through his mediation to the Father also. The ruling principle of the relation is love actively manifesting itself by unreserved devotion, and by following the Divine will. The highest absolute principle of this love is the love of the Father to the Son, and of God to the world. Love is thus the dominant conception from which the Johannine mode of view sets out; and this is the point at which the Johannine doctrine diverges from the Pauline. Lofty as is the apostle Paul's conception of the love of God, yet it results from his view of the law, that love always has righteousness standing over against it. Man cannot get away from the law without satisfaction being rendered to the claim which the law is entitled to put forward against him, without his debt being cancelled, his ransom paid. From the standpoint of the Gospel of John we see that, on the one hand, the law has come to be at such a distance from the present field of vision, that its claims may as it were be regarded as antiquated—there is no occasion for trying to arrive at a definite understanding with the law. On the other hand, the view taken of the whole person of Jesus does not admit of any one feature of his work or personality being insisted on so much more than the rest, as that the whole work of redemption should centre in his death. That death is redemptive only to the same extent as the whole manifestation of Jesus is redemptive. What the fact of the death is with Paul the simple personality of Jesus is here— the person of Jesus in its absolute significance. To gain a correct idea of the relation of the Johannine standpoint to that of Paul, we must consider that all those antitheses, through which Paulinism was obliged to fight its way, were to the author of the Johannine Gospel a part of a far distant past. Faith and works are merged in love, their higher unity. Jewish particularism, with all the antitheses connected with it, disappears in that general antithesis which forms the background of the Johannine view of the world —the antithesis of the two principles, light and darkness, which exercise a determining influence on the moral as well as the religious world.

At this stage the development of the Christian principle has reached its definite goal within the sphere which we are at present considering. Christianity is established as a universal principle of salvation; all those antitheses which threatened to detain it within the narrow limits of Jewish particularism are merged in the universalism of Christianity. This has come about at two different points, at each of which a series of phenomena has run its course, each independent of the other. The one point is to be found in the Church of Rome; the other in the Gospel of John. At both these points the Christian consciousness is working out its freer development, and in both it has the same goal before it, the realisation of the idea of the Catholic Church. In the Gospel of John this process of development presents itself to us on its ideal, in the Church of Rome on its practical side. In the former the development of the Christian consciousness already bears the character of a Christian theology: in the latter the great question is to realise the practical idea of the Church. On the one side the movement proceeds from a definite point: we stand upon the firm ground of historical reality; there are definite antitheses which it is sought to reconcile: on the other side the whole mode of thought floats in the sphere of a transcendental idealism. We do not even know where the Gospel of John came into existence. It is true that it is connected in many ways with the Church of Asia Minor and with the controversies which during the course of the second century made that Church the centre of the ecclesiastical movement; yet both as a whole and in many of its individual features it exhibits such a decidedly Alexandrian stamp, and so close an affinity to the later Alexandrian theology, that we cannot avoid the conclusion that it represents the Alexandrian tendency, and that in whatever part of Christendom it may have come into existence, we have to seek the root out of which it grew chiefly in this direction. In spite of its ideal and theological character it does not lose sight of the practical task involved in the idea of the Church, as when it speaks of the one fold and the one shepherd. It agrees with the Roman Church in its broad anti-Judaistic tendency; its most direct point of contact with that Church, however, lies in the common opposition of the Church and of the Gospel to the Judaism of the Quartodecimans of Asia Minor. The endeavour after unity had already been manifested in the Church of Rome in the brotherly agreement effected between the two apostles Peter and Paul; and the same spirit imposed it on that Church as a necessary task to work out its views of Catholic unity against this relic of the old tenacious adhesion to Judaism. There must no longer be any such declared Judaists as the Quartodecimans still were; and thus another element, which originally formed a link of connection between Christianity and Judaism, but in regard to which Christianity desired no longer to be associated with Judaism, was now eliminated from the Christian Church. Thus it was declared that whoever should cling with the old tenacity to any one of the Jewish elements from which the Christian consciousness in the course of its development had gradually disengaged itself, placed himself thereby outside of the pale of the Catholic Church at least, if not of Christianity. This is the idea which now, from the end of the second century onwards, came to be connected with the term Ebionites. Ebionites at this part of Church history are those Jewish Christians who at this later period, even after a Catholic Church had come into existence, exhibited all those characteristics which had originally found their own place within the Christian community, and had even been regarded as an essential part of Christianity, but which the Catholic Church at a later time no longer sanctioned.[1]

The Ebionites, when we find them as a sect disowned by the Catholic Church, are just what the Jewish Christians were originally, as distinguished from the Pauline Christians. Irenaeus,

[1] Cf. Lehrbuch der Dogmengesch., 2d ed., p. 64.

who is the first to speak of the Ebionites as a sect not belonging to the Catholic Church,[1] and Epiphanius, who gives a description of such remainders of the party as still survived at his time,[2] specify the same features as were originally characteristic of Jewish Christians generally. The account given of them by Irenaeus they worship Jerusalem as if it were the house of God, is a very pointed indication of their view of the absolute importance of Judaism. The Ebionites of Epiphanius held firmly to circumcision; they went so far as to regard it as the seal and characteristic mark not only of the patriarchs and of the just men who lived according to the law, but of the followers of Christ, who (they said) was himself circumcised.[3]

By their hatred toward the apostle Paul and their express rejection of his Epistles, the Ebionites were afterwards distinguished from the more tolerantly disposed Nazarites, of whom at least this is not stated. The accounts we have of the Ebionitic Passover imply that they observed the Jewish festival in the same manner as the Quartodecimans. Epiphanius asserts that the Ebionites did not arise till after the destruction of Jerusalem. This statement, however, is completely unhistorical, and is a mere inference from the assumption that nothing afterwards deemed heretical could have been an original part of orthodox Christianity. The Ebionites did not become a sect till later; even Justin does not regard them as a sect. But an examination of their principles, doctrines, and usages, while it shows us in many points the harsh sectarianism of their attitude, points at the same time to a very close identity and connection with Jewish Christianity. So much is this the case that it cannot be deemed an unjustifiable use of the name to say that Jewish Christianity in general was a kind of Ebionitism. In

---

[1] Adv. Haer. i. 26. [2] Haer. xxx. 1, sq.

[3] Against Ritschl, who (op. cit., 2d ed. p. 172) regards the Testament of the Twelve Patriarchs as a product of Nazaraism, Hilgenfeld maintains (Zeitschrift für wissensch. Theol. 1858, p. 287, sq.) that the Nazarites and Ebionites are not so much two separate sects of Jewish Christianity as rather different modifications of the old hostility against Paulinism as it softened down to a more tolerant attitude towards Gentile Christianity.

the ordinary and narrower sense of the name, however, it denotes that form of primitive Christianity which by no other action than its own came to be detached from the community of the Catholic Church, because its adherents were unable to keep pace with the development of the Christian consciousness in its advance beyond Jewish Christianity.

PART THIRD.

CHRISTIANITY AS AN IDEAL PRINCIPLE OF THE WORLD; AND AS A REAL PHENOMENON EXISTING UNDER HISTORICAL CONDITIONS; OR,

GNOSTICISM AND MONTANISM, AND THEIR ANTITHESIS, THE CATHOLIC CHURCH.

I.—GNOSTICISM AND MONTANISM.

I. GNOSTICISM.

WITH the name and the notion of "Gnosticism" (the reason for coupling it with Montanism in the title cannot be explained till afterwards) we enter upon a totally different field of the history of the early Church from that which we have hitherto been discussing. The question is no longer whether Christianity is a particular or a universal principle of salvation, or as to the conditions on which the Christian salvation is to be obtained. The practical interest is no longer merely that of breaking through and putting aside the barriers that impede the free and more universal development of Christianity. The circle of vision is completely changed. God and the world, spirit and matter, absolute and finite, the origin, development, and end of the world: these are the conceptions and antitheses into the sphere of which we are now transferred. In a word, Christianity is now to be apprehended not as a principle of salvation, but as a principle of the world. The phenomena with which we have now to deal have their own point of commencement, form a circle by themselves, and have a character of their own. So much is this the case, that in fact it is merely the name of Christianity that connects them with the rest of the phenomena which form the history of the early Church. Yet on the other hand they are not without weighty significance for the history of the development of the Catholic Church. It is involved first of all in the very idea of the Catholic Church that she should seek to rise above everything particular, and merge it in the universality of the Christian principle; but on the other hand it is a not less essential part of her office to maintain and hold fast the positive elements of Christianity. In fact, what constitutes her a Catholic Church is that she stands in the middle to harmonise all tendencies together, and rejects the one extreme as much as the other. Had not the idea that developed itself out of Christianity, the idea of the Catholic Church, overcome the particularism of Judaism, Christianity itself would have become a mere sect of Judaism. But on the other side, on the side where it came in contact with heathenism, it was threatened by a danger no less serious, viz., that ideas would come to operate upon the Christian doctrines, under the influence of which they would fade away into vague and general abstractions, so that the Christian consciousness spreading out in limitless expansion would entirely lose its specific historical character. Now this was the tendency of Gnosticism, and the general account which we have to give of Gnosticism in view of this tendency is, that it regarded Christianity not in the first instance as a principle of salvation, but as the principle that determines the whole development of the world. Thus the interests out of which it arose were those of speculation and philosophy rather than religion; and it points back to philosophy as the highest outcome of the human spirit in the Gentile world.

This suffices for a general indication of what Gnosticism is. But when we attempt to give a more particular account of the nature and development of the conception, we find that, even after all the discussion that has taken place on the subject, especially of recent years, this is by no means an easy or simple task. It is still an unaccomplished task, to seize, amidst so much that is indefinite, vague, merely circumlocutory, and only partly true, those points that furnish a clear conception of the thing itself. The most usual course is to conceive Gnosticism as being in the first instance theological speculation. This is Gieseler's[1] account of it. He finds the philosophical basis which serves to explain it partly in the old problem of the origin of evil, and partly in the development of philosophical thought with reference to God. In working out the idea of the Supreme Deity, he says, philosophy found it more and more difficult to regard him as the creator of the world, and became more and more inclined to derive the imperfect good in the world from inferior beings, and the evil from an evil principle. These ideas found support in the Christian view of Christianity, Judaism, and Paganism, as the perfect, the imperfect, and the evil.

Neander[2] starts from the aristocratic spirit of the ancient world, from the distinction drawn between those who know and those who believe, and from the eclectic character of Gnosticism, and goes on to say that, "as soon as Christianity entered into man's intellectual life, it could not fail that a need should be felt to attain to a clear consciousness as to the connection of the truths given by revelation with the previous intellectual possessions of mankind, and also as to the inner connection of Christian truth as an organic whole. Where such a need, instead of being satisfied, was forcibly suppressed, there the one-sided tendency of Gnosticism found its justification." But this is obscure, and Neander's favourite category of reaction is here inapplicable. We look for the solution of the riddle therefore in what follows—"The speculative element in the Gnostic systems is not the product of a reason divorced from history, and resolved to draw everything from its own depths. The void into which a merely negative philosophy invariably sinks had set the human spirit, which ever craves for reality, to seek for a more positive doctrine. In the Gnostic systems we can discover elements of Platonic philosophy, Jewish theology, ancient Oriental theosophy, blended together; but they by no means admit of being explained by the mere mixture and combination of these elements. There is a peculiar living principle which animates most of these

[1] K. G. i. 1, p. 179, sq., 4. N.   [2] Church Hist. vol. ii. p. 1.

combinations. The time in which they appeared stamped them with a peculiar character. In any age there are certain tendencies and ideas which exert a wonderful influence upon everything contemporary with them. Such, in the present case, was the dualistic principle whose influence harmonised with, and, as it were, reflected the prevailing temper of the age. The underlying tone in many of the more earnest spirits of this time was a consciousness of the power of evil; and Christianity operated in a peculiar way upon this feeling." According to this, the origin and nature of Gnosticism are to be explained by the influence of the dualistic principle. Now, unquestionably dualism is an essential feature of the character of the Gnostic systems. But it cannot suffice to explain the nature of Gnosticism; for the influence of this principle is not seen till it becomes apparent in Gnosticism itself. Neander's most pertinent contribution to the understanding of Gnosticism comes to this: "Gnosticism sought to make the doctrine of religion dependent on a speculative solution of all those questions which speculation had been vainly labouring to solve. In this way it was to lay for doctrine a firm foundation, and to provide for the correct understanding of it; so that this was to be the way in which men were to arrive at an understanding of Christianity, and attain to a true conviction, independent of anything external. In a word, then, Gnosticism was a philosophy of religion; but in what sense was it this?[1]

The name of Gnosticism—Gnosis—does not belong exclusively to the group of phenomena with whose historical explanation we are here concerned. Gnosis is a general idea; it is only as defined in one particular manner that it signifies Christian Gnosticism in

[1] Cf. on the notion of Gnosticism my Inaugural Dissertation de Gnosticorum christianismo ideali, Tüb. 1827; and my work die Christliche Gnosis oder die christliche Religionsphilosophie in ihrer geschichtlichen Entwicklung, Tub. 1835. Also my Essays: Kritische Studien über den Begriff der Gnosis, Theol. Stud. u. Krit. 1837, iii. p. 511, sq. Ueber den Begriff der christlichen Religionsphilosophie ihren Ursprung und ihre ersten Formen; Zeitschr. für speculative Theol., edited by Lic. Bruno Bauer, ii. 2, Berlin, 1837, p. 354, sq. Also my Lehrb. d. christlichen Dogmengeschichte, 2d ed., Tub. 1858, p. 69, sq.; and "Die Tübinger Schule," p. 50, sq.

a special sense. Gnosis is higher knowledge, knowledge that has a clear perception of the foundations on which it rests, and the manner in which its structure has been built up; a knowledge that is completely that which, as knowledge, it is called to be. In this sense it forms the natural antithesis to Pistis, Faith : if it is desired to denote knowledge in its specific difference from faith, no word will mark the distinction more significantly than Gnosis. But we find that, even in this general sense, the knowledge termed Gnosis is a religious knowledge rather than any other; for it is not speculative knowledge in general, but only such as is concerned with religion. Thus the apostle Paul uses the word γνῶσις to characterise that view of the eating of meat offered to idols, which claimed acceptance as more liberal than any other, as more enlightened, more strictly in accord with the essence of the matter in question. In 1 Cor. xii. 8 he speaks of a λόγος γνώσεως which, moreover, he distinguishes from the λόγος σοφίας.

The distinction must lie in the greater depth of thought put forward in the former style of address. It is especially noteworthy for our purpose that we find the word γνῶσις, in its more particular sense, used of such religious knowledge as rests on allegorical interpretation of the Scriptures.[1] Gnosis and allegory are essentially allied conceptions; and this affords us a very marked indication of the path which will really lead us to the origin of Gnosticism; for we shall find that allegory plays an important part in most of its systems, especially in those which exhibit its original form.

It is well known that allegory is the soul of the Alexandrian religious philosophy. Nothing else, indeed, can enable us to understand the rise of the latter; so closely is allegory interwoven with its very nature. Allegory is in general the mediator between philosophy and the religion which rests upon positive tradition. Wherever it is seen on a large scale, we notice that philosophical views have arisen side by side with, and independently of, the existing religion; and that the need has arisen to bring the ideas and doctrines of philosophy into harmony with the contents of the religious belief.

[1] Cf. die christliche Gnosis, p. 85, sq.

In such circumstances allegory appears in the character of mediator. It brings about the desired conformity by simply interpreting the belief in the sense of the philosophy. Religious ideas and narratives are thus clothed with a figurative sense which is entirely different from their literal meaning. It was thus that allegory arose before the Christian time among the Greeks. The desire was felt first by Plato, and afterwards still more strongly by the Stoics, to turn the myths of the popular religion to account on behalf of their philosophical ideas, and so to bridge over the gulf between the philosophical and the popular mind; and with this view they struck out the path of allegory, of allegorical interpretation of the myths. It is well known what extensive use the Stoics made of allegory when they wished to trace their own ideas of the philosophy of nature in the gods of the popular belief and the narratives concerning them.[1] But in Alexandria this mode of interpretation assumed still greater importance. Here it had to solve the weighty problem how the new ideas that had forced their way into the mind and consciousness of the Jew, were to be reconciled with his belief in the authority of his sacred religious books. Allegory alone made it possible to him, on the one hand, to admire the philosophy of the Greeks, and in particular of Plato, and to make its ideas his own; and, on the other, to reverence the Scriptures of the Old Testament as the one source of divinely revealed truth. The sacred books needed but to be explained allegorically, and then all that was wished for, even the boldest speculative ideas of the Greek mind, could be found in the books themselves. How widely this method was practised in Alexandria may be judged from the writings of Philo, in which we see the most extensive use made of allegorical interpretation, and find the contents of the Old Testament blended intimately with everything that the systems of Greek philosophy could offer. But it would be quite erroneous to think that it was nothing but caprice and the unchecked play of fancy that called forth this allegorical explanation of the Scriptures, which came to exercise such influence. For the Alexandrian

[1] Zeller, Philosophie der Griechen, iii. p. 123, *sq.*

Jew at the stage of spiritual development which he had now reached, with his consciousness divided between his ancestral Hebraism and modern Hellenism, this allegorising was a necessary form of consciousness; and so little did he dream that the artificial link by which he bound together such diverse elements was a thing he had himself created, that all the truth which he accepted in the systems of Greek philosophy seemed to him to be nothing but an emanation from the Old Testament revelation.

Now the Gnostic systems also, for the most part, make very free use of the allegorical method of interpretation; and this is enough to apprise us that we must regard them under the same aspect as the Alexandrian religious philosophy. As far as we are acquainted with the writings of the Gnostics we see them to have been full of allegorical interpretations, not indeed referring, as with Philo, to the books of the Old Testament (for their attitude towards the Old Testament was entirely different from his); but to those of the New, which were for the Gnostics what the books of the Old Testament were for Philo. In order to give their own ideas a Christian stamp, they applied the allegorical method, as much as possible, to the persons and events of the Gospel history, and especially to the numbers that occur in it. Thus for the Valentinians the number thirty in the New Testament, especially in the life of Jesus, was made to signify the number of their Aeons; the lost wandering sheep was for them their Achamoth; and even utterances of Jesus which contain a perfectly simple religious truth, received from them a sense referring to the doctrines of their system. The lately discovered Philosophoumena of the Pseudo-Origen,[1] who undertook the task of refuting all the heresies, show us even more clearly than before what an extensive use the Gnostics made of allegory. They applied it not merely to the books of the Old and New Testaments, but even to the products of Greek literature,—for instance, to the Homeric poems. Their whole mode of view was entirely allego-

[1] Ὠριγένους φιλοσοφούμενα, ἡ κατὰ πασῶν αἱρέσεων ἔλεγχος. E codice Parisino nunc primum edidit Emmanuel Miller. Oxonii, 1851.

rical. The whole field of ancient mythology, astronomy, and physics was laid under contribution to support their views. They thought that the ideas that were the highest objects of their thought and knowledge were to be found expressed everywhere.[1]

The allegorical mode of thought may be described as being simply the means by which a matter composed of various elements receives a form not unsuitable for itself—a form which makes it easily approachable from a side with which it would naturally have least in common. In trying to understand Gnosticism, then, we have first to ask what is the inner nature of that matter for which allegory provides no more than the outward form of expression. In this respect too, Gnosticism stands in a relation of the closest affinity to the Alexandrian religious philosophy, and must be pronounced to be essentially a mere continuation and development of the latter. Both derived their principal contents from Greek philosophy. The system of Philo may be called a speculative system of religion; and the character of the Gnostic systems is closely similar. Such was indeed the light in which the early doctors of the Church regarded Gnosticism. They declared it to be a different thing from Christianity, to be a purely worldly wisdom, and (for instance Tertullian) reproached philosophy with being the author

[1] Cf. the Philos. v. 8. p. 106. Τούτοις καὶ τοῖς τοιούτοις ἑπόμενοι οἱ θαυμασιώτατοι Γνωστικοί, ἐφευρεταὶ κενῆς τέχνης γραμματικῆς, τὸν ἑαυτῶν προφήτην Ὅμηρον ταῦτα προφαίνοντα ἀρρήτως δοξάζουσι καὶ τοὺς ἀμυήτους τὰς ἁγίας γραφὰς εἰς τοιαύτας ἐννοίας συνάγοντες ἐνυβρίζουσι· iv. 46, p. 81. Ἵνα δὲ σαφέστερα τοῖς ἐντυγχάνουσι τὰ ῥηθησόμενα φανῇ, δοκεῖ καὶ τὰ τῷ Ἀράτῳ πεφροντισμένα περὶ τῆς κατὰ τῶν οὐρανίων ἄστρων διαθέσεως ἐξειπεῖν, ὥς τινες εἰς τὰ ὑπὸ τῶν Γραφῶν εἰρημένα ἀπεικονίζοντες αὐτὰ ἀλληγοροῦσι, μετὰ (leg. ἀπατᾶν or πλανᾶν) τὸν νοῦν τῶν προσεχόντων πειρώμενοι, πιθανοῖς λόγοις προσάγοντες αὐτοὺς πρὸς ἃ βούλονται, ξενὸν θαῦμα ἐνδεικνύμενοι ὡς κατηστερισμένων τῶν ὑπ' αὐτῶν λεγομένων : at v. 20, p. 143, it is said of the Sethiani: ἐστι δὲ ὁ λόγος αὐτῶν συγκείμενος ἐκ φυσικῶν καὶ πρὸς ἕτερα εἰρημένων ῥημάτων, ἃ εἰς τὸν ἀΐδιον λόγον μετάγοντες διηγοῦνται, p. 144. Ἔστι δὲ αὐτοῖς ἡ πᾶσα διδασκαλία τοῦ λόγου ὑπὸ τῶν παλαιῶν θεολόγων, Μουσαίου καὶ Λίνου, καὶ τοῦ τὰς τελετὰς καὶ τὰ μυστήρια καταδείξαντος Ὀρφέως. Of the Gnostic sect of the Peratai it is said v. 13, p. 127, that they ἐπιψευσάμενοι τῷ τῆς ἀληθείας ὀνόματι ὡς Χριστοῦ λόγον κατήγγειλαν αἰώνων στάσιν καὶ ἀποστασίας ἀγαθῶν δυνάμεων εἰς κακά, etc. The whole of the fancies of astrologers about the stars are interpreted by them in their own sense, and from this it may be seen that their λόγοι τῶν ἀστρολόγων ὁμολογουμένως εἰσὶν οὐ Χριστοῦ.

of the heresies.[1] Nor did they derive **Gnosticism** merely from philosophy in general; they sought also to prove in detail from what philosophical systems the Gnostics had borrowed the main ideas and principles of their own. Irenaeus and **Tertullian** opened up this line of argument, but it was the author of the Philosophoumena who gave the most thoroughgoing demonstration of it. This is the design of his whole work. The refutation of the Gnostic heresies which the author proposes to give, consists merely in showing that one Gnostic writer followed one Greek philosopher, and another another; *e.g.* Simon Magus followed Heraclitus the Obscure, Valentinus Pythagoras and Plato, Basilides Aristotle, Marcion Empedocles. With a view to as accurate as possible a demonstration of this agreement, the author of the Philosophoumena sets forth the doctrines of the Greek philosophers in order from Thales downwards. His demonstration is not very convincing, since he deals chiefly with detached points of agreement and with external analogies; but on the whole, he lays before us enough to confirm the general view, that the basis of Gnosticism was the philosophical thought of antiquity: that this was transplanted by Gnosticism into Christianity, with which it was then blended into a system consisting of various elements, but resting on one and the same conception of the universe. In its form and contents Christian Gnosticism is the

---

[1] De praescr. haer. c. 7. Hae sunt doctrinae hominum et daemoniorum, prurientibus auribus natae de ingenio sapientiae secularis, quam Dominus stultitiam vocans stulta mundi in confusionem etiam philosoph'ae ipsius elegit. Ea est enim materia sapientiae secularis, temeraria interpres divinae naturae et dispositionis. Ipsae denique haereses a philosophia subornantur. Inde aeones et formae nescio quae infinitae, et trinitas hominis apud Valentinum: Platonicus fuerat: inde Marcionis Deus melior a tranquillitate; a Stoicis venerat; et uti anima interior dicatur, ab Epicureis observatur; et ut carnis restitutio negetur, de una omnium philosophorum schola sumitur; et ubi materia cum Deo aequatur Zenonis disciplina est, et ubi aliquid de igneo Deo allegatur, Heraclitus intervenit. Eadem materia apud haereticos et philosophos volutatur, iidem retractatus implicantur: unde malum et quare, et unde homo et quomodo? et quod proxime Valentinus proposuit, unde Deus? scilicet de enthymesi et ectromate. Miserum Aristotelem! qui illis dialecticam instituit, artificem struendi et destruendi, versi pellem in sententiis, coactam in conjecturis, duram in argumentis, operariam contentionum, molestam etiam sibi ipsi, omnia retractantem, ne quid omnino tractaverit.

expansion and development of Alexandrian religious philosophy; which was itself an offshoot of Greek philosophy. But if we are to gain a more accurate notion of what Gnosticism was, we must analyse its main ingredients, and ask with regard to each of its characteristic conceptions whether it belongs to pagan or to Christian thought.

The fundamental character of Gnosticism in all its forms is dualistic. It is its sharply-defined, all-pervading dualism that, more than anything else, marks it directly for an offspring of paganism. Pagan antiquity never got past the antithesis of spirit and matter, and was unable to conceive a world produced by the free creative activity of a purely personal will. In the same way in Gnosticism the two principles, spirit and matter, form the great and general antithesis, within the bounds of which the systems move with all that they contain. Now these two principles cannot merely confront each other in an abstract antithesis. Accordingly the main substance of the systems is the process of world-development which is brought about by the action of the principles upon each other. The world is constituted by, and is the sum-total of the relative and restricted antitheses which proceed from the limitation of the absolute antithesis. The fixed path which everything is to pursue in the world is determined on this side or on that according as the shifting balance dips on the one side or the other of the universal antithesis. The activity which initiates this process comes either from the one side or the other. If from matter, matter in its self-originated activity is the principle of evil, and the process of the world-development therefore takes the form of a continuous antagonism, in which two hostile powers act and react on one another. For matter, as the kingdom of darkness, has a natural instinct of enmity to the principle of light. But if the first impulse of the world-development is on the side of the spiritual principle, then this impulse also must be of a spiritual kind. The moving principle is then the process of the spirit with itself: the natural tendency of spirit is to differentiate itself from itself, and in the differentiation of the several momenta which are posited by the thinking activity, to become self-conscious spirit—spirit reflected into itself. From this highest height in the purely spiritual process, the world-development goes forward to the sphere of physical and material life. Matter is itself but the limit of the spiritual being, spirit become objective and external to itself. The conception of matter is thus a very negative one; but the dualistic mode of thought does not fail to maintain here also the absolute antithesis of its two principles; the principle of matter is posited in the very impulse of the spirit to go forth from itself and objectivate itself; the principle of matter lies in the tendency from above downwards of the spirit materialising itself, a tendency which admits of no ulterior explanation. Again, it is an equally essential attribute of the spiritual principle, that spirit frees itself again from the dominion that matter has obtained over it, and rises absolutely victorious over every limitation and obscuration that matter can make it suffer. Thus the whole course of the world-development ends only with the return of spirit into itself as pure spirit. Yet the absolute antithesis of the two principles is not at an end even here. The same process of world-development may at once begin afresh, and again follow the same course. The principle of matter can never be so completely removed, the opposing principles can never be so abstractly conceived, that the possibility or necessity should cease to exist for spirit to be drawn again, in an endless series of worlds, into the same process of world-development. Matter cannot raise itself to spirit, but spirit can always externalise itself into matter, and sink down into matter; and accordingly it is by the emanations and projections ($\pi\rho\sigma\beta\sigma\lambda\alpha\iota$) of the spirit that the infinite abyss between spirit and matter is filled up and the transition from spirit to matter provided for as far as may be. Thus in most of the Gnostic systems an important position is occupied by the Aeons, as the forms of the spirit objectivating itself. In fact it is this conception, that of the Aeons, more than anything else, that identifies these systems with the ancient mode of thought. The Aeons are but the personified ideas, the archetypes of the finite world: in them we are presented with that antithesis of the ideal and the real, or of the upper and the lower world, which also enters into the very substance of the Gnostic systems.

A further leading Gnostic conception is the Demiurgus. The two highest principles being spirit and matter, and the true conception of a creation of the world being thus excluded, it follows in the Gnostic systems, and is a characteristic feature of them, that they separate the creator of the world from the supreme God, and give him a position subordinate to the latter. He is therefore rather the artificer than the creator of the world. But where did the Gnostics get their notion of a Demiurgus? From the fact that he is identified with the God of Judaism, we might be led to think that he simply came from Judaism into their systems, and that the notion was one which belonged only to the standpoint of the Jewish religion. But Platonism also had its Demiurgus, who held the same position as the Demiurgus of Gnosticism.[1] On the one hand indeed the Platonic Demiurgus stands above the θεοὶ θεῶν, the gods of the mythical nature-religion, as the one God and the father of works, which have been made by him, and will not be destroyed as long as he so wills it. But, on the other hand, there is a higher principle above him. The Platonic God can only accomplish his creative work by looking to that which ever remains the same with itself, the ideas, and by taking them for his archetypes, and he must be said to be dependent on the ideas. Now since the Demiurgus holds with Plato the same subordinate position as with the Gnostics, the conception must be fundamentally the same in each case. The Platonic Demiurgus is a mythical form. With Plato the mythical contains an element of truth, in so much as mythus is a necessary form for the setting forth of the abstract philosophical idea; and so the Demiurgus is a mythical personification of the creative power of the ideas. This personification is the form by which alone the mythical view is adjusted to the philosophical consciousness. In the Platonic Demiurgus mythical polytheism passes into a kind of monotheism, the highest truth of which is simply this, that the place of the indeterminate Many is taken by the simple One. This unity on the one hand stands to

---

[1] See my Essay in the Stud. u. Krit., referred to, p. 187.

express the absolute idea, but the mythical element still asserts itself in the assumption that the creator of the world is a personal being free to act, and of the same nature as the gods of the popular mythical belief. We must regard the Gnostic Demiurgus in the same light. When it is said that Gnosticism derived the substance of its thought from Greek philosophy, this is only one side of the matter; the other is that the form in which it sets forth that thought is a reflection of the mythical mode of view of the Greek popular religion. Not only Greek philosophy, but Greek mythology as well, is an essential ingredient of Gnosticism. All the beings that compose the world of Aeons, and present the idea of the absolute in its various relations, are mythical forms. The only distinction between them and the Demiurgus is that the latter stands at a lower stage, and therefore appears in a more concrete mythical form. He reflects and represents the popular mythical consciousness of God. The immediate reason why the Gnostics identified the Demiurgus with the God of Judaism was, that the God of the Old Testament is described for the most part as the Creator and Lord of the world; but the identification serves to indicate to us the view the Gnostics took of the Old Testament religion. They assigned it to a stage of development at which the religious consciousness had not yet risen above an idea so full of sensuous elements as that of the Demiurgus. The Demiurgus proves more than anything else that the contents of Gnosticism were religion rather than philosophy. The distinction between religion and philosophy is, that in religion the philosophical idea, originally abstract, is presented in a more concrete and material form. Now Gnosticism measures the rank which is due to such ideas in proportion to their sensuousness, and reduces them to a lower rank according as they are more material in their character. It thus places its own thinking consciousness above the sphere occupied by the mythico-religious way of thinking, and so is neither purely philosophy, nor purely religion, but both together. The relation in which it places its two elements, philosophy and religion, towards each other, is such that the only way in which we can describe its general character is to call it a religious philosophy.

The Gnostic Demiurgus exemplifies the principle that the relation of religion to philosophy varies according as the two are conceived as more or less identical in form and in substance. When, as we see in Platonism, the Demiurgus is closely united with the absolute idea of God, the mythical personality appears as a necessary form of presentation, inseparably bound up with the matter presented. When, on the other hand, as in the Gnostic systems, the Demiurgus is placed far beneath the absolute God, and sharply distinguished from him, this is a distinct indication that philosophical reflection feels herself to be superior to the concreteness and materiality of the religious mode of presentation, and able to discard it. Gnosticism fixed the relation of all these notions, standpoints, and antitheses to each other, by laying down not merely two, but three principles, and by regarding the psychical, which stands between the spiritual and the material, as the peculiar field of the Demiurgus. These three principles are the elements of all natural and spiritual being : in particular, they divide men into three essentially different classes. If a union of the two principles, spirit and matter, is possible at all, it can only be effected by the mediation of such a form as the psychical coming in between them. The psychical is thus, no doubt, a third principle; but since there are ultimately only two principles, and the true substance of the psychical is the spiritual which it contains, it follows from the constitution of the psychical that it is at last dissolved into the spiritual. It is the finite, the transitory : the whole world of the Demiurgus must come to an end again at last. The distinction between the spiritual and the psychical, into which the distinction between philosophy and religion may also be analysed, rests ultimately therefore on the broad fact that there are different aspects from which our contemplation may set out, so that a matter identical in itself may yet come to appear in various forms.

What the Demiurgus is on the one side of the Gnostic systems, in their direction downwards, Christ is on their other side, in the direction upwards. There being a descent, there must be an ascent as well, and we recognise the Christian character of these systems not only in the fact that they assign this definite place to Christ, but also in the great emphasis with which this side is insisted on. The turning-point of the system as it moves through its various momenta is found in Christ. All that serves in any way to adjust the relations of one part with another, to maintain the connection of the whole, to reunite what has been severed, to bring back what has wandered, to open up the road from the lower to the upper world, to bring everything to the point where the consummation and completion of the whole world's course is arrived at—all this is connected with the names Christ and Jesus, and with the conceptions allied to them. In them is contained the goal towards which the whole world-development is pressing. What was originally only a redemption in a moral and religious sense, becomes in the Gnostic systems the restitution and fulfilment of the whole world-order. Even in the world of Aeons Christ restores the broken harmony, and acts as a maintaining, stablishing, uniting principle; and in the lower world, Jesus who was born of Mary, the Soter in this peculiar sense, has the similar task of $\delta\iota\acute{o}\rho\theta\omega\sigma\iota\varsigma$ or $\epsilon\pi\alpha\nu\acute{o}\rho\theta\omega\sigma\iota\varsigma$, as the Gnostics term their notion of redemption.[1]

Christ is rather a universal cosmical principle than a principle of salvation. On the one side, where the object to be contemplated and comprehended is the procession of the finite from the absolute, the system contained in the Gnostic view of the world takes a direction from above downwards, and descends deeper and deeper, till at last it reaches the point where the general reaction must needs ensue. Christianity comprehends in itself all that lies on the other and opposite side, in the direction from below upwards. We may see, indeed, that even before the Gnostic time the doctrine of Paul contained the suggestions and germs of such a conception of Christianity. With him, Adam and Christ are placed at the head of the two great periods of the world, and stand over against each other as the two principles of the psychical and the spiritual, of death and life. Through Christ, as the conqueror over sin, death, and hell, all is at last subjected to God, so that at last God

[1] Philos. vi. 19, p. 175, vi. 32, p. 190; 36, p. 195, *sq.*

is all in all. Still more closely allied to Gnosticism is the Christology which attains such a high and universal range of view in the two Epistles to the Ephesians and Colossians; though there can be no doubt that this view is partly owing to the influence of Gnosticism itself. But only in the Gnostic systems is Christ placed in such a connection that his manifestation and activity, or Christianity in general, can only be correctly understood in the light of the great process through which the development of the world pursues its appointed course as it is conditioned from the beginning to the end by the conflict of the opposing principles.

Before we can go further in working out the essence of Gnosticism, we must briefly survey its various sects, forms, and systems, in their historical order.

The earliest known Christian Gnostic is the Jewish Christian Cerinthus. From the new source of our knowledge of the Gnostic doctrines,[1] as well as from those previously known, we learn that what may be regarded as the characteristic mark of Gnosticism was a feature of Cerinthus' teaching, *i.e.* that he distinguished between the two notions of God and of the Creator of the world. He is said to have taught that the world did not come into existence through the First Being, but through a power separate from the universal principle, and not knowing the God who is exalted above all. The Christian element in his Gnosticism appears in the assertion, that Jesus was the son of Joseph and Mary by natural generation, and differed from other men only in his greater wisdom and righteousness; that after his baptism Christ, the son of the most high God, descended upon him in the form of a dove; that he proclaimed the unknown Father;[2] but that at last Christ left him again, and that while Jesus suffered and rose again, Christ remained free from suffering.

According to the Fathers of the Church, Simon Magus was the first Gnostic, the forefather of all the Gnostic sects. The groundlessness of this assertion is abundantly clear. If Simon was the originator of all the doctrines which the Fathers ascribe to him, we

---

[1] Philos. vii. 33, p. 256, sq. Comp. Irenaeus, i. 25.

[2] The words in Philos., p. 257, are τὸν γνωστὸν πατέρα; but according to Irenaeus, *loc. cit.*, we have to read ἄγνωστον.

should have to date the rise of Gnosticism at a time when according to all historical indications it was still in the far future. As forefather of the Gnostics, the Simon Magus of the Fathers is an entirely apocryphal and mythical figure, and can only be regarded as a personification of Gnosticism. His assertion that he himself is the most high God shows him to be nothing more than a figure devised to represent the Gnostic idea of the primal Being, of which indeed he is a personification. But the fundamental idea which is meant to be mythically symbolised in him and his companion Helena is the Gnostic idea of syzygy. While seeking to conceive the primal Being according to the absolute notion of him, and as abstractly as possible, the Gnostics were compelled to assume the existence in that Being of a differentiating principle; else it would have been impossible to comprehend how the finite could arise out of the absolute. Accordingly, in their mythical way of looking at things, they represented the highest Being as at once male and female. According to the author of the Philosophoumena, Simon expressed himself with regard to his highest principle in the following way:[1]—From the one root, which is power, stillness, invisible, incomprehensible, proceeded the two branches, which have neither beginning nor end, of the whole of the Aeons. The one branch, which is visible from above, is the great power, the understanding of the whole, pervading all, and male. The other from below, is the great ἐπίνοια, female, giving birth to all. The two come together and form a syzygy, and bring into appear-

[1] In the Ἀπόφασις μεγάλη ascribed to him the words ἀπόφασις μεγάλη are no doubt to be explained by the sense in which he claimed to be the δύναμις μεγάλη. Ἀπόφασις means denial. The great denial is undoubtedly nothing else than the Gnostic process which, moving through affirmation and denial, between above and below, between unity and duality, removes and receives back into itself the forms which have arisen through emanation and projection, and been set forth into the world of outward presentation. The process is characterised in this way in the passages contained in the following note. That Simon Magus is represented as the composer of such a work as the Ἀπόφασις, is but another aspect of the character given to him of an ideal representative of what were thought to be the peculiarities of Gnosticism. And if Simon Magus never really existed, neither were there ever any real Simonians. Those who were called so were simply those who made use of the works supposed to have been written by Simon Magus. Cf. Hilgenfeld, Apostol. Väter, p. 242, sq.

ance the middle space, the infinite air, which has neither beginning nor end. In this is the Father, who sustains and nourishes all that has beginning and end. He is the Ἑστὼς Στὰς, Στησόμενος. The original principle is an ἀρσενόθηλυς δύναμις, because, as the highest δύναμις, it contains in itself also the ἐπίνοια. Thus it is not a simple unity, but such a unity as is at the same time a duality. But the duality does not extinguish the unity, since, though a duality, it is yet but the one principle identical with itself.[1] Since the primal Being is conceived as a spiritual principle, the differentiating principle which it contains is spiritual also: it is the presentative spiritual activity which lives and works in all things seen and imagined in the finite material world. This ἐπίνοια, as the presentative consciousness and as the world of presentation, is mythically personified in Simon's companion Helena: according to the custom of the Gnostics to borrow from Greek mythology the symbolical forms in which their own speculative ideas were to be set forth.[2]

The oldest Gnostic sects are without doubt those whose name is

[1] Philos. vi. 18, p. 173. Ἔστιν ἀρσενόθηλυς δύναμις καὶ ἐπίνοια, ὅθεν ἀλλήλοις ἀντιστοιχοῦσιν, οὐδὲν γὰρ διαφέρει δύναμις ἐπινοίας, ἐν ὄντες. Ἐκ μὲν τῶν ἄνω εὑρίσκεται δύναμις, ἐκ δὲ τῶν κάτω ἐπίνοια. Ἔστω οὖν οὕτως, καὶ τὸ φανὲν ἀπ' αὐτῶν ἐν ὂν δύο εὑρίσκεσθαι, ἀρσενόθηλυς ἔχων τὴν θήλειαν ἐν ἑαυτῷ. Οὗτός ἐστι νοῦς ἐπινοία, ἀχώριστα ἀπ' ἀλλήλων, ἐν ὄντες, δύο εὑρίσκονται. Cf. p. 171: Αὕτη, φησίν, ἔστι δύναμις μία, διῃρημένη ἄνω, κάτω, αὐτὴν γεννῶσα, αὐτὴν αὔξουσα, αὐτὴν ζητοῦσα, αὐτὴν εὑρίσκουσα, αὐτῆς μήτηρ οὖσα, αὐτῆς πατήρ, αὐτῆς ἀδελφή, αὐτῆς σύζυγος, αὐτῆς θυγατήρ, αὐτῆς υἱός, μήτηρ, πατήρ, ἐν οὖσα ῥίζα τῶν ὅλων. "He that stands triply" is meant to set forth the three stages of the primal being, which is self-existent, proceeds out of itself and is received back into itself. He is, as we read, loc. cit., the ἑστὼς ἄνω ἐν τῇ ἀγεννήτῳ δυνάμει, the στὰς κάτω ἐν τῇ ῥοῇ τῶν ὑδάτων ἐν εἰκόνι γεννηθείς, the στησόμενος ἄνω, παρὰ τὴν μακαρίαν ἀπέραντον δύναμιν ἐὰν ἐξεικονισθῇ (when he has objectified himself in a real image, and thus externalised himself, he returns back into the unity of the principle).

[2] In the Philos., vi. 19, it is said of Simon that he οὐ μόνον τὰ Μωσέως κακοτεχνήσας εἰς ὃ ἐβούλετο μεθηρμήνευσεν, ἀλλὰ καὶ τὰ τῶν ποιητῶν. In this feature also Simon fitly represents the character of Gnosticism, its way of bringing everything into its service by means of allegorical interpretation. Cf. Die christliche Gnosis, p. 305, sq. In the following passage of the Philos., vi. 18, p. 175, the two figures, Simon and Helena (whose beauty was the occasion of the Trojan war, all the powers of the world wishing to share her ἐπίνοια), are made to furnish a very characteristic expression of the tendency of Gnosticism to decompose everything positive, and dissolve into general ideas and views: Τὴν Ἑλένην λυτρωσάμενος (Σίμων) οὕτως τοῖς ἀνθρώποις σωτηρίαν παρέσχε διὰ τῆς ἰδίας ἐπιγνώσεως. Κακῶς

not derived from a special founder, but only stand for the general notion of Gnosticism. Such a name is that of the Ophites or Naassenes. The Gnostics are called Ophites, brethren of the Serpent, not after the serpent with which the fathers compared Gnosticism, meaning to indicate the dangerous poison of its doctrine, and to suggest that it was the hydra, which as soon as it lost one head at once put forth another; but because the serpent was the accepted symbol of their lofty knowledge. The serpent first appears at the Fall as the intelligent being which by its dialectic weaves good and evil into each other in such a way that the process of the world's history, worked out as it is from the antagonism of the two principles, at once begins. The first priests and supporters of the dogma were, according to the author of the Philosophoumena, the so-called Naassenes—a name derived from the Hebrew name of the serpent. They afterwards called themselves Gnostics, because they asserted that they alone knew the things that are deepest. From this root the one heresy divided into various branches; for though these heretics all taught a like doctrine, their dogmas were various. According to Irenaeus and Epiphanius, their system was worked out through several successive stages, and much resembled the Valentinian.[1] In the Philosophoumena their doctrine appears simpler. They defined the primal being, as Simon was said to have done, as both male and female, but called it man and the son of man, or Adamas (Adam), and distinguished in it the three principles; the spiritual, the psychical, and the material. The Gnostic perfection was said to begin with the knowledge of man, and to end with the knowledge of God.[2] Jesus was

γὰρ διοικούντων τῶν ἀγγέλων τὸν κόσμον, διὰ τὸ φιλαρχεῖν αὐτούς, εἰς ἐπανόρθωσιν ἐληλυθέναι αὐτὸν ἔφη μεταμορφούμενον καὶ ἐξομοιούμενον ταῖς ἀρχαῖς καὶ ταῖς ἐξουσίαις καὶ τοῖς ἀγγέλοις ὡς καὶ ἄνθρωπον φαίνεσθαι αὐτὸν μὴ ὄντα ἄνθρωπον, καὶ παθεῖν τε ἐν τῇ Ἰουδαίᾳ καὶ δεδοκηκέναι μὴ πεπονθότα, ἀλλὰ φανέντα Ἰουδαίοις μὲν ὡς υἱόν, ἐν δὲ τῇ Σαμαρείᾳ ὡς πατέρα, ἐν δὲ τοῖς λοιποῖς ἔθνεσιν ὡς πνεῦμα ἅγιον. Ὑπομένειν δὲ αὐτὸν καλεῖσθαι υἱῷ ᾧ ἂν ὀνόματι καλεῖν βούλωνται οἱ ἄνθρωποι. Ἐπίγνωσις, Gnostic knowledge, would thus be the knowledge and recognition of the same one religion in all forms of religion, of the same one being in all the spiritual powers of the world.

[1] Cf. Die christliche Gnosis, p. 171, sq.
[2] Philos., v. 6, p. 95. Ἀρχὴ τελειώσεως γνῶσις ἀνθρώπου, θεοῦ δὲ γνῶσις ἀπηρτισμένη τελείωσις.

the counterpart of the primal man. All that the primal man united in himself, the spiritual, the psychical, and the material, descended at once, they affirmed, upon the one man, Jesus the son of Mary. Similar to these are the Perates, of whom hitherto little has been known. It is only the author of the Philosophoumena who has contributed to the history of these heretics a clear account of the doctrine of this sect.[1] They assumed three principles: the first is the unbegotten good, the second the self-begotten good, the third the begotten. Everything is triply divided, and Christ sums up in himself all tripartitions. From the two upper worlds, the unbegotten and the self-begotten, the seeds of all possible powers descended into this world in which we are. From the unbegotten realm, from above, Christ came, to save by his descent all that is triply divided. All that has fallen to the lower from the upper sphere will return through him. The third world is doomed to destruction, but the two upper worlds are imperishable. *Euphrates* the Peratic, and *Celbes* the Carystian, are named as the founders of the Peratic heresy; but the name seems rather to point to the assertion of the Peratics, that since they alone knew the necessary law of that which has come into existence, and the way by which man entered into the world, none but themselves were able to overcome decay.[2] They placed the principle of decay in water. This, they said, is the death that fell upon the Egyptians in the Red Sea. Now, all that are without knowledge are Egyptians: therefore we should leave Egypt, *i.e.* the body. Regarding the body as an Egypt in little, they required that men should pass through the Red Sea, *i.e.* the water of decay, which is Cronos, and betake themselves to the wilderness; that is, attain to that sphere beyond the temporal world, where all the gods of perdition and the God of salvation meet together. The gods of perdition are the stars of the mutable world, which subject to necessity all that rises into being.

[1] Philos., v. 12, p. 123, *sq.* The Perates were already known from Theodoret, Haer. par. i. 17. But Theodoret in his Heresiology only used the summary given in the tenth book of the Philosophoumena. This was shown by Volkmar, Hippolytus und die römischen Zeitgenossen, 1855, p. 22, *sq.*; so that all that we know in detail of the doctrine of the Perates is derived from the above-cited passage of the Philosophoumena.

[2] Philos., v. 16, p. 131. διελθεῖν καὶ περᾶσαι τὴν φθοράν.

Moses called them the biting serpents of the desert, which killed those who believed that they had left the Red Sea behind them. To those who were bitten in the desert he showed the true, the perfect serpent, and whoever believed in it was not bitten in the wilderness. No one can save those who go out of the land of Egypt, *i.e.* this body, and the world, but only the perfect serpent. He who puts his trust in it is not destroyed by the serpents of the desert, *i.c.* by the gods of the temporal world. The significance which the serpent has in several passages of the Old Testament, as where it is the sign of salvation in the wilderness, or the wonder-working rod of Moses in Egypt, Exod. iv. 17, and above all, in the history of the Fall,[1] placed it so high in the eyes of the Gnostics, that they beheld in it one of their highest principles. The serpent was the same as the Son was. Between the Father on the one side, and matter on the other, is the Son, the Logos, the serpent, ever moving, now towards the motionless Father, and again towards matter which has motion. Now it turns to the Father, and takes up his powers into itself; now it turns with these powers to matter, and the formless matter receives upon itself the impress of the ideas of the Son, of which the Son has received the impress from the Father. And as the serpent mediates between the Father and matter, in order to bring the powers of the upper world down into the lower, so the serpent or the Son is the sole saving principle which enables these powers to return.[2] It is thus, in a word, the process of world-development, winding its way dialectically through the antitheses.

The substance of these doctrines, ever concerned with the same problems—unity, duality, trinity of principles, their antitheses, and reconciliation, the descent from the upper world into the lower, and the return from the lower into the upper—is so general, that they may all very well have been in existence long before specific Christian Gnosticism arose, and have received their Christian

---

[1] Philos., p. 133. ὁ καθολικὸς ὄφις οὗτός ἐστιν ὁ σοφὸς τῆς Εὔας λόγος. It is called Catholic as the universal world-symbol; a usage somewhat resembling that in Exc. ex. ser. Theod. par. 47, where the δημιουργὸς καθολικὸς is the Demiurgus in the higher, the universal sense, in contrast to the special Demiurgi.

[2] Philos., p. 135, sq.

colouring and modification only afterwards, when they expanded under the allegorical and syncretistic mode of view. This is what we have before us in the doctrines said to be those of the Simonians, the Ophites, the Gnostici, the Perates, the Sethians (this name belongs to this series of sects); and especially in such a description of them as that of the Philosophoumena. Here we have Gnosticism in all its fluidity and disconnectedness, attaching itself to whatever it can reach, ever seeking, amid the chequered medley of ancient myths and symbols, a new expression for its general fundamental view.

The Gnosticism of more developed structure, of firmer consistence, and which does not shrink from the widest application of its principles, that Gnosticism in which the Christian element is an essential part of the organic system, and cannot be separated from it, meets us first in those systems which are known to us by the names of their authors. The period on which we now enter is the most important in the history of Gnosticism. It begins in the first part of the second century. The chief names which it contains are those of the three famous heresiarchs, Valentinus, Basilides, and Marcion, whose appearance is placed by all the most approved testimonies in the time of Trajan and Hadrian.[1] Basilides is said to have lived at Alexandria about the year 125; Valentinus to have gone from Alexandria to Rome about the year 140. About the same time Marcion came to Rome from Sinope in Pontus: the period during which he flourished at Rome is placed in the years 140-50.[2] Even these outward facts, that Alexandria was the native country of

[1] Hegesippus in Eusebius, Eccl. Hist. iii. 32. Clem. of Alex.: Strom. vii. 17.

[2] As to the chronological statements respecting Marcion and his appearance at Rome, cf. Volkmar, die Zeit Justin's des Märtyrers, in the Theol. Jahrb. 1855, p. 270, sq.: "All the older Fathers, when they speak definitely of the date of Marcion, are perfectly clear that he appeared first in the reign of Antoninus Pius, and at the earliest in the year 135." The Libellus adv. omnes Haereses, undoubtedly not by Tertullian, says, cap. 6, upon the alleged cause of Marcion's leaving his country, Pontus, and going to Rome : Post hunc (Cerdonem) discipulus ipsius emersit Marcion quidam nomine, Ponticus genere, episcopi filius, propter stuprum cujusdam virginis ab ecclesiae communicatione abjectus. It now seems to me, comp. Die Christliche Gnosis, p. 296, that the simplest way of explaining this is to suppose, that the "stuprum virginis" was originally nothing but a figurative way of speaking of his heresy, by which he did violence to the Church, the παρθένος καθαρὰ καὶ ἀδιάφθορος, according to the expression of Hegesippus, Euseb. iii. 32.

several Gnostics, and that two such great heads of sects as Valentinus and Marcion both travelled to Rome, are very noteworthy for the history of Gnosticism.

The profoundest of these systems is also more accurately known to us than any another. It is that which bears the name of Valentinus; though it would perhaps be more fitly termed the Valentinian system, since it is impossible to determine how much of it is to be ascribed to the master, and how much to his disciples. The idea which governs the whole system is that of mapping out the world of Aeons according to its numbers and categories. The total number of the Aeons is thirty; but they are divided into several leading numbers, an ogdoad, a decad, a dodecad. Two Aeons, however, are always connected together, and form an Aeon-pair—for the idea of syzygy is here also one of the fundamental conceptions on which the system is based. Only in the case of the highest Being the followers of Valentinus seem to have given various answers to the question, whether he should be conceived as associated with a female Aeon. Some wished to conceive the Father as simply alone; others thought it impossible that anything should have proceeded from a male alone, and therefore assigned to the Father of the all, in order that he might become a Father, silence ($\Sigma\iota\gamma\eta$) as his $\sigma\upsilon\zeta\upsilon\gamma\sigma\varsigma$. This silence, however, is only an expression for the abstract notion of his absolute unity or of his being alone. But as he was averse to solitude, and was all love, and love is not love if there is not an object of love as well, the Father felt in himself the desire to beget and produce what was most beautiful and perfect of all that he had within him. Alone then as he was, he begot Nous and Aletheia, the duad which is the mother of all the Aeons within the pleroma. Nous and Aletheia themselves gave birth to Logos and Zoe, and from these two sprang Anthropos and Ecclesia. In order that the perfect Father might be glorified by a perfect number, Nous and Aletheia produced ten Aeons; but Logos and Zoe could only produce the imperfect number of twelve Aeons. In whatever way the Valentinians conceived the relation of this decad and dodecad, the principal series of their Aeons is certainly formed by the six primal Aeons, Nous and Aletheia, Logos and Zoe,

Anthropos and Ecclesia. The further development of the system turns mainly upon the well-known myth relating to Sophia. Sophia is the twelfth of the dodecad, the youngest of the twenty-eight Aeons, and as the weakest and the last member of the whole series, is a female Aeon. But if she was separated by a wide interval from the primal principle, she was proportionately conscious of her great remoteness; and this produced in her a longing to overleap all the intervening members, and unite herself immediately with the primal being. She therefore sprang back into the depth of the Father, wishing to produce alone and by herself, like the Father, something not less than what he produced. She knew not that only the unbegotten, as the principle of the whole, as the root, the depth, the abyss, is competent to beget alone. Only in the unbegotten does all exist together: in the begotten the female produces the substance, but the male forms the substance which the female produces. So what Sophia produced was only an ἔκτρωμα, as the Valentinians termed it. Within the pleroma there was ignorance in Sophia, formlessness in her offspring: confusion arose in the pleroma; the whole world of Aeons was in danger of becoming formless and defective, and of finally falling a prey to destruction. All the Aeons fled to the Father, and besought him to comfort Sophia, who was plunged in grief for her offspring.

It is easy to see that the myth aims at explaining the procession of the finite from the absolute. The finite can only derive its origin from the absolute, and yet the finite is inconsistent with the idea of the absolute. Now though, by means of the ideas of syzygy and of begetting, the finite is imported into the absolute itself *ab initio*, still in the Aeon series, in which Aeons are begotten by Aeons, the distinction thus introduced is considered to be one that admits of being reduced again to unity. But at last, if the finite as such is to come into existence, a breach with the absolute must ensue which can no longer be adjusted. Thus in the absolute itself there is a breach, a rent, a division, by which the absoluteness of the absolute is made doubtful. The task now arises, on the one hand, to maintain the notion of the absolute pure and unimpaired, in spite of this breach, and on the other to disengage and eliminate the finite from it. Here is the point where the specific Christian idea of restitution enters to play its part in the system. The Father, pitying the tears of Sophia, and regarding the prayers of the Aeons, commanded a fresh projection; and the number of thirty Aeons was fulfilled, when Nous and Aletheia produced Christ and the Holy Ghost, in order that the ἔκτρωμα might be formed and separated, and Sophia be calmed and comforted. Christ separated the formless ἔκτρωμα from the rest of the Aeons, that the perfect Aeons might not be disturbed by the sight of his formlessness. And that it might cease altogether to be visible to them, the Father caused another Aeon to come into existence, viz., Stauros. He was to be the boundary-mark of the pleroma, to hold together in himself the thirty Aeons, and to be a visible representation of the greatness and perfection of the Father. He is called Horos, because he is the boundary between the πλήρωμα and the ὑστέρημα which lies without; Partaker (μετοχεὺς), because he has part in the ὑστέρημα; and Stauros, because he stands firm and unchangeable, so that no part of the ὑστέρημα can so much as come into the neighbourhood of the Aeons who are within the pleroma. External to Horos or Stauros was the so-called Ogdoad, Sophia, who dwelt outside the pleroma. Christ, as soon as he had formed her, sprang with the Holy Ghost back into the pleroma to Nous and Aletheia, and peace and unity reigned among the Aeons. Thus harmony was restored within the pleroma. But outside the pleroma the same process continued. There Sophia, separated from him who had formed her but had then forsaken her, lay in great fear. Full of longing, she directed her prayer to him in her sufferings, and Christ and the other Aeons all had pity upon her. In the place of Christ comes now Jesus or the Saviour, who is called the common fruit of all the Aeons of the pleroma. Christ and the other Aeons sent him outside the pleroma as the σύζυγος of Sophia who was without, to free her from the pains she suffered in her longing after Christ. He freed her by divesting her of the various affections of which this longing consisted, and out of them he made the Psychical, the kingdom of the Demiurgus. The psychical substance was conceived as fiery. They also called it The Place, the Hebdomad, the Ancient of Days. The Demiurgus also is of a fiery nature, and the words of Moses, Deut. ix. 3, are applicable to him, "The Lord thy God is a consuming fire." The essence of the Demiurgus is composed of all the elements that distinguish the psychical from the spiritual. He is destitute of intelligent consciousness. Sophia, hovering over him in the Ogdoad, works everything in him, while he knows not what he does, and thinks that he himself of his own power effects the creation of the world; as when he says, "I am God, and beside me is no other." Deut. xxxii. 39. The Demiurgus is the creator of souls; he has given them bodies made from material substance, which is diabolic. The inner man, the psychical, dwells in the material body; and the soul is now alone, now in the company of demons, now in that of the λόγοι. The λόγοι, falling from above, from the common fruit of the pleroma and Sophia, are scattered like germs over this world. The Jesus who is united with Sophia outside the pleroma, and is really the second Christ after the first, is distinguished by the Valentinians from a third Christ, the Jesus born of Mary. As the first Christ restored order to the pleroma, and the second to the Ogdoad of Sophia, so the third is to do the same in the present world. This can only be brought to pass, if Christ, who proceeds not only from the Demiurgus, but also from Sophia, reveals that which was concealed even from the Demiurgus. The Demiurgus had been informed by Sophia that he was not the one God, but that there was a higher above him; the great secret of the Father and the Aeons had not remained unknown to him. But he had kept it hidden, and imparted it to none. Thus the revelation of the mystery does not occur within the sphere of the Demiurgus; but when it was time to take away the veil that lay upon the consciousness of psychical man, and to bring all these mysteries to light, Jesus was born of Mary. Placed in this connection, what can Christianity consist in, but in the communication of that knowledge which the Demiurgus possessed indeed, but only abstractly and for himself, so that it should become a part of the common consciousness of mankind? Through Christianity then does man first learn that the Demiurgus is not the highest God, that above him stand the world of Aeons, the pleroma, and the eternal Father; only with Christianity accordingly does the consciousness of the absolute awaken. Now this knowledge is nothing else than the advance from the psychical to the spiritual. The reason why the Demiurgus knows nothing of the higher order of the world above him is that he stands at the stage of the psychical, and the psychical cannot comprehend the spiritual. The discovery through Christ of that which is hidden from the Demiurgus, is the progress from the period of the psychical principle to that of the spiritual. A new and higher consciousness dawns upon humanity: humanity becomes aware of a higher world-order, lying beyond the order of the earthly, grows conscious of that which exists before all change, of the absolute, and its relation to the finite. But it was the spiritual itself that first became the psychical. We have therefore to distinguish two opposite sides of the world-development. On the one side, the spiritual goes down into the psychical; on the other, the psychical rises into the spiritual. The psychical is only a stage of transition for the spiritual; the spiritual divests itself of its own nature and becomes psychical, in order to return from the psychical back into itself. The spiritual ($\pi\nu\epsilon\upsilon\mu\alpha\tau\iota\kappa\grave{o}\varsigma$) principle is the spirit as distinguished from matter; and the series of steps by which the spiritual becomes psychical, and the psychical becomes spiritual, is the process conducted by spirit with itself. Spirit, or God, as essential spirit, goes forth from itself, and in this self-revelation of God the world arises, which, while on the one hand distinct from God, is also on the other essentially one with him. But in whatever way we regard this immanent relation of God and the world, whether as a self-revelation of God or as a world-development, it is a purely spiritual process, arising out of nothing but the essence of spirit. In the Aeons which it sends forth out of itself, spirit produces out of itself and places over against itself its own essence. But since the essence of pure spirit is nothing else than thought and knowledge, the process of its self-revelation can only consist in its becoming conscious of its own essence: the

Aeons of the pleroma are the highest conceptions of spiritual existence and life, the general forms of thought, in which what spirit is essentially, it is for the consciousness determinately and concretely. But with the self-knowledge of spirit, with its self-consciousness as it distinguishes itself from itself, is given not only a principle of differentiation, but also, since God and the world are essentially one, of the materialisation of spirit. For the conceptions which spirit uses in order to reach this consciousness are separate and apart from the absolute principle; and the wider this separation, the more is the spiritual consciousness darkened: spirit divests itself of its own nature; it is no longer clear and transparent to itself; the spiritual sinks down to the psychical, the psychical thickens into the material, and the material is connected at its further extremity with the notion of the demonic and diabolical.[1] But as the psychical belongs in its essence to the

[1] The most important point of the whole system is the transition from the spiritual to the psychical, represented in the sufferings of Sophia. Here we have before us the extremest pain and distress of spirit struggling with itself, despairing of itself, when on the point of being compelled to strip itself of its own nature and to become something different from what it is. On this point compare the following passage in the Philosophoumena, p. 191:—'Ἐποίησεν οὖν ὡς τηλικοῦτος αἰὼν καὶ παντὸς τοῦ πληρώματος ἔκγονος (Jesus or the Soter), ἐκστῆναι τὰ πάθη ἀπ' αὐτῆς, καὶ ἐποίησεν αὐτὰ ὑποστάτας οὐσίας καὶ τὸν μὲν φόβον ψυχικὴν ἐποίησεν ἐπιθυμίαν, τὴν δὲ λύπην ὑλικὴν, τὴν δὲ ἀπορίαν δαιμόνων, τὴν δὲ ἐπιστροφὴν, καὶ δέησιν καὶ ἱκετείαν ὁδὸν καὶ μετάνοιαν καὶ δύναμιν ψυχικῆς οὐσίας, ἥτις καλεῖται δεξιὰ (cf. Christl. Gnosis, 134), ὁ δημιουργὸς, ἀπὸ τοῦ φόβου τούτεστιν, ὃ λέγει, φησὶν, ἡ γραφὴ 'Ἀρχὴ σοφίας φόβος κυρίου· Αὐτὴ γὰρ ἀρχὴ τῶν τῆς σοφίας παθῶν· ἐφοβήθη γὰρ, εἶτα ἐλυπήθη, εἶτα ἠπόρησε, καὶ οὕτως ἐπὶ δέησιν καὶ ἱκετείαν κατέφυγεν.

This suffering appears then in four states; from fear arises the psychical, from grief the material, from despair the demonic; and a fourth stage follows, apparently very different from the three others. Spirit can be degraded no lower than the point where it is at last changed into the demonic; and therefore the fourth stage is the point where all turns and sways round. Arrived at the extremity of its self-divestment, spirit goes into itself and collects itself in order to find a way out of this torture. Can the words ὁδὸς, μετάνοια, δύναμις have any other meaning than this in a Gnostic work, Πίστις Σοφία, published by Petermann, Berlin, 1851, from a Coptic MS.? Sophia's sufferings and μετάνοια form the chief subject of the first part. Jesus descending again after his ascension, for no other object than to impart to his disciples the whole truth from first to last, plain and undisguised, relates the history of the fall of Sophia. When Πίστις Σοφία was in the 13th of the Aeons, the place of all her sisters, the ἀόρατοι who are themselves the 24 προβολαὶ of the great ἀόρατος, then it came to pass at the com-

spiritual, and germs of spiritual life are left everywhere, the spiritual must again pierce through the material obscuration of the spiritual consciousness which takes place at the stage of psychical life : it must throw off the veil that is laid upon it in the world of the Demiurgus. The whole world-development is the continuation of the same spiritual process. There must therefore be a turning-point, at which spirit returns from its self-divestment to itself, and becomes once more clearly conscious of its own essential nature. Such is the Gnostic conception of the Christian revelation. Those who know, in the Gnostic sense, that is to say the spiritual, who as such have also the truly Christian consciousness, mark a new epoch in the general spiritual life, and are the highest stage of the self-revelation of God, and of the world-development. This period of the course of the world begins with the appearance of Christ, and ends at last when through Christ and Sophia, all that is spiritual is received back into the pleroma. Christ in his activity is seen as the principle that re-establishes, that maintains unity with the absolute. He is thus seen at every

mand of the first mystery that she looked up, and saw the light of the καταπέτασμα of the θησαυρὸς of light. She longed to go there, but was not able ; and instead of performing the mystery of the 13th Aeon, she directed her hymns to the place on high. For this all the archons of the 12 Aeons hated her ; because she ceased from her mysteries, and wished to be above them. The great τριδύναμος αὐθάδης hated her most of all ; he who is the third τριδύναμος in the 13th Aeon. He sent forth from himself a great power with a lion's face ; and from his ὕλη a multitude of προβολαὶ ὑλικαί, which he sent to the lower parts, into chaos, to lie in wait for Πίστις Σοφία and take away her strength. When Sophia saw in the depth the light-power that had come from Αὐθάδης, thinking that this was the light she had seen on high, she descended, out of desire for this light, into chaos, and was there put to sore pain by the προβολαὶ ὑλικαί of Αὐθάδης. In her distress she called for help on the light which she had seen at first. She had trusted it from the beginning, and in her unfailing confidence in the power of this light—whence she has the name of Πίστις Σοφία—she addressed to it her μετάνοια. She bewails her distress and pain in 12 μετάνοιαι, and prays for the forgiveness of her sins. The 12 μετάνοιαι correspond to the 12 Aeons, in respect of whom she has erred : and the 12th is followed by a 13th, for the 13th Aeon, the τόπος δικαιοσύνης, is the place whence she descended. With the 13th μετάνοια, her time is fulfilled, the series of her θλίψεις is accomplished : Jesus is sent by the first mystery to help her, and leads her back on high from chaos. Cf. Theol. Jahrb. 1854, p., 1 sq.

stage of the world-development, and in the highest regions of the world of Aeons, in which everything at last comes to rest, and which is arranged from the first with a view to this one great result of the whole. Thus, in the Gnostic view of the world, Christ has quite the significance of an absolute world principle.[1] The Valentinian system affords us a clearer view than any other into the specific character of Gnosticism, its deeper spiritual import, and the inner connection of its view of the world. Nor had any other so large a number of adherents.

The school had many ramifications, and the system was elaborated and developed in various ways by the more eminent disciples and successors of Valentinus, as Secundus, Ptolemaeus, Heracleon, Marcus.[2]

Among the Gnostics contemporary and connected with Valentinus and his disciples, we may mention the two Syrians, Bardesanes and Saturninus; but the most important and the most independent were Basilides of Egypt and his son Isidorus. Our previous knowledge of his system has been much enlarged and modified by the new source of information discovered in the Philosophoumena;[3] and we shall therefore do well to give a brief statement of its main features.

[1] In this statement I have been guided chiefly by the new sources of information contained in the Philos. vi. 29, sq., p. 184, sq. The principal points of the system there appear very distinctly: what is wanting may be easily supplied from the more detailed statement, drawn from other sources, which however agree with this one in all essential points, given in my Christliche Gnosis, p. 124, sq.

[2] Colarbasus, whose name has generally been placed along with that of Marcus, must in future be struck out of the series of Gnostics. Volkmar is incontestably right in the result of his dissertation in the Zeitschrift für Hist. Theol., 1855, p. 603, sq., viz., that "The Gnosticism of Colarbasus may be reduced to the Valentinian Gnosticism of Kol-Arbas, the highest tetrad of the thirty Aeons, as elaborated by the followers of Marcus, who appealed to an immediate revelation of this tetrad, or of the mother of secrets, Sige, in the same tetrad." The only remaining question would be, whether, under the word Kol, we should not understand rather קוֹל, "the voice," i.e. sound in contrast to silence, than כֹּל, "all the four, all four together."

[3] vii. 19, p. 230, sq. Compare: Jacobi, Basilidis philosophi gnostici sententias, etc., Berlin, 1852; Bunsen, Hippolytus und seine Zeit, Leipzig, 1852, i. 65;

The Gnostics, unable to devise terms sufficient to express the idea of the absolute, find themselves obliged to determine it negatively, as that which is exalted above all expression and conception. Thus Basilides places simple nothing at the summit of his system, and thus speaks of God, not as the Being, but as the not-being. There was simply nothing,—not matter, not substance, not what is without substance, not simple, not compound, not man, not angel, not God, simply nothing of all things that can be perceived or imagined. Still, the not-being God made a not-being world out of the not-being: yet every positive attribute is denied of this making, this act of the divine will.[1] Basilides was of opinion that as, generally, the expressions which we use do not really correspond to the things they signify, this must much more be the case in speaking of the absolute; there every positive and negative statement can be but a sign of what we wish to say. We can see clearly that Basilides' great difficulty was to get a beginning. God is and is not, and so the world is and is not; one cannot tell how it came into being; it simply is. In order to get rid of every idea of an emanation or projection from God,[2] Basilides conceived the world, as in the Mosaic book of Genesis, as brought into existence simply and only by the word of him who spoke: though sometimes he did not hesitate to speak of the world as a divine προβολή. Thus the standpoint of Basilides differs from that of Valentinus, inasmuch as what is principally kept in view in his system is rather the return to God than the going forth from God. A prominent con-

Uhlhorn, das Basilidianische System mit besonderer Rücksicht auf die Angaben des Hippolytus, Gött. 1855. Hilgenfeld, Das System des Gnostikers Basilides, Theol. Jahrb. 1856, p. 86, sq. Cf. Die jüdische Apokalyptik 1857, p. 287, sq. My essay: Das System des Gnostikers Basilides und die neuesten Auffassungen desselben, Theol. Jahrb. 1856, p. 121, sq.

[1] Philos. p. 231: Ἀνοήτως, ἀναισθήτως, ἀβούλως, ἀπροαιρέτως, ἀπαθῶς, ἀνεπιθυμήτως, κόσμον ἠθέλησε ποιῆσαι. Τὸ δὲ ἠθέλησε λέγω, φησὶ, σημασίας χάριν, ἀθελήτως καὶ ἀνοήτως καὶ ἀναισθήτως.

[2] Philos. p. 232: φεύγει γὰρ πάνυ καὶ δέδοικε τὰς κατὰ προβολὴν τῶν γεγονότων οὐσίας ὁ Βασιλείδης. He compared the process of emanation to the act of a spider spinning its threads out of itself. He took as his beginning the absolute notion of the not-being, thus opposing the idea of emanation, which assumes the entire reality of the being.

ception of his system is the separation of the powers and elements. Since that alone can be separated which was formerly mingled and connected, Basilides assumed that those elements which afterwards came in the course of development to be separated, and to take up more and more independent positions, were originally mixed, or existed in each other or side by side. And thus the σύγχυσις ἀρχική, which Clement of Alexandria attributes to him,[1] has always been regarded as characteristic of his system, though it has not been satisfactorily shown how it is to be understood. According to the new source of our knowledge, we are obliged to consider it as one of the postulates of his system, which it was necessary for him to make in order to get a beginning of the development. What he says in the exposition of his system is applicable here. Everything seeks to rise from below upwards, from the bad to the better; but nothing is so senseless as to leave the better and go downwards. Unable to explain how a σύγχυσις ἀρχική was brought about, he was yet obliged to presuppose it, if he wished to regard the world-development as a process of separation. He accordingly supposed a σπέρμα τοῦ κόσμου, which contains, as in the smallest germ, all that is comprehended in the whole world.[2]

[1] Cf. Die Christliche Gnosis, p. 211, sq.
[2] Philos. p. 231. Τὸ δὲ σπέρμα τοῦ κόσμου πάντα εἶχεν ἐν ἑαυτῷ, ὡς ὁ τοῦ σινάπεως κόκκος ἐν ἐλαχίστῳ συλλαβὼν ἔχει πάσας ὁμοῦ τὰς ῥίζας—οὕτως οὐκ ὢν θεὸς ἐποίησε κόσμον οὐκ ὢν (ὄντα) ἐξ οὐκ ὄντων, καταβαλλόμενος καὶ ὑποστήσας σπέρμα ἕν ἔχον πᾶσαν ἐν ἑαυτῷ τὴν τοῦ κόσμου πανσπερμίαν. All was in it, but as yet undeveloped and formless. He therefore calls this πανσπερμία an ἀμορφία, p. 229. The σπέρμα is an οὐκ ὄν, as God is οὐκ ὢν θεός, εἶχε γὰρ πάντα τὰ σπέρματα ἐν ἑαυτῷ τεθησαυρισμένα καὶ κατακείμενα, οἷον οὐκ ὄν, ὑπό τε τοῦ οὐκ ὄντος θεοῦ γενέσθαι προβεβουλευμένα, p. 233. The dominant conception of the system is the unity or immanent relation of being and not-being; there is no being that does not include in itself a not-being, and no not-being that does not presuppose a being. This unity, conceived as negatively and abstractedly as possible in the οὐκ ὢν θεός, has developed into a notion of something concrete in the σπέρμα οὐκ ὄν. The relation of God and the world is viewed as the immanent transition from the abstract to the concrete, from the ideality of that which is only conceived to the reality of the actual. The moving principle is the tendency to set forth out of unity the antitheses which, while in unity, are still indifferent, and cause them to confront one another in their pure opposition. This is done when the abstract antithesis of being and not-being becomes the concrete antithesis of spiritual and material.

When this embryo of the world has been once evolved from God as the principle of the world, and not till then, the world-development enters on its determinate course. The divine germs contained in the primal world are called by Basilides the sonship (υἰότης).[1] This again is distinguished into three separate constituent parts as soon as the first projection of the σπέρμα has taken place. The finest part at once returns to the not-being with a swiftness which Basilides characterises by the poetic expression ὡσεὶ πτερὸν ἠὲ νόημα.[2] Every nature in fact strives, one in one way, another in another, to reach the not-being, attracted by its exceeding beauty. The denser part strives to follow the finer, but remains in the σπέρμα; yet it also clothes itself with wings, after the manner of the soul in Plato. The principle that gives the wings is the Holy Spirit: the relation in which it stands to this part of the υἰότης is described by saying that the two are as mutually serviceable as the wing and the bird, neither of which can soar upward without the help of the other. The Spirit rises, indeed, and comes near to that finest part of the υἰότης; but it cannot, from its nature, endure the region of the not-being God and of the υἰότης, the purest region, exalted above every name. It therefore remains behind; but, as a vessel once filled with sweet-smelling ointment keeps the perfume even when empty, so the Holy Spirit has, as it were, a perfume of the υἰότης, and this perfume descending from the Holy Spirit penetrates to the formless under-world. After the first and second soaring of the υἰότης, the Holy Spirit remains in the midst between the world and that which is above the world.[3] After these two parts of the being have been separated by a firmament, the great Archon, the head

---

[1] The ἐκλογὴ κόσμου in Clemens Alex. Cf. Die Christliche Gnosis, p. 223, sq. The expression υἰότης, denoting the spiritual, might seem to refer to the higher grade in which the Son stands in this development from below upwards. So the son of the Archon is more intelligent than the Archon himself. But the expression is to be taken in the sense of the phrase υἱοὶ θεοῦ (Rom. viii. 14, sq.), Philos. p. 238.

[2] Homer. Od. vii. 36.

[3] Hence the πνεῦμα μεθόριον. From the same mediating function (εὐεργετεῖν) the Spirit is described in Clemens of Alexandria as πνεῦμα διακονούμενον.

of the world, tears himself away from the σπέρμα κοσμικὸν (and the πανσπερμία τοῦ σωροῦ), and knowing not that above him there is a wiser, mightier, and better than he, he thinks himself the lord, the sovereign, and the wise architect of the world, and begins to make all the things the world contains. First, not liking to be alone, in imitation of the plan which the not-being God sketched when he laid the foundation of the world in the πανσπερμία, he begot, from the matter of the world which he had ready before him, a son who was far wiser and better than himself. Surprised by his beauty, he set him on his right hand. By his help he made the ethereal world, the kingdom of the great Archon, called by Basilides the Ogdoad. After the completion of this ethereal world, which extended down to the moon, another Archon arose out of the πανσπερμία, who also is greater than all that is under him except the υἱότης, which still remains behind. His place is the Hebdomad, and he too has a son who is more understanding and wiser than himself. From these worlds is now distinguished the region which, as the basis of the whole world-development, Basilides called the σωρὸς and πανσπερμία. It has no governor, arranger, or Demiurgus of its own; but the thought placed in it by the not-being at the creation suffices for it. In it remains the third υἱότης, which has also to be revealed, and to be brought up to the region where, beyond the Spirit, are the two first parts of the υἱότης and he who is not-being. This is the creature, groaning and waiting for the manifestation of the children of God; and we, says Basilides, are these children, we are the spiritual still remaining behind here. When we, the children of God, for whose sake the creature groaned, were to be revealed, the Gospel came into the world. It did not come by the descent of the blessed υἱότης of the inconceivable, blessed, not-being God; but, as naphtha kindles a fire at a great distance, so did the son of the great Archon receive the thoughts of the υἱότης by the mediation of the Spirit. The Son learnt that he was not the God of the whole, but that there was over him the Ineffable, the not-being. He went into himself, was affrighted at the ignorance he had been in up to this time, and how his son sitting beside him—who is now called Christ—instructed him who the not-being is, what the υἱότης is, what the Holy Spirit, how the universe has been disposed and arranged, and whither it is to return. Basilides also applied to the fear which seized the Archon the words ἀρχὴ σοφίας φόβος Κυρίου (Prov. i. 5); and to the penitence with which he confessed the sin of his self-exaltation, the passage Ps. xxxii. 5. The same instruction was imparted also to the whole Ogdoad, and from the Ogdoad the Gospel then came to the Hebdomad. The son of the great Archon caused the light which he had received from above, from the υἱότης, to rise on the son of the Archon of the Hebdomad. Thus enlightened, the son announced the Gospel to the Archon of the Hebdomad; and the impression it produced on him was not different from that produced on the Archon of the Ogdoad. After all these regions with their countless ἀρχαὶ, δυνάμεις, and ἐξουσίαι and the 365 heavens, whose great Archon is Abrasax, had received the enlightenment of the Gospel, the light had to descend also to the ἀμορφία in the nethermost world, in which we are; and the hitherto unknown mystery had to be revealed to that υἱότης which, like an ἔκτρωμα, was left in the ἀμορφία. Thus the light, which had come from the υἱότης through the Spirit to the Ogdoad and thence to the Hebdomad, descended to Mary, and her son Jesus was enlightened by it. The power of the highest which overshadowed Mary is the power of the κρίσις, the separation. The world must continue till all the υἱότης left behind for the aid of the souls in the ἀμορφία follows Jesus, and returns purified. It becomes so fine, that, like the first υἱότης, it soars aloft through its own nature. This κρίσις and the ἀποκατάστασις, which it is to bring about, now come into the foreground of the system.[1] The design of the whole Gospel history from the beginning is to show how Jesus separates and divides all that is mixed without form outside the Ogdoad and the Hebdomad. This separation and

[1] Philos. p. 244. ὅλη γὰρ αὐτῶν ἡ ὑπόθεσις, σύγχυσις οἱονεὶ πανσπερμίας καὶ φυλοκρίνησις καὶ ἀποκατάστασις τῶν συγκεχυμένων εἰς τὰ οἰκεῖα. Τῆς οὖν φυλοκρινήσεως ἀπαρχὴ γέγονεν ὁ Ἰησοῦς.

division takes place with regard to all that is still left behind, in the same way as it had taken place with regard to Jesus himself. His suffering had no other object than the separation of that which was mingled. What suffered in him was the bodily part which he received from the ἀμορφία, and this returned to the ἀμορφία. In the same way the psychical element which came from the Hebdomad returned to the Hebdomad; what came from the higher region of the great Archon returned to him; and what was of the Spirit remained with the Spirit. But the third and still remaining υἱότης soared through all these elements up to the blessed υἱότης. Thus all returns to its place; and when it is there, there it is to stay. For whatever stays in its place is imperishable; but that which oversteps its natural bounds is perishable. It was for this reason that, at the epoch at which Christianity revealed that which was hitherto a mystery, a great ignorance came over the whole world, in order that no unnatural desire might anywhere arise. The Archon of the Hebdomad is prevented from knowing what is above him, in order that he may not desire the impossible, and so suffer pain and sorrow. The same ignorance overtakes the great Archon of the Ogdoad. The universal ἀποκατάστασις, therefore, consists in this, that everything arrives, at the time determined, at the place where, according to its natural constitution, it ought to be; or in this, that it is recognised as being that which it essentially is.[1]

The fundamental idea pervading the system is the same with Basilides as with Valentinus. The spiritual principle divests itself of its own nature, and becomes the psychical and material; and after this self-divestment, it must again be received back into itself. This is the process of world-development which reaches its accomplishment in Christianity. But this accomplishment cannot take place, unless by the spiritual natures attaining a consciousness of their true being; that is, of the spiritual principle which has being essentially, which is absolute and supramundane, with which the

---

[1] Philos. p. 242. Καὶ οὕτως ἡ ἀποκατάστασις ἔσται πάντων τεθεμελιωμένων μὲν ἐν τῷ σπέρματι τῶν ὅλων ἐν ἀρχῇ, ἀποκατασταμένων δὲ ἐν καιροῖς ἰδίοις.

spiritual natures are essentially one, even in that present state in which they are hidden and obscured by the psychical and the material. It is this consciousness of that which essentially is, and is supramundane, that forms the true essence of Christianity. And so accordingly Basilides defines it.[1] Although that which comes to its accomplishment in Christianity has first been undergoing preparation in the earlier stages through which the process of world-development moves, still it does not attain its full reality, till the absorption of spirit into itself has reached its deepest depth. As Valentinus distinguished three different Christs, so in the system of Basilides Jesus cannot appear till after the two sons of the ruler of the Ogdoad and the ruler of the Hebdomad. These three are essentially one; in all the three we have the same principle, which mediates between the several spiritual beings and the primal principle, maintains and restores their connection with it, and recalls them to unity. Both with Valentinus and with Basilides we find the Holy Spirit placed along with Christ, and subordinate to him in the same capacity. The Sophia of Valentinus coincides with the Christ and the Holy Spirit of Basilides; Sophia herself is not found in the doctrine of the latter, since the more concrete idea of syzygy is altogether absent from his system. The Gospel only declares universally that which, though it existed before, existed as a mystery. Before the Gospel, in proportion as any given time was more remote, the deeper was the concealment of this mystery.[2] What was at first shrouded in thick darkness, and then, though declared, was yet, as it were, but a glimmering light,

---

[1] Philos. p. 243. Εὐαγγέλιόν ἐστι κατ' αὐτοὺς ἡ τῶν ὑπερκοσμίων γνῶσις. Only when one knows what is above the world, can one know also what the world itself is.

[2] In this sense Basilides said, p. 238, that the Ogdoad was ἄῤῥητος, the Hebdomad ῥητόν, and that the Archon of the Hebdomad said to Moses: "I am the God of Abraham, Isaac, and Jacob, and the name of the God I did not make known to them" (Ex. vi. 3), i.e. the name of the ἄῤῥητὸς θεός, the Archon of the Ogdoad. In the period from Adam to Moses, the proper period of the ruler of the Ogdoad πάντα ἦν φυλασσό μενα ἀποκρύφῳ σιωπῇ. The two rulers mark two periods of the world.

and was only to break through in the creature which was waiting for the manifestation of the sons of God,—this in Christianity becomes the broad and full daylight of clear and transparent spiritual consciousness. And it is just at this time that God caused a great ignorance to come over the whole world, in order that nothing might strive to overstep the bounds of its nature. The assertion of this ignorance gives us much help towards characterising the standpoint of the system. The ignorance denotes that progress in the march of the world's history, by virtue of which each period is deemed the highest, and regarded as absolute, only so long as spirit in its development has not gone forward to a higher stage. In contrast to a higher stage, the stage preceding appears so subordinate and at so low a level, that all its glory is veiled as by the darkness of ignorance. The two Archons especially are overtaken by this ignorance; but such is the fate also of all that was great and important in its time, and, like the minds of those rulers, believed itself to be the power that governed the world. It is of necessity given over to the darkness of unconsciousness, when the progressing spirit of the world passes beyond it. Therefore, according to Basilides, everything has its determinate limits, its determinate time. Knowledge is ever changing into its contrary. As the process of history is carried further and further, spirit, ever retiring into itself, receives back into itself the forms which it had sent out as of apparently permanent importance. The forms dissolve, and there remains at last, as all that is really before the consciousness, only the abstract notion, the natural law which is immanent in the subsisting order of the world.[1] Here the realism and the idealism of the Gnostic view of the world so interpenetrate one another, that the process exhibited in it is rather the phenomenological process of the spirit than the real one of the world. It is not the real principles of the world's origin in themselves, that are the highest absolute point whence all proceeds, and on which all depends. It is these principles only because

---

[1] The present order of the world, Basilides says, has no governor, such as the Archons were: ἀρκεῖ ὁ λογισμὸς ἐκεῖνος, ὃν ὁ οὐκ ὢν, ὅτι ἐποίει, ἐλογίζετο.

they are the object about which the consciousness of spirit, knowing and thinking, moves, gaining, as it employs itself with these necessary postulates of its own procedure, a clear perception of itself, and being thus enabled to comprehend the antitheses of the subsisting order of the world in all their width. And this is exactly what the genuine Gnostic conception of ἀποκατάστασις amounts to. The main point is, not that something which is not yet, becomes realised in the world of objective existence; but that something which already exists in essence becomes firmly established. That which already has being essentially is to be made to be for consciousness as well, and to be recognised in the consciousness of knowing subjects as that which it already is in essence.[1] The more completely the objective being of things becomes a subjectively known being, and the stricter and closer, therefore, the unity of being and consciousness, so much the more fully is the goal of the world's development attained. It appears plainly from this, that the highest subject with which the Gnostic systems concern themselves, is ever ultimately knowledge and intuition, Gnosis in its peculiar absolute significance. This is what gives the system of Basilides, in the form in which it is now known to us, its distinguished position in the history of Gnosticism. It affords us a deeper insight than any other system into the inner nature of Gnosticism, and the intellectual process carried on in Gnostic speculation.[2]

[1] The ἀποκατάστασις is the third of the successive connected stages after the σύγχυσις and φυλοκρίνησις, Philos. p. 244. The Gnostic addresses himself to his highest task when he determines that the all-important question he has to seek to answer is τίς ἐστιν ὁ οὐκ ὤν, τίς ἡ υἰότης, τί τὸ ἅγιον πνεῦμα, τίς ἡ τῶν ὅλων κατασκευή, ποῦ ταῦτα ἀποκατασταθήσεται, Philos. p. 239. This result is attained when the τῶν ὅλων κατασκευὴ is known and recognised in the consciousness of knowing subjects as that which it essentially is. In this sense it is ἀποκατάστασις τῶν συγκεχυμένων εἰς τὰ οἰκεῖα. All that is comes to stand in its due and proper place, when that which is various in itself is known and contemplated without confusion in its variety of principles. In this indeed all knowledge and intuition consist. Ἄγνοια as above defined is an essential step of the ἀποκατάστασις which is thus accomplished.

[2] Hilgenfeld (in loc. cit.) affirms that the statement of the system of Basilides given in the Philosophoumena is neither fairly consistent with that given by the

We have said that the fundamental character of Gnosticism is its dualistic view of the world. This statement seems at first to receive but slight confirmation from our inquiry into the two systems, which we have described at some length as the two chief representatives of the Gnostic mode of thought. They cannot indeed entirely conceal the dualistic basis on which they are founded; yet this element is not prominent in them, and can scarcely be regarded as their principal distinguishing feature. We should thus be led to say that the peculiar nature of Gnosticism was not fully developed before the appearance of the system of Marcion, which, on account of its more strictly dualistic form, we must distinguish from those hitherto set forth, as marking a new stage of Gnostic thought. Still the distinction is merely relative; for none of the systems, however various their modifications, ever get past the antithesis of spirit and matter. But with regard to this antithesis itself, strict as it seems to be, we nevertheless are able to gather from our inquiries up to this point the very characteristic fact, that the two principles do not form a pure antithesis. The one principle always contains something derived from the other. If spirit is unable to resist its longing to materialise itself, it contains already the principle of matter. And if matter is moved by the impulse to come into contact with spirit, then it has in itself a spiritual element. The two are related as two forces

authorities hitherto known to us, nor derived from original knowledge. For disproof of this position, compare my Abhandlung quoted above, p. 150, *sq*. What Hilgenfeld has further laid down in the Anhang zur jüd. Apokal. p. 287, contains nothing really new. It is clear enough that we are equally unable to determine precisely, in the system of Basilides and in that of Valentinus, how much is due to the founder and how much to the further elaboration of disciples. But, with regard to this question, in a general history of Gnosticism, the form which contains most distinctly the characteristic features of the system is our surest guide. And this form of the Basilidian teaching is undoubtedly to be found in the statement given in the Philosophoumena. The doctrine of Basilides seems to have assumed various modifications; his name is connected with Manichaeism (Das Manich. Rel. Syst. p. 84) and Priscillianism (Gieseler, Eccl. Hist. i. 2, p. 98). It is likely enough that the σύγχυσις ἀρχική, as the duality of principles, appeared more unmistakably at the summit of the system in one of these forms than in the others. But this need not prevent us from regarding the statement of the Philosophoumena as composed of genuine Basilidian elements.

of one and the same substance, and are both attracted and repelled by each other. In their general character, then, the Gnostic systems may as fitly be called pantheistic as dualistic. The antithesis is in any case the same, and all that the difference amounts to is whether the scale falls on the one side or on the other, or whether an almost exact equilibrium is maintained: as one or the other of these alternatives prevails, the system is more or less dualistic. The least dualistic system of all is that of Valentinus, in which spirit and matter are in fact related as substance and accident; spirit is the being, matter the not-being. The same is the case with Basilides, only that the two terms change places: here the spiritual is called the not-being; the material accordingly is the being. The subordination of spirit to matter is carried by Basilides to the furthest point possible. With him they are so immediately one, that in their unity the antithesis turns into indifference, and therefore the development is not from above downwards, as with Valentinus, but from below upwards. It is with Marcion, however, that we meet with dualism in its most genuine form. Here the two principles are placed at the summit of the system in their pure antithesis, although this form too is but a modification of the same fundamental relation.

It is true that the doctrine on which Marcion laid most stress was the sharp dualistic separation of the Law and the Gospel. But it is with perfect justice that he is placed in the series of the Gnostics, since his view of the Law and the Gospel is based on the general antithesis of the two principles, which determine his view of the world. Not only did he assume a matter co-eternal with the highest God, but he also placed the Creator, whom he as well as his predecessors distinguished from the highest God, in such a relation to him and to matter, that he could only be conceived along with matter, under one and the same fundamental notion.[1] The effect of this stricter dualism, however, was to give Marcion's system an essentially different character from that of the other Gnostics. It has nothing in common with them except the four

[1] Compare Die Christliche Gnosis, p. 276, *sq.*

principles, the highest God, matter, the Demiurgus, and Christ. Marcion has no pleroma, no Aeons, no syzygies, no suffering Sophia. Now in the other systems where they appear these principles serve the purpose of setting in motion and helping forward the general process of world-development till it arrives at the point at which in Christianity that which was already in existence comes to full reality and accomplishment. In Marcion's system, therefore, where these principles are wanting, everything takes place suddenly and abruptly, without preparation, without the interposition of connecting links. Everything is arranged so as to sever the connection between Christianity and what went before it. Paganism, according to him, has no affinity with Christianity under any aspect. Even Judaism stands so far below Christianity, that the relation of the one to the other is in his eyes that of the sharpest antithesis. The Demiurgus is not merely a limited and imperfect being, but one who offers opposition to the highest God and Christ.[1] While with Valentinus and Basilides the Demiurgus humbles himself before Christ and returns into himself, with Marcion it is he who compasses Christ's death. It is true that the chief predicate applied to him is righteousness; but in Marcion's view mercy and righteousness stand so far apart, that the latter is nothing but strictness and hardness. The notion of righteousness indeed is only introduced to mark the difference and antithesis between Christianity and Judaism; and this is but one instance of Marcion's strong and decided view of the entire newness and immediateness of Christianity, its incomprehensibleness, and the absence of preparation for it. The God revealed by Christ is a completely unknown God, of whom men had not even a presentiment before, either in the heathen or in the Jewish world. Hence it results, that the Gnosticism of Marcion is in tendency exactly opposed to that form of Gnosticism of which Valentinus is the chief representative. In all the systems that belong to the earlier form of Gnosticism, the common tendency is to bring as

[1] Philos. vii. 31, p. 254. Κακὸς δ' ἐστὶν, ὡς λέγει, ὁ δημιουργὸς καὶ τούτου τὰ ποιήματα.

many intermediate links as possible between the absolute point of commencement and the point when Christianity appears as a new stage of development. They deliberately apply themselves to the task of giving as vivid and concrete a representation as they can of the whole process of development; and Christianity enters into this process in such a way that its whole being and nature can only be comprehended by means of all that it presupposes. All this is quite otherwise with Marcion. With a completely opposite tendency and aim, he seeks to remove from the sphere which those systems fill with their ideal beings, everything that might be thought to be a preparation for Christianity. Only the pure antithesis is to be preserved. And yet, though the two tendencies seem to be opposed, though it seems to be the essence of the one to connect and join, and of the other to tear and cut away every link of connection, still the distinction can be but relative. Such it must be, if the system of Marcion is to be referred to the category of Gnosticism as well as those of Valentinus and Basilides: they are only various forms and modifications of one and the same mode of view. And this anticipation is confirmed by a closer examination. Suddenly and abruptly as the God revealed by Christ appears, and begins to play his part in the history of the world and religion, yet this is merely the mode of his external appearance and revelation to the consciousness of humanity. Even in this appearance the absolute being of the hitherto unknown God is presupposed. The Demiurgus of Marcion, again, may differ from that of the two other Gnostics; but in Marcion's view too, the God revealed by Christ cannot appear and begin to act until the kingdom of the Demiurgus, as the lord of the pre-Christian period, has gone before. The whole history of the world and religion being thus divided into two periods, one of which necessarily presupposes the other; and this relation being incomprehensible except by means of a principle in which unity is bestowed on the antithesis of Christian and pre-Christian: we find this to be the common element between the tendencies of Marcion and that of the other Gnostics, that they make all that is of the essence of Christianity, and belongs to the essential Christian consciousness, dependent on its antithesis to prepare and introduce it. It is thus neither dualism alone, nor the Demiurgus alone, that constitutes the essence of Gnosticism, but the relation in which the Demiurgus stands to Christ, viz., such a relation that Christ himself cannot be, unless the Demiurgus be presupposed. Here then Marcion is as good a Gnostic as any other. Again it is to be remembered that the Gnostic Demiurgus himself is only a mythical personification, one more instance of the general habit of the thought of the ancient world to set forth its conceptions in symbols and personifications. Bearing this in mind, we can see that even when seeking most to assert his Christian consciousness and to know nothing of the pre-Christian world, Marcion is still far from escaping from its modes of thought. He too is unable to conceive the pre-Christian in its distinction from the Christian world, except by the aid of such a figure as the Demiurgus. He too holds a standpoint, at which his Christianity is essentially determined by the general antitheses of his theory of the world. Still, there is a characteristic distinction between him and the other Gnostics; but it is only the consequence of the attitude of strong opposition he takes up towards everything pre-Christian. This distinction is, that he is on the point of passing from the transcendental sphere of an objective world-consciousness in which the world-development moves in the antithesis of spirit and matter, or of the spiritual and the psychical, to that of the subjective consciousness, where the course of the world-development is determined with reference to the ethical ideas of the Law and the Gospel, righteousness and mercy, fear and love. The general Gnostic antithesis of spirit and matter is thrown into the back-ground: instead of it, in order to hold the Law and the Gospel apart in the full width of their distinction, Marcion bases his view of the world or his religious consciousness upon the antithesis of the visible and the invisible.

The Gnosticism of Marcion discards the Aeons, and retains the Demiurgus, but on the other hand sharpens the dualistic distinction. We are led to ask whether there is not a third form of Gnosticism: a form in which the Demiurgus, whose separation from the highest God gives him even with Marcion a heathen aspect, loses prominence, and in which dualism itself is less pronounced; while some at least of the characteristic essence of Gnosticism still remains in this, that Christianity is still regarded from the point of view of the general world-development. Such a system is in fact set forth in the pseudo-Clementine Homilies, and we have now to consider it. It is indeed very different from the systems commonly counted under the name of Gnosticism; and it might quite properly be asked, whether it should be placed in the same series at all. Yet on the other hand we find in it a new and peculiar combination of all the Gnostic notions, and can call it nothing else than a fresh form of Gnosticism.

If we considered that the chief criterion of Gnosticism is to be found in the separation of the Creator from the highest God, in the manner in which it is usually understood, then a system which pronounces against this separation so expressly as the pseudo-Clementine cannot be regarded as Gnostic. But while fully recognising this as a criterion, we can still affirm that the system of the Homilies bears a thoroughly Gnostic character. True, there is not only an antignostic sound, but a really antignostic meaning, in the emphatic statement that the fundamental truth of all religion is, that the highest God is also the Creator of the world. It is the same, when the Homilies carry the idea of the inseparableness of these two conceptions so far as to say, that even were the Creator the worst of all beings, all the worship of men would nevertheless be due to him alone, since from him alone does man derive his existence. Here the two ideas of God and Creator are presented to us as simply identical for man's religious consciousness.[1] But in spite of the identity of these two conceptions, we see that the Homilies set up a separation between them again. First of all, according to them, God is not the creator of matter. A creation from nothing is unknown to them; they, like the other Gnostics,

[1] Hom. xviii. 22.

assume an original matter, which is together with God as his co-eternal body, and whence the four elements and primal substances proceed through the spirit of God, which penetrates the body and transmutes it into various forms.[1] Again, even in so far as God is the Creator, he is so not immediately, but only through the mediation of Sophia. Sophia, always united with God as his soul, is the world-creating principle, by which God goes out of himself and the monad becomes the duad. Sophia is, accordingly, expressly called the Demiurgic hand of God.[2] Thus, the only distinction of the Sophia of the Homilies from that of the Gnostic systems is, that here she is not separated from God, but is placed in the same relation of immanence to his being in which matter also stands to him. A point which contributes still more to establish the analogy between this and the other systems is to be found in what is said of the ruler of the world. The true ruler of the world is not God, but a being holding precisely the place of the Gnostic Demiurgus, merely with the difference that the creation of the world cannot be predicated of him. When the four fundamental substances had come forth from the body of God and had mingled together, there arose from them a being which possessed the impulse to destroy the evil beings. This being has no other origin than God, the origin of all. Its evil nature, however, came not from God, but arose apart from God, by the will of the mingling fundamental substances themselves; yet not against, nay not even without, the will of God; for no being, least of all one that has authority, one that is placed above many others, can come into existence accidentally, without God's will. To this being, described at least thus far as evil, God has delegated the rule over the present world, and the execution of the law, or the punishment of evil. The whole order of the world is accordingly divided into two kingdoms, the present and the future world, or the left and the right hand or power of God. Over against the evil ruler of the present world stands Christ, the good

---

[1] The conclusion of the Homilies, first added in Dressel's edition of them, Gött. 1853. Hom. xx. 5 gives a more detailed explanation of the relation of matter to God. Cf. Uhlhorn, *op. cit.*, p. 179, *sq.*

[2] Hom. xvi. 12. χεὶρ δημιουργοῦσα τὸ πᾶν.

ruler of the future world.[1] This evil being is thus also one who, in the punishment of evil, executes the law, and represents in himself the conception of righteousness, like the Demiurgus of Marcion. But with all that separates him, as evil, from God, and makes him the principle of the demonic, he is not allowed to stand in such an antithesis to God as the Demiurgus of Marcion. The latter, being a creator distinct from the highest God, and a second God by the side of the one and absolute God, is a chief object of the polemic which the Homilies direct against the older Gnostic systems. The general tendency of this system is thus to limit and modify, without absolutely rejecting, the Gnostic ideas, even the Gnostic dualism, in such a way, as to prevent any encroachment upon the fundamental doctrine of God's absolute monarchy, and to reduce the antithesis of two opposite principles till it becomes nothing more than a duality immanent in the being of God. And its character is also analogous to that of the Gnostic systems, inasmuch as it also has a process of world-development: only that it is in the form of its syzygies that it presents that process. The notion of syzygy is held by the Homilies in a sense different from that usually adopted by Gnosticism; it is in virtue of their antithesis that the conceptions which form a syzygy are thus related to each other.[2] The law of the universe is the law of antithesis, or of syzygies. God being himself one from the beginning, divided everything into antitheses, right and left, heaven and earth, day and night, light and fire, life and death. But after man, the order of the syzygies was reversed. At first, the better preceded, the inferior followed; now the worse became the first, and the better the second. Adam, the man made in the image of God, was followed first by unrighteous

[1] Hom. xix. 7, vii. 3, iii. 19. It is only in the conclusion of the Homilies that we find the doctrine of the devil, as the ruler of this world, completed and made clearly intelligible. On the one hand, the devil is not properly an evil, but a righteous, God-serving being; on the other, there is a final transformation of the devil, of the evil into the good. While by reason of his origin from κρᾶσις he has an evil προαίρεσις, he receives through μετασύγκρασις a προαίρεσις ἀγαθοῦ. xx. 9.

[2] God διεῖλε everything at its extreme, διχῶς καὶ ἐναντίως. This is the idea of syzygy, as stated in the chief passage on the subject, Hom. ii. 15.

Cain, and then by righteous Abel. Adam himself was made according to that first divine order: in the syzygy which he forms with Eve, he, the better member, precedes, and Eve, the inferior, follows. The reversal of the syzygies is in this system what the fall of Sophia from the pleroma is in the Valentinian—a rent introduced into the whole world-order, which had to come about sooner or later, but admits of no further explanation. The very existence of syzygies, the duality of a male and a female principle, the division into antitheses, all this is an original defect inherent in the finite nature of the world. This defect, this weak side of the universe, is brought into prominence and becomes predominant, when the female precedes the male, and the worse is always the first, which has to be overcome by the better. Such then is the order in which the process of the world's history is here developed. Its moving principle is not the real antithesis of the spiritual and the psychical, but the ideal antithesis of true and false prophecy. There are two kinds of prophecy, a male and a female, related as truth to error, or as the future to the present world. The relation of the present to the future world is the type of the order in which the members of the syzygies succeed one another. The little is first, the great second; it is thus with the world and eternity. The present world is temporal, the future eternal. First is ignorance, then knowledge. Those who exercise the prophetic gift are arranged in the same way. As the present world is female, and, as a mother of children, gives birth to souls, while the future world is male, and, as a father, takes up the children; so in this world the prophets who appear with true knowledge as sons of the future world, come not first, but follow after.[1] The only application of this law of syzygies to the history of the world and religion is the statement about Adam, that he appeared again at various times under various names, before the flood as Enoch, after it as Noah, Abraham, Isaac, Jacob, Moses. Lastly, he appeared as Christ. In Christ the syzygy is more definitely presented, being plainly seen in the contrast which he bears to his forerunner John

[1] Hom. ii. 25.

or Elias. The relation of the two is that of sun and moon. This relation is seen again in Simon Magus—who was the first disciple of the Baptist, and succeeded fully to his position after his death—and the apostle Peter. The same antithesis then which is exhibited in the relation of the present and the future worlds, is carried on through the present world itself under various forms. The worse, the female, ever comes first; the better, the male, follows after. If, however, we merely find the same antithesis continually repeated, if Christ is at last merely what Adam, Adam who is identical with Christ, was at first, we must ask, what is the general goal of the development? It can only be the dissolution and transition of the present into the future world. This, however, does not take place through such a process of development as that set forth in the other Gnostic systems. The general form of view which underlies the system of the Homilies, is not time and motion in time, so much as space and extension in space. The one true God, who in the most perfect form presides over the universe, and who, wherever he is, is as the heart of the universe in the centre of the infinite, sends forth from himself as centre six dimensions, upward and downward, to the right and to the left, forward and backward. It is true, it is said here that, directing his gaze towards these six dimensions, as a number equal on all sides, he completes the world in six periods of time. Still the fundamental mode of view is concerned with space, with being which rests in space. As that in which all existence comes to rest, he has his likeness, as the beginning and end of all, in future infinite time. For the six infinite directions return to him, and from him everything takes its extension into the infinite: this is the mystery of the number seven. He is the point of rest for all; and if any one within his small sphere imitates his greatness, him he allows to attain to rest in himself.[1] Here, to say the least, there is no state-

[1] Hom. 17, 9. Dualism is lost in the monotheism of this system; and the duality of principles becomes a condition immanent in the nature of God—matter being the body which is animated by the spirit of God, and Sophia, in her unity with God, as his soul, being both monad and duad. But this only shows the more clearly that Gnostic pantheism is the fundamental view of the system. It

ment of a process of world-development carried on in time. And yet the system of the Homilies is true to the fundamental character of Gnosticism; for in this system also it is through antitheses that the whole process of mediation and reconciliation is carried through. We have seen that in the system of Marcion the antithesis of the real world-principles—spirit and matter—merely serves as a foundation and condition precedent of the contrast between the Law and the Gospel; the use of the former antithesis is to render possible a knowledge of the two latter supreme ethical principles in their radical distinction from each other, and of what they actually are in themselves. In the system of the Homilies we have the same genuinely Gnostic striving after positive knowledge. The cosmogony and the metaphysics of the system are subsidiary to the great end of raising the moral and religious consciousness to the standpoint of absolute knowledge. False and true prophecy or religion are here what the Law and the Gospel are with Marcion. There is a true, and there is a false prophecy; and together, they constitute the essence, and they guide the course, of the history of the world and of religion. Now, since the distinction between them is so infinitely great, and nothing can be more important for man than to be acquainted with it, there must be a test by which man can distinguish the two, and know absolutely what is false in the false prophecy and true in the true. For this reason, God has founded the whole order of the world upon the law of syzygies. As a teacher of truth, that the knowledge of that which is might be possible to man, God has clearly revealed the canon of syzygies in the nature that He has made.[1] By this supreme and most universal test truth may be known and error distinguished. In accordance with this canon, Simon Magus is known for a false

is simply Gnostic pantheism that we have before us in the immanent relation of God and the world. The relation of God to the world is that of centre to circumference, οὐσία to μετουσία, 17. 7.

[1] Hom. ii. 15. ἔνθεν γοῦν ὁ θεὸς διδασκαλῶν τοὺς ἀνθρώπους πρὸς τὴν τῶν ὄντων ἀλήθειαν, εἷς ὢν αὐτὸς διχῶς καὶ ἐναντίως διεῖλεν πάντα τὰ τῶν ἄκρων, ἀπαρχῆς αὐτὸς εἷς ὢν καὶ μόνος θεός, ποιήσας οὐρανὸν καὶ γῆν, ἡμέραν καὶ νύκτα, φῶς καὶ πῦρ, ἥλιον καὶ σελήνην, ζωὴν καὶ θάνατον. Cf. iii. 16.

prophet: for Peter did not come till after him; Peter follows him as light follows darkness, knowledge ignorance, recovery sickness. The false Gospel must first come by a deceiver; then, and not till then, the true one can be spread abroad for the refutation of future heresies. After him again, Antichrist must come first; then only will the true Christ, Jesus, appear; and thereupon eternal light will dawn, and all darkness disappear.[1] Antithesis thus follows antithesis, that the knowledge of truth to be brought about by means of the antitheses may more and more be deep and universal. Now truth is from the beginning one and the same; there is no essential distinction even between Mosaism and Christianity, their contents being really the same; and so the goal of the whole development must be to make truth known, and to introduce it into the general consciousness of humanity. The only reason why Christianity marks an epoch is, that in virtue of its spreading the Gospel even among the Gentiles, it is the completion of universalism. Another point in which this system coincides with Gnosticism is, that Christ is with it a universal world-principle. What gives unity to the whole process of the world's history, whose moving principle is the law of syzygies, is this; it is ever the same one true prophet, the man made by God, and endowed with the Holy Spirit of Christ, who from the beginning of the world's course passes through all its periods, changing at each stage both his name and form, and at last, after times appointed for him, receives his recompense for the work that he has undertaken, when he arrives, anointed with the mercy of God, at everlasting rest.

The ultimate distinction between the system of the Homilies and the older Gnostic systems may be thus expressed. In the former a strict adherence to the principle of unity makes Gnostic dualism appear as a thing immanent in monotheism. From the transcendental metaphysics of the Gnostic cosmogony, we here descend to the history of the world and religion, there to follow out the antitheses through which the knowledge of the essentially true and the self-existent is rendered possible. In the older systems

[1] Hom. ii. 17.

there was already some preparation for this transition; namely, in the idea of the "spiritual." The element of the spiritual natures is knowledge; they are spirit freed from all material or animal darkening of its consciousness, self-conscious, knowing, ever rising to the knowledge of that which is essentially true. Gnosticism in all its forms is the knowledge of the absolute, absolute knowledge; only, the object which it places before itself varies. In the older systems it is the absolute, generally, with the antitheses of the principles; with Marcion it is the antithesis of Christian and pre-Christian, or of the Law and the Gospel; in the Homilies that of true and false prophecy.

The three forms of Gnosticism with which our discussion has now presented us may also be distinguished according to the three forms of religion whose multifarious elements go to make up the Gnostic doctrines. In the earlier systems the symbolic and mythical mode of view proper to heathen antiquity prevails; the pre-Christian is the prelude of Christianity, and the distinction between the two is wavering and unfixed. The system of Marcion concerns itself with the pure conception of Christianity, disengaged from all foreign elements. In the Homilies, Christianity is only purified and expanded Judaism. While the earlier systems placed Judaism at a very subordinate stage, and Marcion even denied it all religious value, in the Homilies it is the absolute religion. In order to hold this position, however, the Homilies were driven to employ an arbitrary method of dealing with the Scriptures. The depreciation of Judaism by the earlier Gnostics was founded on certain passages of the Old Testament, in which they found the chief proofs of their assertion that the Demiurgus, as the God of the Jews, was only a weak and limited being; the Homilies declared all these passages to be spurious interpolations. Thus one form of Gnosticism is the denial of the other; and the opposition they bear to each other is according to their historical order. The ancient Gnostics built many of their doctrines on allegory; Marcion rejected allegory. His doctrine again was opposed by that of the Homilies; for there can be no doubt that the false doctrine, which the Homilies combat in Simon Magus as a new form of heathen polytheism, is Marcion's Gnosticism. These several forms, then, not only succeed one another historically, but are intimately connected with, and supplementary of, one another; and in these several stages, Gnosticism has worked out its idea and accomplished its course. The essence of Gnosticism is the endeavour to comprehend the stages of religious history, as that which they are in their true nature, or philosophically. It could thus take up its absolute standpoint either in a form of Christianity approaching as closely as possible to Paganism, or in pure Christianity, or in a Christianity identical with Judaism.[1]

[1] Another peculiar form of Gnosticism, which without doubt belongs to a later time, when the influence of Manicheism was felt, is the system of the above-mentioned (p. 211) Πίστις Σοφία. To establish a clear connection between the several leading ideas of this work, and to give an intelligible and comprehensive view of the whole system, was a difficult task, and the manner in which Köstlin addressed himself to the work, in his Dissertation in the Theol. Jahrb., 1854, Das gnostische System des Buches Πίστις Σοφία, deserves grateful acknowledgment. The Πίστις Σοφία, according to Köstlin, is distinguished from the other Gnostic systems by its monistic character and its practical religious tendency. With respect to its fundamental mode of view, it is still occupied with the antithesis of spirit and matter. But matter, though impure, is not originally an evil principle. The whole universe has arisen by emanation. In the highest region of the divine realm of light, infinitely exalted above all worlds and heavens, the Ineffable of his free will sends forth from himself the beings, of luminous nature, that rest in his bosom and strive to go forth to an independent reality of their own; this region is such a purely spiritual realm of perfect law and harmony, that Sophia is deposed from the seat which she holds in the Valentinian pleroma to a more distant sphere. The idea of a fall from the infinite and a return to it is the subject treated throughout. It is so treated that the fate of Sophia, her fall, penitence, and redemption, become types prefiguring what is afterwards to be realised in mankind in exactly the same way. The world has been made, i.e. has come forth from the Ineffable, by means of the first mystery, only in order that the latter and the other mysteria purgatores and remissores, i.e. the hidden powers of the Deity, which preside over the purification of the world by conversion and penitence, may be able to translate into action their tendency to a purifying activity. Through the whole range of the boundless universe, itself brought forth by means of these powers, their activity is to extend, overcoming even the fall and the opposition offered to good. The mysteries are finally to make manifest the eternal exaltation of the divine over all that is finite, the infinitely reconciling and blessing power and life of the good principle. A peculiarity of the system is its doctrine of mysteries. The idea of the mysteries includes all on which the welfare and permanence of the world and mankind depend.

Another phase of Gnosticism, usually termed Docetism, still remains to be examined. Docetism involves a question which goes deeply into the nature of Gnosticism, and is of considerable moment for our view of the latter. The more universal, comprehensive, and transcendent the point of view from which Gnosticism regarded Christianity, the more pressing became the question, what was the relation of Gnostic to historical Christianity? did not Gnosticism cast doubt upon the historical facts of Christianity,

The mysteries generate, rule, reconcile, and save the beings who stand under them. The whole of Christianity is thus that introduction or leading down of the mysteries to the world, which, effected by Christ, is to make the world and the realm of light known to one another, to reconcile them and unite them for ever. The two fundamental ideas of the system, alike essential, are those of righteousness and grace. Either through conversion and amendment, or through utter annihilation, evil is to disappear, and the final goal of the whole world-process to be reached, viz., the purification of the universe from all that is unworthy and perverted. Here, on the one hand, the question of practical religion is placed first, and the one aim is to bring before man, in all its extent and gravity, the finiteness of his nature, his dependence on the lower and worldly powers, his incapacity to raise himself above them without the help of some higher redeeming power; and, at the same time, to give him the assurance that a redeeming power is really present in the universe, and has appeared in Christ. But, on the other hand, the mode of attaining this practical aim is conditioned by the foundations of the system, which are laid in Gnostic metaphysics. Not until a view of the infinite exaltation and glory of the supra-celestial region of light and its principles has been gained, is it possible to comprehend the manner in which the finite returns to the infinite, or rather, is taken back into itself and united with itself by the infinite from which it proceeded. This system, therefore, bears a very close affinity to those that are classed under the first of the chief forms of Gnosticism, especially to Ophitism; but it is raised above them by its moral spirit and its comparative freedom from dualism and from the spirit of particularism. According to Köstlin, p. 188, sq., the Πίστις Σοφία affords a convincing proof, not only that the later epoch of Gnosticism was a period of decay and dissolution, but also that many attempts were then made to bring back Gnostic doctrine to greater harmony with the spirit of Christianity and the demands of the moral consciousness, to maintain interest in it by bold speculations concerning the world beyond the grave, and to combine it with all available elements of other existing systems. This appears most clearly (says Köstlin) in that part of the book from which it derives its name, the passages setting forth the doctrine of Sophia. Notwithstanding the Ophitic basis of thought, Sophia is conceived, as with Valentinus (though in a yet more spiritual manner), as the representative of the finite spirit's longing for knowledge of the infinite; and with the addition of the ethical element, she becomes also the type of faith, penitence, and hope.

and upon its historical character generally, in a way which the Christian consciousness could not possibly allow? The name Docetism, as used to designate the Gnostic view of Christianity as more or less docetic, informs us that this question really arose. By this name we understand the assertion that Christ, as it is said even in 1 John iv. 3, had not really come in the flesh, that is, had not had a true and real body, like another ordinary man.¹ Now the body is the material basis of human existence. It follows immediately, therefore, from this assertion, that, Christ having had no real body, the reality of the facts historically connected with his person, and the historical character of Christianity, are also brought into question. All the events in which his body was supposed to be concerned, and notably his passion, are not anything that really happened: it is merely thought that they so happened; they are only something represented, only δοκήσει or κατὰ δόκησιν, something docetic.² The comparative deviations of

---

¹ Compare the Epistles of Ignatius. Ep. ad Smyrn. cap. 5: τὸν κύριον βλασ-φημεῖ, μὴ ὁμολογῶν αὐτὸν σαρκόφορον.

² Ignat. loc. cit. cap. 2. "Ἄπιστοί τινες λέγουσιν τὸ δοκεῖν αὐτὸν πεπονθέναι, αὐτοὶ τὸ δοκεῖν ὄντες. Though Docetism is a part of the general character of Gnosticism, the Docetae are sometimes spoken of as a particular Gnostic sect. Clement of Alexandria mentions (Strom. iii. 13) Cassian, a pupil of the school of Valentinus, who shared with Tatian the principles of the Encratites, as the ἐξάρχων τῆς δοκήσεως. The author of the Philosophoumena, without naming a founder, speaks of the Docetae as a peculiar sect which had of itself assumed that name; introducing them in company with Monoimus, Tatian, Hermogenes, the Quartodecimans, the Montanists, and the Encratites. They conceived God as the first principle, under the figure of a seed, containing the infinitely great in the infinitely small. The world grew out of God as the fig-tree from the seed. As the fig-tree consists of stem, leaves, and fruit, so from the first principle there arose three Aeons; and these, by reason of the perfection of the number ten, multiplied themselves tenfold to thirty Aeons. The Redeemer is the common product of all the Aeons, the expression of their unity; he is the unity of the principle which, identical with itself, is in all things that have come into being. As there are thirty Aeons, so the Redeemer assumes thirty forms (ἰδέας). Hence it comes that every heresy has a different idea of the Redeemer, and each takes the Redeemer, conceived according to its own idea, to be the only true one (διὰ τοῦτο τοσαῦται αἱρέσεις ζητοῦσι τὸν Ἰησοῦν περιμαχήτως, καὶ ἔστι πάσαις οἰκεῖος αὐταῖς, ἄλλη δὲ ἄλλος ὁρώμενος ἀπ' ἄλλου τόπου, ἐφ' ὃν ἑκάστη φέρεται, φησὶν, καὶ σπεύδει δοκοῦσα ταύτην εἶναι μόνον, ὅς ἐστιν αὐτῆς συγγενής, ἴδιος καὶ πολίτης, etc., 8, 10, p. 268). This doctrine of the Docetae then is merely an expression of the general

the Gnostic systems from historical Christianity may therefore be measured according to their various views with respect to the nature of Christ's body. The position of Basilides seems to have been nearest to the common idea of the body of Christ and his birth from the Virgin Mary.[1] Valentinus and other Gnostics, however, supposed that he was not born of Mary, but only through (διά) Mary; that he passed through her as through a channel; that his birth was only a birth in appearance.[2] The Valentinians certainly held that Christ possessed no more than a psychical body, but the question was very much disputed among them, and was the occasion of their being divided into two schools: the Anatolian and the Italiot. According to the latter, to which Heracleon and Ptolemaeus belonged, Jesus had a natural body, and for that reason the Spirit descended on him at his baptism. The former, and here we may name Axionicus and Adresianes, considered that the body of the Soter was spiritual, because the Holy Spirit, *i.e.* Sophia and the demiurgic formative power of the Highest, had descended upon Mary. The most decided Docetism was taught by Marcion. According to him, Christ's whole manifestation was a mere appearance and phantasm. Not even the slightest contact with the kingdom of the Demiurgus and its material life was to be admitted. Christ was therefore not even born in appearance, but descended directly from heaven to earth.[3]

character of Gnosticism, a fundamental view of which it is that, as opposed to the one objective absolute principle, all that has come into being is but a subjective idea, fashioned according to the variety of aspect under which it is imaged in the idea-forming consciousness. In a word, Gnostic Docetism is that side of Gnosticism which may be called idealism; and since it speaks of ἰδέαι, this term is especially appropriate. While Gnosticism endeavoured to comprehend the absolute, or to enable the consciousness to approach that which is in itself, there was forced on it the perception that the process on which it was employed was purely phenomenological; that its metaphysics could never conduct it beyond subjective consciousness. Exactly where the elements of its structure should have met and exhibited concrete reality of existence—as in the person of the Redeemer—there being was dissolved into a mere δοκεῖν.

[1] In the Philos., vii. 26, p. 241, it is in accordance with the doctrine of Basilides that Jesus is directly called ὁ υἱὸς τῆς Μαρίας.
[2] Comp. Tert. adv. Valent., cap. 27. Theod. Haer. fab. v. 11.
[3] Comp. Die christliche Gnosis, p. 255, *sq.*

Comparing these various opinions, we see plainly the close connection of the docetism and the dualism of the Gnostic systems. Redemption, according to Gnostic doctrine, consists in the liberation of the spiritual from the material and psychical; and thus it is inherent in the idea of the Redeemer, that he must come as little as possible into contact with the psychical.[1] It is true that a human body, to be substantial, must contain a material element; but the strong repulsion of the two principles of spirit and matter makes it essential to give such a preponderance to the spiritual as to exclude everything material. The inevitable conclusion is, that the body of the Redeemer had not the concrete reality of human existence. If he nevertheless appeared with a human body, that body was a mere presentation corresponding to no reality. And what is true of the body of Christ is true of his personality in general. The body of Christ has no material substratum, and so his personality is destitute of the concrete contents of a human existence. The Gnostic Christ is too immaterial to plant his foot firmly on the earth, or to be bound up with the organic system of human life. His self-consciousness has its centre of gravity in the transcendental region of the world of Aeons; and he suddenly floats down from on high, in order to pass a brief existence in a human form and presence. This cannot be said to be a human being. In addition to this there is nothing left by Gnostic doctrine that can be regarded as the effect of the personal activity of the Redeemer. The work of the Redeemer is redemption; but what redemption is in the view of the Gnostics is plainly shown by their well-known assertion of a φύσει σώζεσθαι. If those who are saved are saved by nature, *i.e.* because as spiritual natures they are under a necessity of returning back at last into the pleroma, then it does not appear how their salvation requires a Redeemer at all. In the Gnostic view, salvation does not depend on action and moral performance, but consists simply in a mode of being. Knowledge as such, the knowledge of the absolute, is itself

---

[1] Philos. vii. 31, p. 254: διὰ τοῦτο ἀγέννητος κατῆλθεν ὁ Ἰησοῦς, φησὶν (Μαρκίων) ἵνα ᾖ πάσης ἀπηλλαγμένος κακίας.

redemption and salvation.[1] When then in spiritual natures the original spiritual principle, which can never be wholly quenched, in its gradual development breaks through the material and psychical elements by which it is obscured, and illuminates the man's consciousness in such a way that he rises above the world of the Demiurgus, and becomes aware of his unity with the pleroma, then is reached the highest stage of spiritual life, which as such is also the life of salvation; and redemption is accomplished. It is true that the Gnostic systems regard the process as the work of the Redeemer. But all that this means is that they see in his appearance and action an outward representation of that which is in itself an inner process of spiritual life. That which is constantly taking place in the same way in the endless number of spiritual beings, that one act of the spirit which in every life, after going out of itself, goes back into itself, and rises to its original being, is here summed up in its unity in Christ; Christ being the universal principle and upholder of spiritual life. The concrete, the individual, the personal, is in every case lost in the generality of the idea; the Gnostic Christ merely represents a principle, the spiritual principle which underlies all forms and stages of development. The system of the Homilies is distinguished from the other Gnostic systems by its greater unity of character. And the principle which the other systems fail to keep a hold of consistently, so that with them Christ assumes a variety of forms, the Homilies fix and state distinctly in its unity, when they lay down that it is the same one prophet of truth who appears in all ages of the world, only under various forms and various names. Even in this case, what significance is left for the external manifestation and human birth of Christ? It looks as if in the system of the Homilies, Gnostic supernaturalism was about to throw off the mask completely, and to declare in so many words, that outward revelation is nothing but the immanent self-revelation of spirit. The prophet is a prophet, we are told, through his ἔμφυτον καὶ ἀέννaov πνεῦμα;[2] and this πνεῦμα is said to belong not only to the prophet but to

---

[1] Cf. Die christliche Gnosis, p. 139, sq., 480, sq. [2] Hom. iii. 15.

all pious men. For, it is laid down generally, truth springs forth from the pious man's pure indwelling spirit. In this sense the apostle Peter is made to say, "So was the Son revealed to me by the Father: therefore I know of my own experience the meaning of revelation. For as soon as the Lord questioned me (Matthew xvi. 14), it rose in my heart, and I know not what came upon me, for I said, Thou art the Son of the living God. He who for this called me blessed, told me first that it was the Father who had revealed it to me. After this I perceived what revelation is; to learn a thing without outward teaching, without visions and dreams; and this is the case, for the germ of all truth is contained in the truth which God has implanted in us. This truth is concealed or discovered by God's hand alone; God working according to his knowledge of the worthiness of each." The place of the outward revelation, then, is taken by the inward: the former can only bring to consciousness the germ and principle of truth already deposited in the spirit of man. Here we obtain some insight into the deeper connections of a view which lies at the root of, and is the inner principle of, all the Gnostic systems, however various their outward forms. If the same divine spirit which was in Adam appeared also in Christ, then, since after being thus imparted to Adam it must have passed also to those descended from him, the divine principle in Christ is not essentially different from the divine in all other men; consequently, it is not anything that positively passes the bounds of the natural. It is the same divine spirit of man, the holy spirit of Christ, which, in the seven pillars of the world, goes through all the periods of the world's history, but which also dwells as an inmost principle in all men. The only distinction is that while in these two it appears in the strength and purity of its substance, as the pure archetypal man, in all other men it is more or less obscured. Yet even in them it is not so eclipsed and darkened, that it cannot, whether through the inward energy of the principle or by some incitement from without, break through the darkness which obscures it, and regain the full light of its self-consciousness. This Adam-Christ is as it were the male principle. What obscures and weakens it in particular individuals is only that there is a female principle bound up with it, and that the latter has obtained the ascendant. The former is the spiritual and reasonable; the latter the sensual, and weak side of human nature, the side subject to error and sin. Hence even the phenomena wherein false prophecy or demonic heathenism manifests itself, have their ultimate source, according to the Homilies, in a principle dwelling in man himself. The two principles of reason and sense are thus for the individual man and for human nature regarded in its essence, what on a larger scale Judaism and heathenism are for the world's history. In each case appears the same duality—a male and a female principle. Thus we have only to strip off the symbolic mythical clothing in which Gnostic supernaturalism wraps itself, and to take the forms in which it personifies its conceptions for what they are in themselves, and we have the true kernel of the Gnostic view of the world in a very transparent rationalism, founded on the immanent relations of the self-consciousness of the spirit. Even if there was no very direct consciousness of this rationalism, still its principle is essentially involved in the notion of Gnosticism; and it thus appears that Docetism was merely the point at which this rationalising tendency—present, whether more or less developed, in all Gnosticism—reached its clearest and most unmistakable outward manifestation. It lies in the nature of the case and is unavoidable, that, in proportion as stress is laid on general speculative or religious ideas, the historical reality of the facts of Christianity should be thrown into the background. In the presence of the idea the element of fact receives only a secondary importance, or may even become a mere figurative reflection of the idea. Such is the true significance of Gnostic Docetism. It makes an assertion with regard to the body of Christ which is essentially true of Gnosticism as a whole. The body of Christ lacks the concrete reality of a human body; and in the same way, it is the general character of Gnosticism to refine and generalise away the positive contents of historical Christianity. Christianity becomes a part of the general view of the world; it is interpreted as one stage in the universal process of world-development. The Gnostic Christ is a universal principle, which conditions, as in the earlier systems, the real process of world-development, or at least, as in the system of the Homilies, the knowledge of truth generally. Christianity (according to the Gnostics) is concerned, not with the mere question of salvation—how is man saved? but with one more universal—what is the beginning, the course, the goal, of the world-development? or, how is it possible to attain to absolute knowledge of the true, of that which is in itself? When occupied with the question of salvation, Christianity was in danger of withering away into Jewish particularism. In the same way, when occupied with the problems raised by Gnosticism, it was on the point of dissolving into the thin element of a general transcendental view of the world. Both dangers needed to be met by the catholic tendency of Christianity, as worked out in the realisation of the Church. But before we turn to this side of the development of the Church's history, Montanism claims our attention.

II.—MONTANISM.

GNOSTICISM AND MONTANISM have this in common that they are both concerned with questions which go back to first principles, questions relating to nothing less than the course of the world in general. The difference between them is, that while Gnosticism contemplates the point of commencement, whence all proceeds, the absolute principles that condition the process of God's self-revelation and the course of the world-development, in Montanism the cardinal point round which everything revolves is the end of things, the catastrophe towards which the course of the world is moving on. They also differ widely from each other in respect of the range of ideas with which they are conversant. Gnosticism enters into broad views of the universe, such as had been opened up, and made attractive by the boldest speculative ideas of the philosophy of the age; Montanism does not advance beyond the Jewish Messianic idea. These differences however, do not take away what the two systems have in common. Indeed, the two phenomena which we have coupled together may both be traced up into the primitive Christian mode of view. The elements of both are to be found there. Paul approaches the Gnostic view of the world, when in speaking of the two world-periods, the pre-Christian and the Christian, he regards them in the light of general principles which determine the development of humanity, and when he distinguishes separate steps in a course of the world that returns into the absolute unity of God. Montanism, again, is derived entirely from the primitive Christian idea of the immediate coming of Christ, a belief which Paul also shared. Before going on to Montanism then, we may appropriately consider this belief which is so marked a feature of the original Christian consciousness. The belief in the second coming of Christ, and the reaction against a view of the world which had lost its hold upon this belief, are the two leading momenta which serve to explain the origin and character of Montanism.

What connected Christianity with Judaism most directly and most intimately was the Jewish Messianic idea; though from it also there arose the sharpest antithesis by which the two faiths came to be separated from each other. It had been thought that Jesus was the promised Messiah, who had appeared with a view to the fulfilment of the Messianic expectations. His death seemed to leave these hopes unfulfilled, and to destroy them for ever: the disciples, as Jews possessed with the Messianic belief, felt that such an event made it impossible to apply the belief to him. But the gulf lying between idea and fact was only too soon filled up. He had not, as the living Messiah, fulfilled what was hoped of him; but as the risen Messiah, exalted to heaven, he might return from heaven again, now at length to accomplish all that had not yet come about. The Parousia of Christ became a necessary postulate of the faith of the first disciples; the old belief had assumed a new form, but it was impossible to renounce the substance of it, and it seemed to be a necessity that it should be fulfilled without delay. Many passages of the books of the New Testament show with what power this belief reigned in the minds of the first Christians. So much was this the case, that in this respect there was no essential difference between the apostle of the Gentiles and the author of the Apocalypse. If any of the first publishers of Christianity was capable of discerning that its destiny—its exaltation into the universal religion—was only to be fulfilled in the distant future, it was Paul. Yet even he, as he thinks on Christ's coming, firmly believes that all is now approaching its end, and that he will himself live to see the great catastrophe. Such a belief, however, too surely brought its own refutation to last long in all its strength and vividness. The longer it remained unfulfilled, the more inevitably it tended to lose its hold on the mind of the age. Even within the New Testament itself, we can trace the various modifications which it gradually underwent. Compare the two books which vary most widely in their manner of stating it; what a discrepancy of tone do we find between the Apocalypse, where it blazes out in its brightest flame, and takes its most concrete form in the idea of the millennium, and the Second Epistle of Peter. The author of the latter speaks of scoffers who shall come in the last days, walking after their own lusts, and saying, "Where is the promise of his coming? for since the fathers fell asleep, all things continue as they were from the creation;" and instead of questioning the facts on which the scoffer proceeded, he merely seeks to refute him by substituting for the belief itself a recognition of the general truths that lie at its base. This shows us pretty plainly what the state of belief on the subject was at this time. But though it had ceased, at least in its original form, to be a universal article of Christian faith, still there could not fail to be some, who in contrast to the increasing worldliness of the Christian mind which was manifested in the decay of this belief, quickened it in themselves even to a stronger life, and held it fast with fresh enthusiasm. Such were the Montanists; and this is one of their most prominent traits. Even though it be admitted that millenarianism was at the time a universal Christian belief, still the Montanists were the most pronounced of all millenarians. It was this doctrine that especially kindled their enthusiasm: their prophets announced, in language like that of men inspired, the judgments which were impending with the coming of Christ, the reign of a thousand years, and the end of the world, and depicted all that was coming in the most vivid colours. How much they were occupied with the thought of the immediate end of the world, and how real the thought was to them, is shown by the saying of the prophetess Maximilla, "After me comes nothing but the end of the world?"[1] Soon as the consummation might come, it could not approach too quickly for their millenarian spirit. In their daily prayer, to ask that God's kingdom might come was to give utterance to their millenarian view of the world; the kingdom of God and the end

---

[1] Μετ' ἐμὲ οὐκέτι προφῆτις ἔσται, ἀλλὰ συντέλεια.

of the world were with them the same idea.[1] Even then, though the whole generation for which the coming of Christ was supposed to have been promised, had but looked for it in vain, still the belief itself that in the immediate future Christ would appear, and the kingdom of God begin, was not abandoned. The Montanists knew the spot where the heavenly Jerusalem would descend; they had even had a vision foreshadowing the descent from heaven. With other Christians, coldness and lukewarmness had laid hold of millenarianism; but for that very reason it became all the stronger and livelier with them. And this shows us how close was the connection between the millenarian belief of the Montanists and another no less characteristic part of their system, ecstatic prophecy. If they were living entirely in the thought of Christ's coming and of the future, and saw close at hand the events that were to introduce and accompany the impending catastrophe, this contemplation of the future in the present inevitably gave rise to prophecy. Prophecy with the Montanists assumed the form of ecstasy; a fact very characteristic of the sect, though ecstasy itself was by no means an uncommon thing. Ecstasy is merely prophecy intensified. By a natural analogy, as millenarianism among the Montanists advanced to fresh energy, prophecy also, as the expression of their millenarian inspiration, soared with a loftier flight, and became ecstasy. Here the finite subject became absolutely passive under the divine principle. Hence the saying of Montanus, in which he compares man to the lyre, the Paraclete to the plectrum, and calls the former a sleeper, the latter a watcher; and the belief that the special organs of the Holy Spirit were women, prophetesses such as Maximilla and Priscilla. The one belief naturally gained

---

[1] Compare Tertullian, De Orat. c. 5; where he says of the *veniat regnum tuum ; Itaque si ad Dei voluntatem et ad nostram suspensionem pertinet regni dominici repraesentatio, quomodo quidam pertractum quendam in seculo postulant (how can so many ask, that the kingdom of God should further prolong itself into secular time? millenarianism was then no longer a universal belief); quum regnum Dei quod, ut adveniat, oramus, ad consummationem seculi tendat ; optamus maturius regnare et non diutius servire. Etiam si praefinitum in oratione non esset, de postulando regni adventu, ultro eam vocem postulassemus, festinantes ad spei nostrae complexum.*

strength together with the other. The believers in Christ's coming did not feel their belief disturbed by the long lapse of time to which they had now to look back. On the contrary, the longer the past period, the nearer they thought they must be to the great catastrophe. For the same reason, since everything was now in its last stage, in the καιρὸς συνεσταλμένος, the spirit too, the πνεῦμα ἅγιον, the principle of the Christian consciousness, must gather its energies more powerfully together, must give forth more immediate, more unequivocal utterances. Both beliefs were involved in the consciousness of living in the dies novissimi. Thus, Tertullian's theory of the various periods of development is, that as first the plant arises from the grain of seed, and lastly the fruit from the blossom, so justitia was first in the state of nature, then advanced to childhood under the guidance of the Law and the Prophets, next through the Gospel blossomed into youth, and now is brought to maturity by the Paraclete.[1] All this is but an analysis of the idea of the novissima. What is sought to be done is to bring out what is the last in the last things, by striking out of them all that is not the last, but must at once be followed by the last. But according to the Montanist opinion, the more nearly everything approached its end, the more everything converged in the novissimi dies, the more concentrated and intense, the more filled with compressed energy did everything become. Everywhere, says Tertullian, the later forms the conclusion, and that which goes before is outweighed by that which comes after. This is a universal law alike of the human and the divine order of things; and especially of the novissimi dies,[2] in which the prophecy of Joel (often cited by Tertullian), that the spirit should be poured out on all flesh, was to be fulfilled. In this period, when tempus est in collecto, when every force gathers itself together and prepares all its keenness, the spirit likewise enters into the mind of the Christian with unwonted power, and fills it with its own divine all-

[1] De virg. vel. c. 1.
[2] De Bapt. c. 13. Compare the Praef. Act. Felic. et Perp., and Epiphanius Haer. 48, 8, in Schwegler's Montan., p. 39.

illumining essence. The Apocalypse gives virtually the same account of the relation between the novissima and the working of the spirit in connection with it. The several stages of the great catastrophe of the world are the subject of the book; the author is merely the instrument of the divine inspiration that has come upon him, he too is ἐν πνεύματι, i.e., in a state of ecstasy (i. 10). Prophecies and visions form the whole contents of the Apocalypse; prophecy and vision were the shapes assumed by the ecstatic condition of the Montanists. The spirit which from the first was the animating principle of the Christians, and awoke their prophetic inspiration and ecstasy, is also the principle of Montanism. At this time it was generally termed Paraclete, perhaps because in the distress and affliction of the last days it was to be not only the guide that should lead into all truth, but the intercessor, the support and comfort of all those whom it swayed with its rich and abundant power; in any case, this particular name, as applied to the Holy Spirit, was intended to mark its special and peculiar function during that last period, in which the Montanist saw everything pressing towards its end.

It is in the moral sphere that the Paraclete carries on his actual operations. He speaks with his full energy in prophetic ecstasy in order that the secrets of the future may be searched, and all the obscurities of consciousness made light. But he also insists emphatically on the moral requirements of practical Christianity. As the spiritus sanctus, ipsius disciplinae determinator, institutor novae disciplinae, he is the strict spirit of moral severity, the declared foe of all laxity and indifference in moral things. What he is, he is for one end only, viz., that he may in the field of morals realise that which he is; thus Tertullian, when he sums up all the features which belong to the idea of the Paraclete, gives the first place to his practical task. He opens the Scriptures, purges the understanding, raises the Christian to a higher stage of perfection, but above all, his practical aim is to give discipline its right direction.[1] The Montanists increased the severity of Chris-

---

[1] De virg. vel. c. 1.

tian discipline by several ordinances peculiar to themselves, as by the xerophagiae, by the extension of the dies stationum to the evening, and by their requirements with regard to marriage and martyrdom. But their fundamental idea, the source of all these regulations, was that the Christian lived in the last times, and stood at the end of the whole course of the world. This thought filled the Montanist's mind as a belief, and could not but determine his behaviour. He lived in the one thought that the end of the world was at hand, and discerned in all around him nothing but the signs of the advancing catastrophe. It was necessary then, that inwardly as well as outwardly he should have completely broken with the world; and his outward actions could have no other aim than that of carrying out this breach with the world in every direction, and wholly sundering the bonds by which his flesh still joined him to the world. It has been very correctly observed,[1] that in its moral requirements Montanism set up nothing new; that it was only new in so far as it was reactionary; that the only question between the Montanists and their adversaries in the Church concerned an increase of strictness in enforcing an old ordinance which was on the point of becoming obsolete; that their laws upon marriage and fasting merely aimed at the carrying out in practice of that which they recognised as a divine and eternal command, the old law laid down in both Testaments. Still the cause of this reactionary tendency was the Montanist's belief that he understood better than others the time in which the Christian was living, that he recognised it for what it was, for the last time. Further, how much must that original Christian frame of mind, resting on the belief in Christ's immediate coming, have changed and degenerated, when the duty of martyrdom was so little thought of, that whole churches purchased exemption from persecution with money and wholesale, and when bishops and clergy gave their sanction to the cowardice, and encouraged it by their example.[2] We may well conclude that in other respects

[1] Ritschl, Enstehung der Altkath. Kirche, 1st ed., p. 513; 2d ed., p. 497, sq.
[2] Tert. de fuga in persec., cap. ii. 13.

also there had been a falling off from the strictness of the primitive custom. The Church had entered into friendship with the world. The tendency which gave rise to Montanism may therefore justly be regarded as a reactionary one. For though it was the ever-growing worldliness of Christianity against which it fought with such energy, yet its resistance was grounded on the principle of a return to that primitive standpoint at which the Christian mind, believing in the coming of Christ and the immediate end of the world, had cast itself off from all worldly interests. Accordingly, this motive tendency is continually seen in Tertullian, and appears as the basis of every precept and admonition.[1] The same tendency must be borne in mind when we seek an answer to the question—which could not before be usefully asked— What is the relation between the Paraclete and the Spirit that worked in the apostles? The Paraclete attempts to bring in no dogmatic or moral novelty; as Tertullian says, he is restitutor potius quam institutor. Nevertheless, his requirements exceed those of Christ and the apostles; what they had declared to be morally allowable he can no longer concede to the weakness of the flesh. But the reason of this also is to be found in the Montanist expectation. The nearer the world draws to its end, the less can the weakness of the flesh be spared. Everything that prevents the flesh from becoming holy must be utterly rooted out.[2] In the age succeeding the apostles, the spirit comes with stricter requirements than theirs; not that the apostles desired anything else; only their demands were not so openly and directly made. Tertullian states it as a general view that strictness is always accompanied by a certain lenity which only admits of being explained on the principle of accommodation. The Paraclete also makes use of this accommodation as the apostles had done. Christ, if his meaning be rightly understood, would have prohibited even first marriages. Only from indulgence, from accommodation to human weakness, did he refrain from totally forbidding marriage, as properly he

---

[1] Compare, e.g., Ad Ux., i. 5.
[2] De Monog. c. 3. Caro docetur sanctitatem, quae et in Christo fuit sancta.

should have done. In this view, the whole history of the world is a progressive accommodation; what is at first permitted and freely granted has afterwards to be more and more restricted and withdrawn. What Moses commanded, Christ disallowed, because from the beginning it was not so; and so the Paraclete may now disallow what Paul permitted, if only the new provision is worthy of God and Christ. Formerly it was worthy of God and Christ to put down hardness of heart, when its time was past; it is worthy of them now to root out the weakness of the flesh, for the time is now rapidly becoming shorter. Hardness of heart prevailed till Christ came; and the weakness of the flesh had its time, till the operation of the Paraclete began. The Lord had deferred until this period what could not be borne at that earlier period. Although the Paraclete does no more than carry out the intentions of Christ and the apostles, yet, because his action comes after theirs, it is possible for him at this later period to effect what was impossible before. Everything has thus, as a general rule, its appointed time. Strictly speaking, the flesh, the material part of humanity, has no moral justification; what is permitted to it is a mere concession—a concession that becomes more and more inappropriate, as with the approaching end of the world the relation of the spirit to the flesh inevitably becomes more and more strained, inharmonious, and repellent. As the present order of the world is broken up, the two principles of the spirit and the flesh diverge to the full breadth of their opposition. The material principle must give way to the spiritual, and be unconditionally subordinated to it; for, from the beginning it was only allowed to have scope in the world in order that the spiritual might display upon it its absolute power. It may be compared to a wood which is allowed to grow only that the axe may at last be laid to its root.[1] The last, the end of things, the time in which the finite is made manifest in its finiteness—this is the standpoint. The Paraclete, then, is spirit drawing back into itself as it becomes aware of the world's finiteness, and coming, in its self-consciousness, to the knowledge of its power over the flesh

[1] Tert., De exhort. castit., chap. vi.

and the world. In this exaltation of the self-consciousness of spirit by means of the Paraclete, all deceitful illusion, with which the flesh surrounds it, at once disappears; rapt from the world, it sees with clear vision the temporal order of things even now collapsing in its vanity The moral doctrine of Montanism is thus summed up in one simple requirement—to break with the world, as the world itself to the eye of the Montanist is breaking to pieces and collapsing; to dissolve the bonds by which the spirit and the flesh were held together, as the world is itself in process of dissolution.

When we have once clearly conceived the idea on which Montanism is based, and so seen what its essential nature is, we recognise the justness of the parallel that has been drawn between it and Gnosticism. Each adopts a transcendental mode of view. Each conceives the true essence of Christianity as lying far away, beyond the actual present. The Gnostic, however, looks back to a past whence all derives its first absolute beginning; the Montanist looks forward to a future wherein all reaches its end, and the present world vanishes before the world beyond. For both Christ is the absolute principle of the world; but while the Gnostic uses this principle in order to construct a whole world-development, its operation with the Montanist is only the destruction of the world. Christ has appeared as the Messiah only in order to bring all to an end, and to introduce the great catastrophe through which the present passes into the future order. In both systems, Christ, as the principle determining the process of world-development, is the turning-point, to which everything leads up in such a way that the end unites with the beginning; but while Gnosticism allows all its processes to continue through a limitless period, Montanism sees the final catastrophe arriving as soon as possible. As soon as Christ has appeared—and he is to appear in the immediate future—the world is at its end; by the mere fact of his appearance, the present order disappears and makes way for the future one. The final goal is with each system an ἀποκατάστασις, in which the principles, separating and taking up their relative positions, confront each other in their purity; in Gnosticism these principles are spirit and matter, in Montanism spirit and flesh. Different as the notions were which the Gnostics and the Montanists associated with the terms spirit and spiritual, in both systems what was sought after was that Christians should be pure organs of the spiritual principle. The Gnostics considered themselves to be pre-eminently the spiritual natures, and assigned all other Christians to the stage of mere psychical life. The Montanists found in their distinction of the πνευματικοὶ and ψυχικοὶ a vantage-ground from which they could look down with disdain on the catholic Christians who did not confess their doctrine of the Paraclete. The same antithesis comprises both systems; but in the case of the Montanists its sphere is much more limited.

When we know what Montanism is, the question concerning the external circumstances of its origin becomes of less importance: its peculiarity is precisely this, that the elements from which it sprang existed from the beginning of Christianity. Least of all is any elucidation afforded by its alleged derivation from Montanus. It is therefore hardly worth while to imitate Neander in his anxiety to refute those who have even doubted the historical existence of this apocryphal personage. In the earliest Greek writers the Montanists are not spoken of under this name, but are called Cataphrygians (οἱ κατὰ Φρύγας) after the place where they lived and awaited the descent of the heavenly Jerusalem. All that can be said of Montanus is that he appeared as a prophet in the time of the two well-known prophetesses, Priscilla and Maximilla, or even earlier.[1] The only ground for the supposition that he spoke of himself as God the Father, or the Paraclete, is, that according to the character of ecstasy, the speaking subject was not the ecstatic prophet, but God himself, or the Holy Spirit. Montanism appeared about the middle of the second century, and after that

---

[1] The Philosophoumena do not make him the founder of a sect, but merely say (S. 19, p. 275), καί τινα πρὸ αὐτῶν (Priscilla and Maximilla), Μοντανὸν ὁμοίως δοξάζουσιν ὡς προφήτην.

time attracted more and more observation, as the circumstances of the growing and developing Church, and practical life, were more deeply affected by the questions which it raised. To follow its history further, therefore, it is necessary first to consider the phenomena which occupy the other side of the history from that hitherto investigated.[1]

[1] What has been said above upon Montanism forms the chief contents of my dissertation in the Theol. Jahrb. 1851, p. 538, sq.; Das Wesen des Montanismus nach den neuesten Forschungen; in which is also contained a critique of the recent views on Montanism put forth since the time of Neander and Gieseler. Schwegler's work, Der Montanismus und die christliche Kirche des zweiten Jahrhunderts, Tübingen, 1841, first set the example of more thorough research into this subject. Neander's view of Montanism is also very one-sided. His principal source of error is that he allows himself to be misled by the vague statements we have about the person of Montanus, and consequently explains the character of Montanism by the nature-elements of the ancient Phrygian religion, and the Phrygian temperament, as manifested in the ecstasies of the priests of Cybele and Bacchus. To follow him is only to allow ourselves to be diverted, at the outset of our inquiry, from the right point of observation.

www.ingramcontent.com/pod-product-compliance
Lightning Source LLC
Chambersburg PA
CBHW031252250426
43672CB00029BA/2298